IN THE[...] THE BIB[...]URCE OF UNCHA[...]GED AUTHORITY.

The Pilgrims and Puritans of Plymouth and Massachusetts Bay were zealots who envisioned a society based on the Testaments rather than the laws of man; their austere heritage is a vital part of our American history.

This book is a fascinating study of that heritage. Joseph Gaer and Ben Siegel trace the work of the Puritan divines, men such as Cotton Mather and Jonathan Edwards, through the great Transcendentalists — Emerson, Thoreau, Hawthorne — as they analyze the impact of biblical concepts upon the growth of American institutions. They show how biblical injunctions guided the relationship of state and church; Bible precedents led to an equitable judiciary system; biblical practices sanctioned enlightened medical procedures; and how the unparalleled imagery, language, and style of the Old and New Testaments inspired a great national literature.

The Puritan Heritage is an engrossing and provocative work that tells much about America and Americans —a book that helps explain why we are a nation entirely unique in the history of the world.

Other MENTOR Books of Special Interest

Democracy in America (abridged)
by Alexis de Tocqueville
The classic critique of freedom and democracy in 19th century America by a brilliant Frenchman.
(#MT362—75¢)

America in Perspective *by Henry Steele Commager*
Commentary on our national characteristics by 21 perceptive observers from Tocqueville to Brogan.
(#MT424—75¢)

A Documentary History of the United States (revised, expanded) *edited by Richard D. Heffner*
Important documents that have shaped America's history, with commentary.
(#MP479—60¢)

The Life of Abraham Lincoln *by Stefan Lorant*
A unique text-and-picture biography of the great and beloved American President, with hundreds of illustrations.
(#MT323—75¢)

The
PURITAN HERITAGE

AMERICA'S ROOTS IN THE BIBLE

by

JOSEPH GAER and BEN SIEGEL

A MENTOR BOOK
PUBLISHED BY THE NEW AMERICAN LIBRARY

Grateful acknowledgment is made to the following for permission to quote from the works listed:

Anderson House for an excerpt from *Winterset* by Maxwell Anderson, Copyright 1935 by Anderson House, Copyright renewed 1963 by Gilda Anderson, Alan Anderson, Terence Anderson, Quentin Anderson and Hesper A. Levenstein; and for an excerpt from *Key Largo* by Maxwell Anderson, Copyright 1939 by Maxwell Anderson.

Norma Millay Ellis for an excerpt from "To Jesus on His Birthday" from *Collected Poems* by Edna St. Vincent Millay, published by Harper & Row. Copyright 1928, 1955 by Edna St. Vincent Millay and Norma Millay Ellis.

Alfred A. Knopf, Inc., for an excerpt from "Sunday Morning" from *The Collected Poems of Wallace Stevens*.

The Macmillan Company (New York) for an excerpt from "Heart of God" from *The Collected Poems of Vachel Lindsay*, 1930; and for an excerpt from "Calvary" from *Sonnets 1889-1927* by Edwin Arlington Robinson, 1928.

Random House, Inc., for an excerpt from "Dear Judas" from *Dear Judas and Other Poems* by Robinson Jeffers. Copyright 1929 and renewed 1957 by Robinson Jeffers.

Charles Scribner's Sons for an excerpt from "Sonnets at Christmas" from *Selected Poems* by Allen Tate, 1937; and for an excerpt from "The Children of the Night" from *The Children of the Night* by Edwin Arlington Robinson, 1914.

Library of Congress Catalog Card Number: 64-25081

MENTOR TRADEMARK REG. U.S. PAT. OFF. AND FOREIGN COUNTRIES
REGISTERED TRADEMARK—MARCA REGISTRADA
HECHO EN CHICAGO, U.S.A.

MENTOR BOOKS are published *in the United States* by
The New American Library of World Literature, Inc.,
501 Madison Avenue, New York, New York 10022
in Canada by The New American Library of Canada Limited,
156 Front Street West, Toronto 1, Ontario,
in the United Kingdom by The New English Library Limited,
Barnard's Inn, Holborn, London, E.C. 1, England

PRINTED IN THE UNITED STATES OF AMERICA

AUTHORS TO READERS

The Puritan Heritage is a beginning. It attempts to trace the cultural impact of biblical and postbiblical concepts upon the American settlement, government, law, education, medicine, and literature. There is not, to our knowledge, another study that draws together between a single set of covers these varied and complex materials.

We have been preceded, of course, by a great number of specialists in the above and related fields. Our debt to them is indeed large, and apparent on every page. We wish to acknowledge a special indebtedness to the writings of Samuel Eliot Morison and Thomas Jefferson Wertenbaker in colonial history, Perry Miller in Puritan theology, George Lee Haskins in early Massachusetts law, and Walter Fuller Taylor and Randall Stewart in American literature.

We do not intend that this modest volume written for the general reader be viewed as the definitive study of so vast a subject. Many volumes would be needed to accomplish such a task. Our hope is merely to make the interested reader aware of America's indebtedness—in certain aspects of its culture—to the Judeo-Christian beliefs, customs, and writings.

Our opinion of the "interested reader" is a high one. We have based our study, therefore, upon the most reliable and respected sources available to us. Our practice has been to work from the original document whenever feasible, and when it was not, to rely upon what seemed the most reliable secondary source. After much discussion, and soul-searching, we reduced all documentation to a fairly extensive bibliography, yet included only those titles that had proved the most useful in preparing each chapter. These not only indicate the major source materials, but should guide the interested reader to further reading. The date given in each entry signifies the edition consulted, rather than first publication.

Another question arose from our use of quotations from seventeenth-century writings. We came, finally, to rather an unscholarly decision: to quote verbatim where we felt the language posed the modern reader no problem; to modernize spelling completely where we had some doubts on this point. We ruled out, for the most part, the currently popular practice of slightly altering archaic language.

Many friends and colleagues merit more than casual acknowledgment for their advice and encouragement. To avoid omitting even one, we herewith tender them a collective thanks. Yet more specific appreciation must be offered those extremely cooperative and patient reference librarians at the Honnold and Scripps libraries of the Claremont Colleges, the University of California (Los Angeles), the Los Angeles Public Library, and far from least, the California State Polytechnic College (Pomona).

Thanks are extended also to Messrs. Victor Weybright and Edgar Doctorow of The New American Library for unsparing but penetrating editorial guidance. And special medals of valor should be cast for two gallant ladies, Fay Gaer and Ruth Siegel, not only for their editing and typing, but simply for putting up with us. A final thanks to Helen Beckett for producing a legible typescript by means of her magic typewriter and unfailing good humor.

For all errors of omission and commission, the authors unavoidably (albeit reluctantly) accept full responsibility. What else can we do?

SPONSORED BY THE JEWISH HERITAGE FOUNDATION

JOSEPH GAER
BEN SIEGEL

Santa Monica and Glendora,
California
November, 1962

CONTENTS

INTRODUCTION

American civilization rose in a new world. It was a civilization nourished by many sources and shaped by various forces.

Its chief strength was the land. It was a land vast in length and width, and rich in soil and forest and stream. Two great oceans protected and isolated its coasts in the east and west. In a setting so blessed with resource and promise, the new civilization was destined to flourish.

The land had waited long for its new inhabitants. Time and events transformed the virgin wilderness into a sprawling agricultural community. The community soon developed into a highly complex industrial society, a society evolving from the vigor, imagination, and determination of those who had taken possession of the land. For the newcomers had proved equal to the challenge and the promise.

Shaping the new civilization from the start and influencing its growth was the religious heritage the settlers transplanted to its soil. This religion was principally Christianity, and from the beginning it was Bible-directed. Its adherents—in New England especially—attempted to create in the new land a Bible commonwealth that would fulfill God's plan for man.

The religious, political, and economic factors motivating these first New Englanders were varied and often contradictory. Yet the settlers' prime goal was always a society more perfect than the one from which they had come. Always the Bible was the majority's unchallenged authority. Biblical and post-biblical injunctions guided the evolving relationship of church and state. Bible precedents led to an equitable judiciary and to an elaborate system of public-supported schools and colleges. Biblical, talmudic, and early Christian practices gave sanction to enlightened medical and sanitation procedures.

Biblical imagery, language, and style inspired much of the new nation's literature.

The theocratic dreams of America's early Pilgrim and Puritan inhabitants were ultimately frustrated by unpredictable circumstances. The theocracy that had proved ideal for a tiny Near Eastern country nearly 2,000 years before proved ill-suited for a young society in a vast new land. But America had planted its religious roots with zeal and sincerity, and they proved hardy. As for the Puritans and their Bible—they have left a lasting impression upon the American character and the American culture.

Why and how they did so comprise the themes of this study.

The

PURITAN HERITAGE

One: Settlement

PILGRIMS, PURITANS, AND THE NEW ISRAEL

THE PURITAN TEMPER   Much of what is now recognized as distinctively American in thought, culture, and tradition is derived essentially from four very different sets of values. These begin with seventeenth-century Puritanism, and go on to the eighteenth-century fusion of liberalism, federalism, and the Southern aristocratic code. Then follow nineteenth-century New England transcendentalism and, finally, the western frontier's "rugged individualism." Most historians agree that, of all these influences, Puritanism has proved the most sustained. Not to understand Puritanism, they insist, is not to understand America.

The philosophic patterns of the Puritans, in turn, are rooted in the images, principles, and laws of the Bible. America's roots lie deep in biblical soil, planted there from the country's very beginnings.

The scripturally oriented Puritan creed motivated the reforming and separatist movements in the Anglican Church. It inspired England's seventeenth-century Puritan Revolution and Commonwealth, caused the migrations to Plymouth and Massachusetts Bay, and guided the transformation of these settlements into a theocracy. Even today, despite new knowledge, changing beliefs, and earth-shattering events, Puritan ideals, although greatly modified, still contribute to those fundamental ideas, practices, and goals the rest of the world regard as peculiarly American.

The Protestant Reformation, which rent and divided sixteenth-century Europe, made the Bible Christianity's prime spiritual and moral authority. It would be difficult to exaggerate the Bible's importance in shaping the European mind in the sixteenth and seventeenth centuries. England was deeply affected. John Richard Green, the popular nineteenth-century English historian, has stated that from the middle years of Elizabeth's reign the English were rapidly to become the people of a book, and that book was the Bible. In fact, most English readers were scarcely aware of any history, romance, or poetry (with the possible exception of Chaucer's) when the Bible began to be used for home prayer and to be read to crowds gathered at St. Paul's.

The Bible exerted its influence upon all English society, but it had particular significance for the Puritans. These were English Protestants who in the late-sixteenth and early-seventeenth centuries adopted John Calvin's creed and his reinterpretation of Pauline theology. Calvin accepted and extended Luther's belief in "justification by faith" (that man could attain salvation primarily by believing in God), provided this faith was strengthened by daily Bible study and meditation. He rejected confession, intercession, and mortification. Calvin's ideas, as presented in his *Institutes of the Christian Religion* (1536), became a keystone of the Protestant Reformation. During the next hundred years his ideas were little changed by his followers, and Calvinism remained essentially the religion propounded in his book, one based upon a strongly literal interpretation of Scripture.

The Bible thus became the Puritans' principal theological authority and made them the Reformation's direct representatives within the Church of England. They opposed the episcopal hierarchy, the prayer book, all ritual vestments, the sign of the cross in baptism, kneeling at communion, bowing at the name of Jesus, use of the ring in the marriage service, the observance of saints' days, and the celebration of Christmas. They accepted the new English version of the Bible in its most literal sense. It molded their speech, their thoughts, and their lives. Every biblical allusion, precept, or sentiment became a divine command and rule of life.

The Puritans had no awareness of the attitude of their Jewish contemporaries toward the sacred writings. There was only a handful of Jews scattered throughout England during the entire Puritan period. The Puritans relied upon a literal application of many beliefs and laws long reinterpreted by Judaism. For example, Western Jews discarded any belief in witchcraft long before English courts stopped meting out death sentences to witches.

The Puritans also looked upon themselves as God's chosen people, comparing their state to that of the ancient Israelites.

From Old Testament accounts of the Hebrew tribal struggles and wanderings the Puritans borrowed their imagery and formed their thinking patterns. Their attitude moved James Russell Lowell, the distinguished nineteenth-century American man of letters, to comment that "Those fierce enthusiasts could more easily find elbow-room for their consciences in an ideal Israel than in a practical England."

For Calvin and his followers the Old Testament's central theme was the covenant between God and man. The Puritan's acceptance of Calvinist theology made his life a relentless struggle against Satan's temptations. Even when church membership, material prosperity, and good health indicated election, the "saint" was not totally free of the possibility of sin. He could not relax for a moment. For was there not —as John Bunyan was to point out—a gateway to Hell even at the foot of the Heavenly Mountain? Hardly surprising then that the Puritan developed an almost morbid interest in his spiritual health.

But added to the possibility of salvation there lay before him and his fellows the prospect of an earthly triumph in the form of a community of worthy souls—a Bible commonwealth. The Bible provided not only the Puritan's spiritual beliefs but his philosophic and political concepts as well. The scriptural concern for the poor, orphaned, and mistreated contributed much to the Puritan view of the equality of all men before God—at least of all men within the brotherhood of elected "saints." These middle-class Englishmen had little use for those bearing the taint of worldliness, and this included most of their non-Puritan countrymen. They rejected too the rigid social distinctions that were characteristic of Elizabeth's age.

In the spiritual tradition common to Judaism and Christianity, the Puritans found constant recognition of and respect for individual dignity. For both Hebrews and Puritans, God was the only true monarch; no man could be more than His chosen agent. And to God the humblest slave equaled the mightiest prince. How else explain Moses' defiance of Pharaoh, Nathan's rebuke to David, Elijah's challenge to Ahab, Jeremiah's opposition to Jehoiakim? The Puritans, however, had little general interest in either religious or political democracy. Their prime concerns centered on their right to worship God as they saw fit and to have properly acknowledged their political privileges as free Englishmen.

English Puritans considered themselves devout members

of the Church of England, stating repeatedly their desire to prevent any ecclesiastical schism. But when they insisted upon greater "purification" of Anglican creeds and rituals, and the lessening of the bishops' authority, they immediately found themselves opponents of the state and embroiled in a civil controversy that was not to be resolved completely for one hundred and twenty-nine years—until the Bloodless Revolution of 1688.

Differences over church ceremony and scriptural interpretation were evolving into a political dispute between the crown and Parliament—that is, between arbitrary government by the crown and landholding aristocratic Episcopal Church followers, on the one hand, and the assertion of popular rights by the rising middle-class Puritan tradesmen and merchants who made up Parliament, on the other. The situation grew acute under Charles I. He came to the throne in 1625 and launched a policy of uncompromising suppression. Throughout England dissenting clergymen were ousted from their pulpits. Parliament, in turn, became the voice and protector of the Puritan movement.

What had started as a religious dispute now flared into a death struggle between monarchism and republicanism. Puritan pamphleteers immediately interpreted the struggle as a spiritual war between good and evil. They identified their Cavalier opponents as representatives of Amalek and Philistia, as well as sons of Satan, Belial, or Darkness.

THE GREAT MIGRATION In spite of the increasing ferocity of their civil struggle with the crown, English Puritans were far from presenting a united front. While the majority aimed at control of Parliament, others, disheartened by unfolding events, began looking westward. In the New World lay the prospect of a "wilderness Zion" and an Anglican Church free of bishops, vestments, altars, organs, and stained glass. When Charles dissolved Parliament in 1629, the Puritans began leaving the country in large numbers. The Great Migration to America had begun.

Serious differences developed also within Puritanism. No longer a purely religious phenomenon, Puritanism took on the characteristics of a revolutionary party struggling for political control. And like all such parties, it had its internal divisions.

Most English Puritans favored a national church embracing the entire population and backed by the state. Like Calvin's system in Geneva and in the Church of Scotland, the church was to be Presbyterian. In it, the hierarchy of archbishops, bishops, and priests would be replaced by one of governing bodies—from the national assembly down through the regional classis to the presbytery of the parish church (consisting of the minister and the elders). Others favored the Congregational approach. They viewed each church as "particular" and founded on a covenant entered into by those willing and able to confess their faith, swear to the covenant, and abide by its dictates. Looking upon a national church as "the last stronghold of Antichrist," they rejected any idea of bishop, classis, or synod, and insisted every congregation be self-governing and choose its own pastor and officers.

Yet both Presbyterians and Congregationalists advocated use of civil authority to prevent heresy or the rise of competing ecclesiastical proposals. These "solid Puritan" groups were equally horrified by the Brownists, a band of religious independents who rejected alike pope, bishop, and presbyter. Having little sympathy for the Puritan view that religious unity was essential to national unity, the Brownists (taking their name from Puritan radical Robert Brown) denounced the established church as contrary to the Bible and separated from it. History knows them as the Pilgrims. Puritans and Anglicans combined to make Pilgrim life in England untenable, causing the Pilgrims to flee to Holland and then to the New World.

The Pilgrims were a small, radical Calvinist group of humble tenant farmers from the countryside surrounding the community of Scrooby in west England. Accepting Calvinism with a zeal equal to that of the other dissenters, they believed each congregation should determine its own spiritual course without the guidance and domination of a priesthood. Pilgrim preacher John Robinson put it pointedly: "In what place soever . . . two or three faithful people do arise, separating themselves from the world into the fellowship of the gospel and covenant of Abraham, they are a church truly gathered."

Despairing of accomplishing their purposes within the

Church of England, they seceded and established independent churches modeled on the Congregational pattern. Hence they were not Puritans in the strict sense of reforming Anglicans but one of the many unaffiliated congregations cropping up in early-seventeenth-century England. Fully realizing the risks, they were determined to "shake off the yoke of anti-Christian bondage . . . whatsoever it should cost them."

It cost them a great deal. They were immediately harassed by the king's officers. Shortly after his accession in 1603 James had announced he would "harry" all nonconformists to the established church out of the land. He soon made good the first part of his threat but reneged on the second, refusing the petitioning Pilgrims (a name they were to apply to themselves in Holland) permission to leave England. By autumn of 1607 the Pilgrims found conditions so intolerable that they decided to flee the country. Betrayal and arrests followed. Yet, led by minister John Robinson and William Brewster, the Scrooby postmaster, more than one hundred men, women, and children scattered into small groups and made their way to Holland. After assembling in Amsterdam, they decided to move on to the university town of Leiden.

In liberal, progressive Holland they found too many encroaching heresies that threatened the purity of their Calvinist creed and practices. Life also was economically difficult. For twelve years the Pilgrims led a tenuous existence in Holland. Finally they decided to brave a voyage to America. Permission was obtained from the Virginia Company to settle in its territory, and financial backing was sought and received from a group of London investors known as the Merchant Adventurers. The plan was to add fresh English recruits and then sail for the New World.

The Pilgrims left for England in July, 1620. But it was September before they took their last look at the Devonshire port of Plymouth. The delay exposed them to bad weather and a difficult crossing. Sickness took a heavy toll, and storms and faulty navigation brought them not to Virginia, but New England. In November, 1620, they sailed wearily into Cape Cod Bay. A month later they made their way to Plymouth Harbor. They were finally "home."

If America's first English settlers, at Jamestown, were motivated by mercantile rather than religious reasons, just the reverse was true for this handful of their impoverished countrymen. The Pilgrim saga represents not only man's conquest of nature, but also his self-conquest in search of an ideal.

The Pilgrims disembarking from the Mayflower at Plymouth had risked their lives to cross the sea and establish for themselves and their posterity a Bible-based society in a wilderness harboring hostile and—to them—savage peoples. They naturally had additional hopes of material gain in land and commerce—as did certainly their merchant backers. However, the Pilgrims were motivated primarily by an unassailable determination to worship God according to their own conscience. This determination enabled them to combat the hunger, loneliness, and disease experienced in the New World. Only deep religious devotion can account adequately for the survival of the Plymouth Colony and for the existence of the later Massachusetts Bay, Rhode Island, Maryland, and Pennsylvania colonies.

At Plymouth, far removed from England's political strife, the Pilgrims devoted themselves wholeheartedly to the Bible's letter and spirit, and to their own interpretation of God's will. Attacked and despised within and without the Puritan movement, exiled far from their homeland, their minds filled with scriptural events, the Pilgrims found obvious identification with the ancient Hebrews. Had they not also in establishing their church entered into a "covenant of the Lord"? Were not Israel's experiences strikingly similar to their own? Did not their exodus to the New World's wilderness indicate they too were God's instruments destined to spread His truths among the heathen? Had not England been their Egypt? James I their Pharaoh? The Atlantic their Red Sea? Were not several of their judicious community and military leaders men of deep spiritual convictions and therefore worthy counterparts of Moses and Joshua?

The Pilgrims brought to the New World a special leaning toward the Hebrew language and learning. A knowledge of Hebrew was basic to the Protestant Reformation, but it seems to have held particular fascination for Pilgrims and Puritans. How else explain a concern for Hebrew in the midst of a pioneer community's hardships and dangers? Elder William Brewster, for example, was a serious Hebraist with a small but choice collection of Hebraica. Even his tombstone carried a Hebrew inscription. Governor Bradford prefaces his *History of Plymouth Plantation* with the ex-

planation that he has undertaken Hebrew at an advanced
age because

> Though I am growne aged, yet I have had a longing de-
> sire, to see with my own eyes, something of that most
> ancient language, and holy tongue, in which the Law,
> and oracles of God were write; and in which God, and
> angels, spake to the holy patriarchs, of old time; and
> what names were given to things, from the creation.
> And though I cannot attaine to much herein, yet I am
> refreshed, to have seen some glimpse hereof; (as Moses
> saw the Land of canan afarr of). My aime and desire is,
> to see how the words, and phrases lye in the holy texte;
> and to dicerne somewhat of the same for my owne
> contente.

The Pilgrims were not content to draw figurative analogies
to the Bible. They made Scripture a political and religious
guide, deciding their social organization should be modeled
as closely as possible after Israel's twelve tribes under Moses.
Their American theocracy persisted for almost the rest of the
century, terminating only in 1691 with the Plymouth Colony's
absorption by Massachusetts Bay.

Their encounter with various religious forms in Holland
had freed the Pilgrims to a considerable degree from the
bigotry and intolerance then sweeping England. Despite their
plan for a strongly patriarchal society based upon the Bible,
they believed ecclesiastical censures should be entirely spiritual, without temporal penalties. This caused their subsequent
history to be much more liberal than that of their fellow
Calvinists at Massachusetts Bay. Most clearly reflecting this
liberal attitude was the now famous seventeenth-century social
covenant, the Mayflower Compact. John Quincy Adams was
to describe it as the "genesis of American democracy," claiming it was "perhaps the only instance in human history of that
positive, original social compact which speculative philosophers have imagined as the only legitimate source of government."

Drafted "in the name of God" and based upon His covenant with Israel, the compact was completely democratic in
character. Entered into by the forty-one male adults physi-
cally able to attend the meeting, it represented the first application of a religious covenant to civil government in the New
World. No social, religious, or political distinctions were

drawn between the Dutch and English groups, or between masters and servants. The government was to promote "ye generall good of ye Colonie."

The compact proved the model for the series of significant social contracts leading to the Declaration of Independence and the Constitution. In fact, these later documents are not truly comprehensible without an awareness of the Pilgrims' religious and civil attitudes. Describing the Plymouth Colony as dedicated to "the glorie of God, and the advancemente of the Christian faith," the compact declares its members now covenanted and combined together "into a civill body politick . . . to enacte, constitute, and frame . . . just and equall lawes" to which all pledged "due submission and obedience."

Accepted as the colony's fundamental law, the compact not only enforced equal rights but established a long-lived respect for scriptural precedent. The revised Pilgrim Code of 1656 states that the laws given ancient Israel were "for the mayne so exemplary, being grounded on principles of moral equitie as that all Christians especially ought alwaies to have an eye thereunto in the framing of their politique constitutions."

God was no abstraction to these early New Englanders. Passionately God-centered, their lives and thoughts were filled with a moral fervor reminiscent of the Hebrew prophets. Whenever possible, the Pilgrims modeled their lives close to the Hebraic pattern. Their first Thanksgiving celebration, in 1621, was not the day of joyous feasting it has since become, but a day of religious fasting and prayer, according to Jewish custom.

Their laws, which could carefully govern individual conduct and still safeguard religious and civil liberties, resulted primarily from a social conscience shaped by scriptural ideas and events. And so deeply did the Pilgrims etch their personalities and ideas upon modern history that two centuries later James Russell Lowell, with considerable justification, could write: "Next to the fugitives whom Moses led out of Egypt, the little shipload of outcasts who landed at Plymouth . . . are destined to influence the future of mankind."

PILGRIM AND PURITAN MERGE But the Pilgrims were not to dominate and shape New England life. This fell to the wealthier, better-educated, more forceful Puritans who refused to forfeit their legal standing in the Anglican Church.

These courageous, hardworking, home-loving Englishmen had so intense a desire for spiritual liberty that they too were willing to hazard all they possessed by journeying to the New World. Charles I's dissolution of Parliament in 1629 convinced them that reform of the Anglican Church *in England* was impossible. Led by the formidable John Winthrop, and armed with a 1629 charter issued to the Massachusetts Bay Company, they gathered a select group of 406 emigrants —all of whom had been carefully screened for piety and character—and in April, 1630, headed for New England. There they would institute their much desired reforms.

The parting sermon was delivered by the fiery John Cotton, who was later to come over and play an important role in the new Puritan commonwealth. Cotton declared that like the ancient Israelites the immigrants were God's chosen, headed for the land He had promised and prepared. In this new land they would be able to work undisturbed for God's greater glory.

Arriving in 1630 (John Endecott had led an advance party of sixty in 1628 to prepare a Puritan community at Salem), a decade after the Pilgrims, the Puritans were determined to establish a new Israel on the North American continent, to create in Massachusetts a Bible commonwealth. Described by literary historian Moses Coit Tyler as "the greatest company of wealthy and cultivated persons that have ever emigrated in any one voyage from England to America," the Puritans believed their community should exist primarily to glorify God. In the decades following they bent every effort toward that end.

Within ten years the Massachusetts Bay population was about twenty thousand. Many among this number had immigrated more for economic than religious motives, having little sympathy with an all-powerful theocracy. Yet such strong-willed leaders as Winthrop, Cotton, John Norton, and John Wilson forced all to conform to Puritan doctrine. This doctrine was not only a religious creed but a complex and subtle patterning of the individual's total emotional and intellectual life.

During the first years in New England the Puritan elders, exerting most of their influence through the pulpit, shaped the general pattern of Puritan life as much as the modern teacher, novelist, journalist, television producer, and political commentator combined. "Instead of reading about it in the Sunday papers, as we do today," Professor Herbert Schneider has written, "the old Puritans had a quaint custom of making history six days a week, and on the seventh, 'going to meeting' to hear the minister explain it."

Once safely established in the New World, the Puritans, like the Pilgrims, adhered to the Congregational rather than Presbyterian form of church polity. However, they continued to reject the principal of separatism. They viewed themselves as unequivocal Church of Englanders destined only to transplant the established church in New England.

In spite of frequent and sincere declarations of church loyalty, the Puritans did hope to attain a complete—and reformed—uniformity of their own. Certainly the gentle, much persecuted Pilgrims, who wanted only to be left in peace, were no match for their militancy and expansiveness. Once firmly established, the Puritans easily dominated and finally drew the Pilgrims into their orbit.

Differences between Puritan and Pilgrim were greatly diminished and then obliterated by the American migration. Separated from royal and ecclesiastical control by three thousand miles and more than seven weeks of difficult travel, the reforming and separatist Anglicans developed similar social and religious views. "Differences of social condition and of wealth," historian R. B. Perry points out, "lost much of their importance under pioneer conditions. The common environment, the common needs and hazards, the common Bible, and above all the common Calvinistic creed, filled a much greater place in their lives than the abstract issue of Separatism or the circumstances of their migration."

Whatever economic and political motives influenced the Plymouth and Massachusetts Bay settlers to unite, the primary bond was an awareness of a common faith. This was underscored by the striking differences in belief between them and Virginia's Anglican inhabitants. In 1643 the Plymouth Colony became part of the New England Confederacy, and in 1691 lost all "separateness" by merging with Massachusetts Bay.

THE NEW ENGLAND MOSES AND JOSHUA The New England clergy was completely sympathetic to the Bay Colony's political oligarchy and to its view that freedom of conscience was only for the few "visible elect." Although the total community—including hundreds of artisans, laborers, and servants—was expected to attend and support the church, only church *members,* that is, the elect or "saints," could vote.

To become a member, not only did an applicant have to be a man of substance, but he had to make public confession of sin and conversion, and to pass a rigid examination posed by the pastors and church officials. "This was an ordeal not to be undertaken lightly," historian William Miller has recently pointed out, "especially given the social penalties that would accompany failure in a community such as Massachusetts Bay." Lacking a political voice, the overwhelming majority of New Englanders were forced to express their bitter frustrations by widespread but harmless parodies of the Puritans; one such parody proclaimed, "the world belongs to the saints, and we are the saints."

The Puritans tended frequently to be narrow, selfish, and bigoted, but they had come to the New World solely to establish colonies where their own worship would be protected by civil law from innovation and contradiction. They constantly reiterated this point: "We came hither because we would have our posterity settled under the pure and full *dispensations* of the gospel; defended by rulers that should be of ourselves." Everything else was secondary. "It is never to be forgotten," thundered later Salem minister, John Higgenson, "that our New England is originally a plantation of religion and not a plantation of trade. . . . Let Merchants and such as are increasing Cent per Center remember this." Nonbelievers simply were not welcome.

The Puritan leaders were primarily clergymen. And for fifty years theirs tended to be the important names in Massachusetts history. They believed they had been divinely chosen for their tasks. They were convinced that only through the church and its spokesmen could the individual become aware of his sinfulness, his social function, or God's unfolding plan for mankind. While Anglican England's progress might be measured by a shift from the "divine right" of the Pope to that of the king, that of Massachusetts equally could be gauged by a shift from the "divine right" of the king to the "divine" privileges of clergy and magistrates.

Living as he did in a wilderness where he hoped to establish a civilization devoid of Old World corruptions, the American Puritan had special need not only of a "perfect Rule of Faith" but of a divine law book to guide daily actions. For him the Bible was a daily, deeply felt source of spiritual and emotional sustenance and the basis for that initiative, determination, and resourcefulness for which he was to become famous.

The Puritans drew repeatedly on the covenant idea, embodying it in religious and secular dealings. Like the ancient Hebrews and contemporary Pilgrims, they believed the spiritual contract existed not only between God and the individual but also between God and the entire group, and that the group was to act as one in fulfilling God's laws. In return, the group received God's favor and protection, and any luck or misfortune befalling the entire community was indicative of how this obligation was being fulfilled. Days of general thanksgiving or "humiliation" were held in formal recognition of God's persistent interest. "If we keep this covenant," stated John Winthrop, "wee shall finde that the God of Israell is among us"; however, "if wee deal falsely with our God . . . wee shall be consumed out of the good land He has promised."

The Puritans had every reason to be confident that their holy commonwealth had a better chance of success than that of their embattled English brethren. All New England life consisted of settlements tightly organized into congregations in which the clergy were the leaders and the magistrates their willing officials. Little significant religious disagreement occurred during the first few decades, and the Puritan ideal was less an ideal than "the professed rule of practice." Disillusionment and failure were in the future.

As had the separatist Pilgrims, the American Puritans—in thought, language, and action—came to look upon themselves as a new Israel fighting Satanic forces in a land of

wickedness and paganism. "The Christian Church so called,"
declared clergyman John Stevens, "is only a continuation and
extension of the Jewish church." As minister William Brattle
put it, "the covenant of grace is the very same now that it
was under the Mosaical dispensation. The administration
differs but the covenant is the same."

In searching Scripture for relevant texts to support their
views and needs, the Puritans easily discovered numerous
similarities between themselves and the Israelites. They (again
like the Pilgrims) viewed England as their Egypt, James I
as their Pharaoh, the Atlantic as their Red Sea. They also
were an embattled people obviously chosen to carry out
divine plans for the world's redemption. They too had been
driven from their homes, not as punishment, but to build a
promised land. The only significant difference they could see
between ancient Israel and themselves was that they were
expected to convert the very wilderness to a promised land.

And in such figures as Winthrop, Cotton, and Norton,
the Puritans felt they had leaders comparable to Moses and
Joshua. Cotton Mather makes this clear in eulogizing John
Winthrop:

> Accordingly when the noble design of carrying a colony
> of chosen people into an American wilderness, was by
> some eminent persons undertaken, *this* eminent person
> was, by the consent of all, chosen for the Moses, who
> must be the leader of so great an undertaking: and in-
> deed nothing but a *Mosaic spirit* could have carried him
> through the temptations, to which either his farewell to
> his own land, or his travel in a strange land, must needs
> expose a gentleman of his education.

John Cotton's tomb inscription compared him to Moses, and
gave surprising mention of a "living Joshua," John Norton:

> But let his mourning flock be comforted,
> Though Moses be, yet Joshua is not dead:
> I mean renowned Norton; worthy he
> Successor to our Moses is to be,
> O Happy Israel in America,
> In such a Moses, such a Joshua.

American Puritan society developed then as biblically
oriented and theocratically organized—dominated by God's

elect, who alone were full church members and enabled to vote. The holy covenant and civil covenant literally were one. The civil covenant became merely the physical enforcement of the church's desires. And religion, rather than just an aspect of social life, became the ultimate standard and goal to which all institutions were subordinated.

Of course Puritans were not the only colonials motivated by biblical doctrines. So too were Virginia's Anglicans, though they were not as bound by Scripture as the Puritans. Equally directed by biblical doctrines were the unsmiling Scottish Presbyterian followers of John Knox, who presented the Bible as the final law. The Quakers were another group. Such Quaker leaders as George Fox, Robert Barclay, and William Penn strongly opposed many aspects of Puritanism, yet their lives and teachings exemplified the extremes of the Puritan spirit. The Quakers also conceived their church in terms of the Hebrew "remnant" and insisted that God's message could be understood only by living in the biblical spirit. But they rejected Puritan intolerance. When Pennsylvania's founder, William Penn, arrived in 1682 with a land charter from Charles II, he found the Pennsylvania region already settled by Swedes, Dutchmen, and other Englishmen. Granting them immediate civil and religious freedom, he issued in 1701 his Charter of Privileges, which remained in effect until 1776. Despite its startling contrasts and paradoxes, its frequent neurotic and morbid outcroppings, the Quaker spirit created in Pennsylvania a colony that soon rivaled Rhode Island as a refuge for religious rebels.

The Puritans then were not alone in believing the Bible to be God's inspired word and revealed will. Most of seventeenth-century America shared this view. But the Puritans regarded the Bible as their civil and social authority as well. "Creeds, characters, and customs were all tried by this unfailing test," Joseph Banvard has written, "and all was rejected which, in their opinion, did not stand this ordeal. Laws and regulations adopted by them, which, at the present day, are stigmatized as singularities, were, in many instances, the legitimate fruits of their strict adherence to the teachings of the Bible." Any irreverance toward the Bible, or failure to adhere to its dictates, brought a rapid fine or whipping.

Congenial to Puritan thinking, especially in the midst of trying economic conditions, was the scriptural admonition that both the rich and poor accept their stations cheerfully. To that end Reverend Joseph Morgan could argue that "a more comfortable Life here . . . [meant] far less danger as to the next Life." Still the "Rich Man has a *miserable* Life; for he is always full of Fear and Care. . . . We need to *pity* and *love* Rich Men." Undoubtedly the good reverend's argument was received with varying emotions among the less well-to-do. Puritans were hardly alone in utilizing biblical doctrines to sanctify these and other concepts of private property, individual enterprise, and profit. Most religious groups were doing the same. Early Moravian leaders even employed biblical warrants in their communal experiments in Pennsylvania to encourage their members to multiply and replenish the earth.

The Puritans found nothing in the Bible contrary to nature or reason. They were convinced that reason, properly employed, could prove anything in nature to be God's work or intention. Neither they, nor the next century's revolutionary leaders, implied anything atheistic or antireligious in speaking of "nature's laws" or "natural rights"—as has often been assumed. Numerous seventeenth- and eighteenth-century election-day sermons stressed the lack of contradiction between God's will as revealed in nature and His will as revealed in the Bible. Other groups—the Anglicans for instance—might attempt to harmonize reason and religion by reducing scriptural doctrines to a minimum but the Puritans stretched Scripture to cover all existence.

Jonathan Edwards, America's greatest Puritan theologian, not only saw no conflict between Bible and reason, but even argued that philosophy and science were identical, thereby managing to strengthen Calvinism, temporarily, against the tide of hostile eighteenth-century rationalism. Nevertheless Edwards and all other Puritan divines were quick to urge one important qualification—that revelation precede reason. The Bible was not to be tested by nature, they insisted, but nature by the Bible. For reason does not illuminate Scripture, but Scripture's clear sense strengthens reason.

The Puritans' impassioned devotion to the Bible overflowed their thought and colored their daily lives. The ethical idealism they derived disciplined their minds, fortified their wills, and confirmed their principles. Their belief in a divine mission, as much as any practical factor, enabled them to triumph over difficulties that defeated other colonists. It gave them a tenacity and courage that helped them cope with the rigorous life of the American wilderness during the early-seventeenth century.

"PSALM BOOK. SHOT AND POWDER-HORN" Like
their English brethren, American Puritans viewed theocracy
as the most desirable political structure. They made a valiant,
if not quite successful, attempt to establish a new Canaan in
New England. They searched the Old Testament for appropriate precedents, being much more concerned with religious
ideals and values than with either political or social democracy. Had not the Hebrew ideal been essentially theocratic?
"The days when 'there was no king in Israel,'" Millar Burrows writes, "when 'every man did that which was good in
his own eyes,' were regarded in retrospect . . . as a time
when God ruled his people directly." Neither prophet nor
scribe had looked with sympathy upon human rulers, particularly those who might usurp God's prerogatives.

At no time did America's Puritan leaders intend to establish a government representing the people's views and desires.
Each congregation reserved the right to admit, censure, or
expel members. Each also elected its own officers—two ministers (a pastor and a teacher) and two ruling elders. These
leaders worked zealously to prevent entrance into their new
Zion of any who disagreed with them. They had risked life
and property to worship according to their conception of
Christianity and to establish a religious commonwealth. As
each congregation constituted a separate covenant, only
those who shared its views and accepted its leadership were
welcome. Anyone else could find plenty of space available
outside the community. Increase Mather derided these
"hidious clamours for liberty of Conscience," while John
Norton viewed liberty of worship as "a liberty to blaspheme,
a liberty to seduce others from the true God. A liberty to tell
lies in the name of the Lord." T. J. Wertenbaker sums up
their attitude: "The Puritan community thought that heretics
should have only the liberty to leave."

The Puritans established a theocratic oligarchy in which
the civil magistrates were mere spokesmen for the church
and its ministers, who held no public offices but remained
the colony's unquestioned final depository of power. The
franchise was carefully controlled. Only church members—

hand-picked by the clergy—were able to vote. Of course only the "visible elect"—those owning property, whose private lives were deemed blameless and who completely accepted the established order—merited church membership. Women were excluded automatically from church government in keeping with Scripture.

The "chosen" ruled, with all others spiritually and politically excluded, and with church and state so interlaced as to be practically the same. In bending the Bible to meet their peculiar needs, the Puritans resorted to an arbitrary primitivism that often contradicted the scriptural spirit.

Several commentators have seen Puritanism as essentially a fusion of the Hebrew spirit, early Christian conscience, and Reformation values. Certainly Puritanism rejected anything suggesting Rome or the Anglican episcopacy. The Bible, Calvin had insisted, recognized no ecclesiastical officer higher "than a preacher of the Word of God, called to govern the church." Puritans denied bishops superiority over other ordained ministers, insisting that the entire ministry should enjoy identical privileges and powers.

For this, as well as for their belief that each congregational majority should elect its pastor without answering to king, archbishop, or higher body, they found scriptural precedent. Had not every synagogue been an independent entity, with formal ranking of the rabbinate unknown? In the Salem congregation "every fit member wrote, in a note, his name whom the Lord moved him to think was fit for a pastor, and so likewise, whom they would have for teacher; so the most voice was for Mr. Skelton to be Pastor, and Mr. Higginson to be Teacher." The Salem ministers were then ordained by the congregation officers' laying on of hands. This lay ordination represented a clear break from episcopal practices.

Thus, in spite of restrictive theocratic practices, the Puritan majority, like the Hebrew, often had occasion to assert itself. And though Puritan exclusiveness is often criticized, it should be remembered also that even New England's limited republicanism allowed greater general participation in church and political matters than had been possible for centuries in Europe. For the elect, at least, even theocracy was an assertion of liberty and democracy.

The Puritan minister often resembled his Judaic counterpart. Both rabbi and minister based their spiritual authority entirely upon learning, piety, and interpretation of the divine law—a source open to all. Their social roles also were similar. Neither held an official administrative position, deriving his social authority from strength of character, ability, and training. In New England, only the minister could "open" the "rule of God's word," then buttress his views by Scripture. Consequently, he served the civil magistrates not only as religious adviser but as political, social, and administrative guide as well. Garbed usually in black skullcap and Geneva cloak, his arrival at the meetinghouse brought the Puritan congregation to its feet, where it remained until he had seated himself in the pulpit. Many Orthodox Jewish congregations still pay their rabbi this respectful tribute. The significant Puritan changes (decentralizing the church, abolishing the episcopal hierarchy, and bringing together minister and congregation) followed Jewish precedent.

And except for the change from Saturday to Sunday, the Puritans treated the Sabbath in the Jewish manner. They began the day of worship and prayer the previous sundown, refraining for twenty-four hours from any sort of work, including shaving, sweeping, making beds, washing dishes, and cooking. There was to be no travel (except to attend worship) or amusement of any sort.

Stringent legislation enforced Sabbath laws. Constables and tithing men arrested all Sabbath-breakers, upon whom severe penalties were imposed. A public "cage" for noisy offenders was constructed, and playing children and strolling youths and maidens were warned they were engaging in "things tending much to the dishonor of God, the reproach of religion and the prophanation of the holy Sabbath." One Massachusetts law of 1653 actually prohibited as a waste of time Sunday walks or visits to the ships lying in the harbor. In 1670 John Lewis and Sarah Chapman were brought before the New London court for "sitting together on the Lord's Day, under an apple tree in Goodman Chapman's orchard." James Rogers, for sailing in a vessel on the Sabbath, was fined twenty shillings, while Steven Chalker was chastized for driving cattle on the day of rest. John Cotton refused even to study for a sermon on the Sabbath for fear of "wearisome labour to invention or memory."

One striking difference between Judaie and Calvinistic Sabbath codes did exist: even the most orthodox Jews will relax Sabbath strictures for health reasons. Not so the early New Englanders. When, shortly after their arrival, a fire destroyed the Pilgrims' "commonhouse" roof on the Sabbath, they refused, despite an icy downpour, to repair it until the next day. Many of them—including Governor John Carver and his successor, William Bradford—were already ill from the difficult ocean voyage, bad food, and subsequent exposure. This hardheaded piety resulted in an epidemic of influenza, pneumonia, and consumption which took thirty lives during the next two months. Only twenty-three adult Pilgrims were left to enjoy their first New England spring.

But the Puritans were forced by the physical dangers that surrounded them to relax their laws enough to permit the carrying of a gun on the Sabbath. They were careful to give this act religious justification, in the Hebrew halakic or legalistic sense, and to stipulate that the gun was to be discharged only upon the appearance of an Indian or a wolf. A striking picture is evoked, suggests Professor Abraham Neuman, by the thought of either Pilgrims or Puritans walking to Sabbath services "three in a row, reverent but armed, each man equipped on Sunday morn with psalm book, shot and powder-horn."

Many parallels of form and principle existed between the Puritan social pattern and the Jewish medieval *kahal,* or communal organization. Both peoples centered their religious and communal activities about the meetinghouse (synagogue means literally "meeting" or "assembly"). Synagogue and meetinghouse interiors offered interesting similarities. Both rejected the "dim religious light" for as much bright daylight as possible, and both stressed an almost barren simplicity and no musical instruments. But in contrast to the synagogue, the meetinghouse was never heated; as a result, the Puritan elders unbent to the point of allowing ministers to wear mittens while preaching and even permitted the womenfolk to use footstoves during services. In spite of such "luxuries," the freezing Massachusetts winters provided a demanding test of Puritan fortitude. The calls to prayer in meetinghouse and synagogue were by drum and horn, and both had separate seating for the sexes.

The Puritan tithing man was in many ways analogous to the Hebrew *shamus,* or beadle. One of the tithing man's tasks was to keep all awake during services. "Equipped with a long staff, which had a heavy knob at one end, and at the other a long foxtail or a hare's foot, he strutted during meeting," states Neuman, "waking the drowsy sleepers by rapping the masculine heads with the heavy knobbed end, but using the furry end to tickle the Priscillas into gentle but startled wakefulness." One resourceful minister, the Reverend Mr. Moody, scorned such aids. He resorted instead to a rabbinic device, interrupting his sermon to shout, "Fire, fire!" Awakened so rudely, the bemused listeners cried out, "Where?" The angered preacher then thundered, "In hell, for sleeping sinners."

The New Englanders were inordinately fond of biblical allusions, expressions, and especially, names—for invective as well as compliment. Naturally those earning their contempt were identified with the Bible's less praiseworthy characters. Anne Hutchinson, the noted liberal heretic, for example, was a "wretched Jezebel," while a reckless coach driver became a "Jehu." Conversely, names of admired biblical figures such as Daniel, Jonathan, Esther, Enoch, Ezra, and Rachel were used repeatedly for their young.

The Bible was also a never-ending source of American place-names. Some of the more obvious examples are Salem, Bethel, Bethlehem, Canaan, Carmel, Eden, Gilead, Goshen, Hebron, Jaffa, Jericho, Jordan, Nimrod, Palestine, Pisgah, Rehoboth, Sharon, Shiloh, and Zion.

That the Puritan reverence for Scripture frequently degenerated into literalness is undeniable. That their interpretations were often arbitrary, biased, and colored by contemporary needs is equally true. The Puritans more readily concentrated on the Bible's harsher, more militant aspects than on its incentives to tenderness and humanity. They also were more likely to employ the Bible to support undemocratic than democratic principles. Their social values were essentially autocratic and authoritarian. To Puritans, God's word provided divine license for the "chosen" to dominate all social thoughts, actions, and relationships, to identify their religious ideals with public policy, and to enforce this policy by whatever civil pressures seemed necessary.

The Puritans were convinced that holy writ was to be interpreted and expounded by learned leadership alone and that the less educated farmers, merchants, and laborers were to accept and obey this leadership unquestioningly. Their overriding desire, whatever the cost, was to be pure, unyielding, and worthy. Was not a holy commonwealth at last within reach? Hadn't they succeeded in transplanting the "true belief" to New England? Hadn't they rid their regions of past idols and contemporary contaminations and obstacles? Wasn't their God Jehovah, the God of ancient Israel, "a God of battles" who fought on behalf of His people and made their enemies His? Wasn't He with them in a way in which He could not be with those who differed with them? Were not their chances of salvation, therefore, better than those not sharing the covenant?

The Puritans valued this "primitive Old Testament particularism" much more than they did the later "broad universalism" of the second Isaiah. Yet this intolerance constitutes only part of the Puritan heritage. For it became clear even before the turn of the eighteenth century that within the Puritan code itself lay the democratic seeds of its own limitations—if not destruction. Puritanism could persecute various religious sects, forcing them beyond its boundaries, but it had itself engendered and nourished the sectarian spirit. It had insisted repeatedly that divine truth lay within reach of anyone who would read the Bible and accept God's grace, and that each was morally obligated to adhere to this truth he had personally discovered.

The Puritan's concern for the total community's moral and spiritual well-being repeatedly developed into charitable civic groups, like Cotton Mather's "friendly societies." Even so thorough a non-Puritan as Ben Franklin was to admit that Mather's *Essay To Do Good* had helped imbue him with a sense of communal participation, service, and humanitarianism. Nor did Puritans limit their concern to their own. Roger Williams tried to educate and assist the New England Indians, and so did, among others, John Eliot and the Mayhews. Judge Samuel Sewall's deep sense of justice caused him to renounce publicly his own role in the Salem witch trials and to publish in 1700 a tract condemning slavery as un-Christian. Much of the Puritan's gravity and intolerance resulted from his intense desire to master his own impulses and lead an orderly, disciplined existence. Harsh with others, he always was even harder on himself.

The Puritans, it is true, often turned the "compact" idea, or holy covenant, to their advantage. Yet such dissenters from oligarchy as Roger Williams, Thomas Hooker, John Wise, and Jonathan Mayhew also used it to defy authority, by arguing that a compact limits both civil and ecclesiastical relationships. It was within Puritan thought after all that Williams found the principle of religious tolerance and introduced it into the American tradition. Believing firmly in clear separation of church and state, he opposed the state's right to dictate anyone's religious or political beliefs. In 1663 he saw this idea expressed in Rhode Island's royal charter.

No individual, the charter stated, was to be in "any wise molested, punished, disquieted, or called in question, for any differences in opinione in matters of religion," provided he didn't "disturb the civill peace." Such minority religious groups as the Quakers, Mennonites, Dunkers, and Amish obviously did not enjoy full citizenship in communities dominated by Puritans or Anglicans, but they were quick to seize upon the steadily evolving liberal ideas and to turn every religious contest into a political battle for increased concessions. Though there were early setbacks, they soon won significant victories.

It should be remembered also that colonial New England's economic structure, unlike that of Virginia, was fundamentally anti-aristocratic. Both the more well-to-do and the many unskilled laborers, servants, and slaves were rapidly outnumbered by a large middle class of small freeholders and skilled artisans. Compelled to produce most of New England's needed articles, this class constituted the basis of the region's sound economic system. And any evaluation of Puritan New England's influence upon American political freedom should consider this very valuable legacy—her "democracy of labor."

The Puritan's faults, though serious and numerous, are overshadowed by his virtues and achievements. His insistence that the elect could do no wrong made him susceptible to the temptations of bigotry and hypocrisy. His equally strong insistence upon faith, dignity, and self-discipline imposed upon himself and his community high standards of conscience, morality, and behavior. He made few concessions to human nature, being convinced that men are neither free agents, perfect, nor even essentially good; yet his views come close to modern psychological and sociological findings. And his view of man actually convinced the Puritan of the inevitability of God's continual intervention in human affairs.

In addition, his private reading of the Bible encouraged personal interpretation and convinced him that every man is endowed with certain inalienable moral and spiritual obligations. Thus the Puritan became literally his own churchman, replacing the authority of confession and creed with a sense of spiritual covenant.

Further, the Puritan's constant probing of mind and soul combined with his disdain for religious, social, and political trappings to produce this country's rich flowering of diverse doctrines and sects. His belief provided him with the courage, energy, and self-discipline to overcome a wilderness and implant those ideas of government, law, education, philosophy, and literature that made New England the nation's intellectual center for more than two centuries. Fully aware of their personal and political faults, Ralph Waldo Emerson grudgingly referred to the Puritans as "great, grim, earnest men" who had "solemnized the heyday of their strength by the planting and liberating of America."

These then were the principal religious and social ideas directing our country's founders, the ideas forming, as Clarence Manion puts it, the very "bloodstream of our constitutional system." Certainly to Puritanism must go much of the credit for our constitutional guarantee of religious freedom in preference to that mere assurance of "tolerance" that assumes a privileged church. All of us now enjoying the rights and pleasures of American religious, social, and intellectual freedom owe those courageous, tough-minded, passionately devout Puritans—and their Bible—an incalculable debt.

Two: Government

BIBLE, CHURCH, AND STATE

THE NEW CANAAN   Both Pilgrims and Puritans arrived in their new Canaan prepared for an ideal theocracy. That these hardheaded Puritan autocrats should have instead contributed so much to the formulation and development of American democratic principles is one of history's anomalies. Especially ironic is their painful forging of a republican structure at the cost of the very Bible commonwealth they had crossed the sea to establish.

From the beginning they chose their magistrates, framed their laws, and established their general legislative procedures according to Scripture. They rejected the authority of both English magistrates and established church. Mosaic law provided New England's judicial system with its one irrefutable source of supreme spiritual authority and legal precedent. The fundamental Puritan premise was that God's law had "an everlasting equity" and should guide all future legal activities.

This attitude persisted and is evident even in present American legal codes. The Pentateuch's principles are seen in such early documents as the Mayflower Compact and Salem Covenant. The first New Haven general assembly of 1639 also leaned heavily upon Scripture. Convened to establish a civil government, the assembly heard frequently from the Reverend John Davenport, who was determined "to drive things . . . as near to the precept and pattern of Scripture as they could be driven," and who made clear his conviction that the Scriptures represent "a perfect rule for the direction —and government—of all men in all duties." Precedent having been established, the Mosaic law came to dominate New

England's legislative procedure. In 1641 a proposed Body of
Liberties was drafted consisting of two laws drawn from the
New Testament and the remaining forty-six from the Old.

Usually magistrates and clergy cooperated fully. But differences occasionally did arise as to which group more clearly
embodied divine authority. Most disagreements, however,
flared between magistrates and the elected deputies. One
such dispute resembled the modern Congress-Supreme Court
struggle over the issue of judicial review. Here a dispute
over a sow's ownership quickly evolved into the question
whether a handful of judges had the legal right to negate the
decision of a larger body of deputies. In describing the
incident, the theocratic John Winthrop marshaled Old Testament precedents to declare that were the magistrates forbidden to veto the deputies' action, the colony would be a
democracy and, he argued with finality, "there was no such
government in Israel."

Winthrop's view represented that of most Puritan leaders, church and judicial, who were convinced their divine
covenant made them responsible to God rather than to
bishops, kings, or populace. For if such a compact was binding in religion, they held, it was equally binding in government.

In the early days of Puritan settlement, therefore, the
church elders drew little practical distinction between church
and civil administration. Assembled in town meeting, those
inhabitants empowered to vote concerned themselves with
both religious and civil affairs. Certainly no candidate for
public office could expect election unless sanctioned by ministers, elders, and other congregational leaders. And before
any officials were selected or elected, appropriate verses were
read from Scripture describing the council of elders established by Moses.

If an early settler was doubtful as to the proper relationship of church and state, the *Platform of Church Discipline*
(1646) set him straight: "It is the duty of the magistrates to
take care of matters of religion. . . . Moses, Joshua, David,
Solmon, Asa, Jehoshaphat, Hezekiah, Josiah are much com-
mended by the Holy Ghost for . . . putting forth their
authority in matters of religion." On the other hand, "Church
government stands in no opposition to civil government . . .
nor any way intrencheth upon the authority of civil magistrates in their jurisdiction . . . but rather strengthening them,
furthereth the people in yielding more hearty . . . obedience

unto them." Church and state, therefore, were to help each other "in their distinct and due administrations."

This division of authority between clergy and magistrates has raised the question as to whether the New England government was a theocracy in the biblical sense. For in a theocracy the ministers themselves hold public office, and the Massachusetts clergy was careful not to do so. Whether or not the term "theocracy" should be applied is of little importance. The New Englanders were striving to reproduce the Hebrew theocratic laws and political structure as closely as possible. They viewed their own trials and tribulations with the land's natural elements and savage inhabitants as similar to those of the ancient Israelites. And in the struggle with the crown over the Massachusetts charter, the ministry frequently cited the Bible's disparagement of human monarchy.

This basing of all actions upon direct biblical authority persisted throughout the century. John Davenport could cite Isaiah to defend publicly several high-ranking Puritan refugees from the 1660 Restoration: "Hide the outcasts, betray not the fugitive; let the outcasts of Moab sojourn among you; be a refuge to them from the destroyer." Or minister William Brattle could insist that "the covenant of grace is the very same now that it was under the Mosaic dispensation. The administration differs but the covenant is the same."

The reverence of the Puritan leaders for the divine covenant—as well as their unhappy experiences with the English government and its laws—caused them to substitute Old Testament rulings for English common law. So for the ten years of the Bay Colony's Confederacy with Connecticut, New Haven, and Plymouth, its judicial system lacked the authority of either a coherent system of statutes or that of common law. Thus the magistrates, historian J. G. Palfrey points out, dispensed law relying solely upon "their own reason and conscience, instructed by Scripture."

Though there was growing unrest and increasing opposition to their autocratic rule as the century came to its close, the Puritan elders harbored no doubt as to their divine mandate. A Boston ministerial convention in May, 1698, still could reach almost unanimous agreement that their church remain operative under the Old Testament covenant. The very sincerity and depth of their conviction made them difficult men to deal with or to change.

A part of biblical history holding special interest for New England's founding fathers was that dealing with the Hebrew commonwealth. For it was during the five centuries from the Egyptian exodus to Saul's appointment as king that there developed those principles of individual rights and liberties that they found relevant to the American experience. Like the American colonists, the Israelites had been forced to throw off a tyrannical ruler and then evolve a new government. They too had no monarch or previous government of their own to discard; they had no privileged aristocracy to replace, no outmoded institutions to refashion. Both Hebrews and Puritans were strikingly fortunate in having the opportunity to select and establish for themselves the governmental structure holding the highest promise and appeal. And both arrived at the political structure of a democratic federal republic.

Yet New World democracy was not to emerge overnight. Many complex and far-flung factors were involved. English Puritanism's military victory under Cromwell was a mixed blessing for New England's Puritans. During the two decades following Cromwell's victory, New England expanded its population, economic trade, and ecclesiastical authority without fear of foreign interference. In fact, only New England enjoyed the special mercantile privileges—and revenues—of the Navigation Acts. On the other hand, the steady stream of wealthy, educated, and devout refugees fleeing royal tyranny was replaced at this time by an increasing number of unsanctified poor, arriving as indentured servants, tradesmen, and laborers. Communication between the two Puritan communities weakened in victory, for English Puritanism became progressively more liberal, whereas the American branch increased in bigotry and rigidity.

While the New England Puritans accepted the Bible's democratic premises in theory, they refused repeatedly to put them into adequate practice. This not only weakened their moral position but insured the need of a new approach to social polity. And their rigidity and self-righteousness—at a time when the world was beginning to change, especially in America—provided the seeds of their self-destruction.

Some historians have pointed to the reliance of the Puritans upon Scripture as the prime cause of their political and religious rigidity. The reverse was true. The Bible actually encouraged the multiplication of political factions and religious sects, being "sufficiently vague to stimulate rather than settle argument." Inviting individual interpretation, the Bible, far from cramping New England's intellectual life, encouraged free thought and discussion. But whenever such activities threatened the authority of the Puritan leadership, it hastily was quashed.

Because Puritan theocratic ideals managed to persist into the eighteenth century, many have assumed they encountered little opposition. Not so—forces of dissolution were early at work. Within a few years of its settlement the holy commonwealth was torn by impassioned theological and political disputes. Demands by the general populace for increased participation in Massachusetts Bay's administration were heard from the very beginning. Shortly after settlement, in October, 1630, the eight Puritan magistrates were confronted with a demand from 118 fellow settlers to be recognized as freemen. These petitioners were not to be wholly denied, and a series of small but significant concessions followed.

These first cracks in the structure became larger in 1634, when freemen gained the right to elect deputies and to assist the governor and magistrates in imposing taxes, making laws, and appointing other freemen. Other dissenting and important voices soon were heard urging more democratic procedures. Hartford's liberal leader, the Reverend Thomas Hooker, rejected Winthrop's warning about the danger of referring political or legal questions to the people. He replied that for political authority to rest with judges and counselors not answerable to the people could lead only to tyranny and confusion. "A general counsel chosen by all," Hooker declared, is "most suitable. . . . This was the practice of the Jewish Church, directed by God."

The scholarly, irrepressible Roger Williams was in New England by 1631 voicing from the pulpit his displeasure with the union of church and state, and denying the magistrates' right to punish violators of the Sabbath and the Commandments. Williams was this nation's earliest advocate of complete religious freedom, or what he termed "soul liberty." For this "heresy," and for his total rejection of the holy commonwealth, he earned the distinction of being New England's first rebel, and was banished. He became dependent for some time upon the Indians. No spiritual good, Williams insisted, could be expected from a civil state employing "a civil sword in spiritual matters." You "pretend liberty of conscience," he once wrote the Puritan theocrats, "but alas, it is but self, the great god self," which truly interests you. He was to remain until his death an outlaw from Massachusetts.

But for all his "heretical" views, Williams based Rhode Island's social and political structure upon biblical principles. He believed that God, working through human agents, manifested His presence in all civil activities. He saw nothing in Scripture to prevent his establishing as a basic law the principle that every man has an absolute right to "a full liberty in religious concernments." And he did this before John Locke had promulgated his principles of tolerance, before Milton had written his *Eikonoklastes* and Algernon Sidney his *Discourses Concerning Government*. Williams viewed the people as the source of political authority: God had not granted anyone control over another's conscience; thus men were not empowered to grant each other this authority. Certainly men do not gather in civil society to have their consciences regulated. "The fountain and original of all authority and rule," he was later to declare in *The Examiner Defended,* "is the People consenting and agreeing in their several combinations by themselves or their deputies, for their better subsistence."

For Williams civil government was the people's servant rather than master. In June, 1636, he founded the community of Providence as a "shelter for persons distressed for conscience"; through its Social Compact he required its settlers and joiners to accept all laws arrived at by majority consent —but "only in civil things." Rhode Island's constitution is the first recorded American civil document not only tolerating but also recognizing the legality of all religions and absolute liberty of conscience. Most Puritan leaders exhibited little tolerance toward their Jewish contemporaries, but Williams, although cautiously, could state:

> I humbly conceive it to be the duty of the civil magistrates to break down that superstitious wall of separation . . . between the Gentiles and the Jews, and freely without their asking to make way for their free and peaceable habitation amongst us.

Williams' attitude paved the way for later recognition of Jewish civil rights in Rhode Island as well as in all American colonies.

Williams saw his principles again take tangible form in

1647, when Rhode Island's first general assembly adopted a legal code restricted to civil matters and promising all men freedom of conscience and worship.

Shortly after their difficulties with Williams, the Massachusetts Bay inhabitants became divided over the "heresies" of Anne Hutchinson. Like Williams, Mrs. Hutchinson and her followers were purged (in 1638) and the theocracy maintained, but the resultant bitterness lingered long. The Quaker persecutions followed, and New England remained turbulent. Loud rumblings of discontent were sounded in the 1650's. Many among the nonelect and unfranchised were prospering with slight regard for relating work and worship. Seeing little connection between eternal salvation and the right to vote, they were growing dissatisfied with the elect's ecclesiastical and political domination; they were becoming aware of the Enlightenment, the Royal Society, and the ideas of Newton and Locke, Pascal and Descartes.

The Puritans, who had transformed a wilderness into fertile farms, expanding villages, and thriving towns, now were anxious to preserve their gains by stringent laws and regulations and a proper reading of the Bible. At about the time when the Puritan Commonwealth in England was collapsing, the New Haven court could reject a nonfreeman group's demand for extension of the franchise with the declaration that it couldn't commit "weighty civil or military trusts into the hands of either a crafty Achitophell or a bloody Joab." Those suggesting such a procedure were to be considered "troublers of our peace and disturbers of our Israell," for to grant nonchurch members the vote would be to defeat the holy commonwealth's main end, from "which we cannot be persuaded to divert."

But in falling back upon biblical laws the Puritans failed to consider more than 3,000 years of social evolution and to realize that Hebrew law could not be reapplied without considerable modification. Nor did they realize that despite its apparent severities the Mosaic code was relatively mild when compared to preceding and contemporary laws.

During the seventeenth century's last decades the Bible commonwealth's failure became all too clear. By then the church's direct power over the state had faded, although the pulpit's political influence—now aimed at the people—was far from dead. It was simply limited and indirect. And the ministers had still much to say about New England's religious life—as the witch trials indicate. The elders had suffered defeat principally because they had set themselves against those "natural instincts" that couldn't be suppressed permanently. They had chosen to ignore until too late the nonelect's growing unrest and economic power. Those few Puritan leaders who had advocated greater tolerance and equality had been quickly purged. The rising note of desperation in sermons echoed clearly the changing times, revealing a growing awareness of imminent theocratic failure and the need for some form of compromise.

It was a painful admission. Professor Perry Miller states that the sermons "tell the story, and tell it coherently, of a society . . . founded by men dedicated . . . to . . . eternal and immutable principles—and which progressively became involved with fishing, trade, and settlement." Economic necessity had forced the Puritans to adopt a liberal land policy, granting newcomers large tracts to encourage settlement. Immigrants from England, the West Indies, and the other American colonies streamed in. These newcomers contributed much to New England's economic prosperity, but they also weakened its intellectual and moral unity.

Time and change were against the Puritans. Rationalism, liberalism, and individualism were to guide the approaching eighteenth century. These principles the unyielding Puritans found extremely distasteful. Compromise did not come easily to them, and their belated attempts were futile.

Actually, the roots of secular individualism were embodied in Puritanism itself, in its concern for the individual's spiritual and moral well-being. The very industry and zeal so strongly advocated by the pulpit wrecked that Puritan class structure that had assumed that "men would remain forever in the stations to which they were born, and inferiors would eternally bow to gentlemen and scholars." The witch trials were the old guard's last desperate act. Calvin's ideas and words would be heard again in those of Jonathan Edwards and the revivalists, but these men would dominate individuals rather than communities. In 1691 the king issued a new charter for Massachusetts; it instituted a royal governor and a representative assembly. More significantly, the charter based the right to vote on property holdings rather than church membership and promised all Protestants religious freedom.

The charter merely culminated the series of successive Puritan setbacks that were marked by the general struggle for representative government, the specific heresies of Roger

Williams and Anne Hutchinson, the Quaker persecutions, the loss of the original Massachusetts Bay Charter, and the witchcraft scandals. Like Virginia, Massachusetts Bay was now a crown colony, and the Bible commonwealth was legally destroyed.

NEW NEW ENGLAND CONCEPTS As the eighteenth century began, the Boston merchants—long a patient buffer between clergy and lower classes—tipped the scales against their former allies. Merchant Thomas Brattle, for example, was the major organizer in 1698 of Boston's liberal Brattle Street Church, in which a public description of religious experience was not required for membership. With William, his minister brother, Brattle led the fight to break the Mather hold upon Harvard College. In 1701 Increase Mather was forced to resign the college presidency. The clerical autocracy's unchallenged power was officially terminated.

More in keeping with the new century's intellectual realism were clergyman John Wise's liberal views. Discerning ecclesiastical parallels in every type of civil administration, Wise concluded that the form most basic to civil and church government was clearly democracy. "Government was never established by God or nature," he declared, "to give one man a prerogative to insult over another."

Historians have pointed out that the strivings and sufferings of such religious reformers as Roger Williams and Anne Hutchinson—and of such minorities as the Baptists and Quakers—had been far from futile. The very ideas of religious freedom for which they had been persecuted were accepted and advocated not only by Wise—whose liberal *Vindication of the Government* (1717) was constantly reprinted, becoming "one of the bibles of the American Revolution"—but by Thomas Jefferson and other political leaders who would inscribe them upon the Declaration of Independence and Constitution.

Thus seventeenth-century Bible Puritanism—directly and indirectly—prepared eighteenth-century America for such cataclysmic social and intellectual changes as the separation of church and state, the evolving of an optimistic view of human nature, and the spread of democratic liberalism.

The enlightened eighteenth-century American no longer thought of himself as Puritan. He was interested in rationalizing away Puritan theology and discovering a new secular basis for individual freedom. He envisioned a nation dedicated to such principles. Yet while he strove for increased individualism and although he rejected Puritan theology, he retained many of Puritanism's values and basic beliefs. Above all, the American rationalist retained the Puritan dependence upon the Bible.

When England began encroaching upon colonial liberties, the political leaders—as might be expected of enlightened rationalists—pursued at first a course of logic and reason. They petitioned the king and Parliament for relief in accord with established English principles of right and justice. This failing, they resorted to force to defend their liberty and property. Their goal was the Englishman's acknowledged constitutional rights secured in the Bloodless Revolution of 1688 and guarded jealously by the House of Commons. But as mere "crown dependencies" within a mercantile structure, the colonies lacked both parliamentary representation and an official instrument for redress of grievances. They possessed only that restricted and unspecified liberty the English enjoyed before achieving their bill of rights.

The arrogant, slow-witted George III proved uncooperative, choosing to follow James I and Archbishop Laud in insisting upon his divine right and demanding the colonists' unlimited submission. The colonists, in pressing for greater political freedom, attempted to give their arguments as much scriptural authority as possible, hoping in this way to gain the support—at home and abroad—of those to whom the Bible was an infallible political, as well as religious, authority.

The Old Testament continued to be New England's prime source for sermons, letters, civil documents, and political pamphlets. Though ideological, political, and social changes had destroyed Puritanism's theological domination, its moral code—the Bible—proved amazingly durable and influential. Preachers continued to preach from Scripture, and congregations continued to listen. The New England theocracy no longer existed as a political or social force, but it persisted in the popular mind, even becoming the basis for the brief Puritan revival known as the Great Awakening.

It would be difficult to exaggerate the pulpit's part in stirring up and maintaining the growing anti-England agitation. To ministerial eyes the increasing political differences seemed a continuation of ancient Israel's struggles against her idolatrous neighbors. Most early Americans had no source of information or knowledge other than the pulpit. Newspapers were few. Books were expensive. Many could not read. The pulpit constituted a vital and direct intellectual force.

New England had been the center for seventeenth-century Puritanism's religious and political conservatism. It proved to be home also for the eighteenth century's revolutionary religious and political concepts. Here in the early 1700's evolved a liberal outlook and tenets quite different from the rigid dogmas of the Winthrops, Endecotts, Cottons, Davenports, and the Mathers. Yet the basic Puritan values survived. And new churches were built "on the old rock." Indeed, New England's strong moral and religious tradition attracted and stimulated the newly developing religious and political movements.

In Boston, the fiery Sam Adams and other early revolutionaries started their political agitations. Here abolitionists, Unitarians, and Christian Scientists first flourished. In this most Protestant of communities America's second largest Roman Catholic population was to develop. Here, in the new century's opening years, evolved those affirmations of man's "new dignity" later to find their way into the Declaration of Independence. Such phrases as "nature's laws," "nature's God," "equality," "unalienable right," and "life, liberty, and happiness" were common in the Boston churches well before the Revolution.

But the Bible remained the prime political and judicial authority. Led by their clergy, the New Englanders discussed and debated, analyzed and interpreted the divine law. These tough-minded New England ministers were no mere pulpit orators. They were distinguished scholars and active patriots and legislators. They had encouraged New England to support the English Revolution of 1640 with preachers, soldiers, and supplies for Cromwell's armies. They had given asylum to three of the tyrannicides. They had lent their voices to the spirit of the Bloodless Revolution of 1688. Now they placed themselves in the forefront of American Revolutionary events by opposing absolutism and by loudly advocating colonial separation from England.

Utilizing biblical phraseology, imagery, and concepts whenever possible, they made resistance—and ultimately independence and war—"a sacred duty" for a people who were still, on the whole, religious. They pointed to the Hebrew commonwealth as irrefutable evidence that "Rebellion to Tyrants is obedience to God" and that the divine preference was clearly for democracy. "No one can fully understand the American Revolution and the American constitutional system," states A. M. Baldwin, a recent commentator, "without a realization of the long history and religious associations which lie back of [them] . . . without realizing that for a hundred years before the Revolution men were taught that these rights were protected by divine, inviolable law."

The hostile charge that the colonial leadership's masterstroke was gaining the clergy's support was obviously true. The effect upon the aroused audience must have been striking indeed as they heard the ideas and principles voiced by their political leaders repeated on Sundays from the pulpit in deeply religious terms and the most solemn tones.

Thus did New England's ministers, in the century preceding the American Revolution, lend divine authority to contemporary political concepts. No matter what individual phraseology or arguments were used, the inevitable conclusion of countless sermons and pamphlets was that government should be established by the people and subject to its consent. For between leaders and people there existed a natural "compact." Had not the Hebrew commonwealth, the ministers asked, rested on compact? Were not New England's theology, church structure, city charters, and town covenants essentially compacts? Was not the compact idea to be found in the writings of the best minds, past and present?

Magistrates and people thus were bound by a divine law designed to safeguard individual rights and liberty. Acting in majority, the people were empowered to alter the law and to select leaders whose actions were limited and who could be removed for a moral or legal infraction. So rather than being able to please themselves, the leaders were to devote themselves to a careful study of God's law, "both natural and revealed," as described in the Bible. Even when dealing directly with the Hebrews, had not God instructed the leaders to record the law so that it could be constantly reread?

These principles were actually Locke and Rousseau's social contract given religious context and justification; for this reason they carried considerable weight even with the most secular-minded. That they were sometimes ignored in practice and difficult to attain made them all the more attractive. Thus did Puritan theology take on political coloration. In the years preceding, during, and following the Revolution, the Boston pulpits resounded to ringing defenses of "reason," "nature," and "freedom."

These views were not merely the shouts of excited patriots; they were rooted in the previous century's religious convictions. The clergy had from the American settlement's beginnings equated God, state, and nature. John Davenport, for example, had declared civil rule to be "God's Ordinance" which, in turn, equals "the Law of Nature." And, as men are "combined in Family-Society," he had reasoned, they also are necessarily "joyned in a Civil-Society." These theories provided the eighteenth-century clergy with a well-established precedent for deriving political theories from nature and Scripture. If some among them differed in their interpretations, few questioned the authority of the Bible, or that civil and religious liberty constituted its all-pervasive theme. Nor did any find cause to doubt that a government, ruler, or administrator not devoted to the people nor protective of their inviolable rights lacked divine sanction.

It seemed clear to all that proper government secured the life, liberty, and prosperity God had ordained for man. Harvard's president, the Reverend Samuel Langdon, summed up the entire pre-Revolutionary climate when he declared, in 1759, that any political constitution protecting the people's life, liberty, and property was clearly in keeping with nature's laws and God's "perfect pattern."

The eighteenth-century intellectual and political changes did relatively little to diminish the Bible's influence. Both during the early colonial period and again in the exciting time preceding the break with the mother country, New England's ministers drew their civil creeds from biblical history. The biblical distaste for monarchy became increasingly important, providing as it did a religious justification for rebellion. Ironically enough, before British-colonial relations so deteriorated, both the Puritan and Anglican clergies in America had used the Bible to argue that "British patriotism was a Christian duty." The Dutch- and German-speaking Calvinists and Lutherans among the colonists had never harbored much enthusiasm for Britain, but still they were Protestants, with deep-rooted hatreds for Catholic France and Spain, the Empire's major enemies. So they had proved generally amenable to the views of their fellow Protestants. Now they could enter wholeheartedly into the pulpit's increasingly vociferous outcries against England.

As the gap widened between the two peoples, New England's ministers intensified their "political preaching." Most now rejected Cotton Mather's rigid theology, yet they still agreed with his view that New England's peculiar "ecclesiastical circumstances" required its ministers to engage in politics. And they continued to be active in all aspects of public life. Many were soon to serve in the various state legislatures and continental army, and almost all used their pulpits to denounce "unlimited submission and non-resistance" as slavish distortions of scriptural spirit and meaning. They quoted Moses, Joshua, Samuel, and various judges and prophets to emphasize God's sole monarchy. They bore down hard on the condemnation of human monarchy in Samuel. History testifies to the impression these ideas made upon American political leaders. The American Revolution's highest glory, John Quincy Adams later declared, was that it indissolubly connected civil and Christian principles.

Under the intellectual leadership of such vigorous firebrands as Jonathan Mayhew and Charles Chauncy, Boston became the headquarters for ardently progressive young Whigs and religious liberals. The Puritan concern with God's glory was transformed there into a moral and social concept. At Boston's West Church the first Mayhew, later described as "the Father of Civil and Religious liberty in Massachusetts and America," was infusing his theology with political radicalism and leavening his politics with theological arguments. For him true religion meant love of country and freedom, and hatred of tyrants and oppression.

As war drew closer, the churches (Quakers excepted) played their expected militant parts. Descendants of the colonizing Puritans proclaimed their allegiance to the "only king," the Almighty, and swore to defend His "Zion wilderness." (Anglicans were equally fervent in their exclamations of loyalty to the divinely appointed George.)

In an election sermon before Massachusetts Bay's third Provincial Congress, on May 31, 1775, the Reverend Samuel Langdon took for text Isaiah 1:26, "And I will restore thy judges as at the first." Revealing the additional influence of Algernon Sidney and John Milton, he declared:

The Jewish government, according to the original con-

stitution . . . was a perfect republic. . . . Let them who
cry up the divine right of kings consider that the only
form of government which had a proper claim to a
divine establishment was so far from including the idea
of a king, that it was a high crime for Israel to ask to
be in this respect like other nations; and when they were
gratified, it was . . . a just punishment for their folly . . .

He continued with a sentiment the Declaration of Independence was to echo the following year:

Every nation . . . has a right to set up over themselves
any form of government which . . . may appear most
conducive to their common welfare. The civil polity of
Israel is doubtless an excellent general model, allowing
for some peculiarities; at least, some principal laws and
orders of it may be copied. . . .

Langdon's sermon was printed and widely distributed among
the Massachusetts ministers and representatives.

On May 17, 1776, a national fast day, Presbyterian minister George Duffield, addressed a Philadelphia audience that
included John Adams. He compared George III to Egypt's
Pharaoh to emphasize that the same divine providence that
had freed the Israelites was favorably disposed toward the
colonies. Mayhew, in a Boston sermon, about a week later,
on the "Repeal of the Stamp Act," declared monarchy
"unbiblical and unHebraic."

God gave Israel a king (or absolute monarchy) in his
anger, because they had not sense and virtue enough to
like a free commonwealth, and to have himself for their
king,—where the spirit of the Lord is there is liberty,—
and if any miserable people on the continent or isles of
Europe be driven in their extremity to seek a safe retreat
from slavery in some far distant clime—O let them find
one in America.

The Reverend Samuel West delivered that year's election
sermon before the Massachusetts Bay Council and House of
Representatives on May 29. This was five weeks before the
Declaration of Independence. West—like Langdon—took
Isaiah 1:26 as his theme to insist "magistrates have no authority but what they derive from the people." West then
praised Jethro's advice that Moses appoint a council of

leaders, and concluded with David's statement that all who rule must do so "in the fear of God."

The Puritan clergy's Revolutionary role should have destroyed the false image of all Puritans as unfailing political reactionaries. Popular misconceptions, however, are a long time dying. Much more valid was the claim that the Declaration of Independence failed to assert any right that the New England clergy had not discussed before 1763—if not earlier. Years later, in 1822, John Adams restated this view. Apparently irritated by the acclaim accorded Jefferson's literary gifts, Adams wrote that the Declaration lacked one idea that had not "been hackneyed in Congress for two years before." Jefferson was quick to agree, asserting his intention had not been "to find out new principles" but to express the "American mind." The Declaration's authority, he added, rests on its "harmonizing sentiments of the day."

Not all colonials, however, favored rebellion. Feelings of being permanently linked to the mother country ran deep, and advocates of unqualified divine right and nonresistance were many. In addition to Virginia's numerous Anglican Church members, there were sizable and influential Episcopalian groups in New York, New Jersey, Maryland, and Pennsylvania. Other Loyalists were scattered throughout the New England colonies. Most of them gave their complete obedience to the Church of England, which had faithfully identified itself with the monarchy since the 1660 Restoration. In any event, the sermons of leading colonial clergymen definitely indicated that acceptance or rejection of divine right and nonresistance doctrines clearly separated Loyalists and Whigs.

One colorful exemplar of Loyalist sympathy was Jonathan Boucher, Anglican rector of St. Anne's in Annapolis. Boucher was loudly contemptuous of the doctrine of equality and the "demagogues and independents of the New England provinces"; he harbored special dislike for Philadelphia and that "old scoundrel Franklin." Believing himself in danger from the "republican demagogues," Boucher took to carrying two loaded pistols into the pulpit. It is doubtful that tears were shed on either side when the good Reverend Boucher returned to his native England.

A better known and more eloquent Tory sympathizer was John Wesley, Methodism's founder. His pamphlet *A Calm Address to American Colonies* (1775) heatedly reversed his earlier expressed sympathies for the colonial position and greatly embarrassed American Methodists. So great was the countering torrent of newspaper and magazine attacks that Wesley felt compelled to defend his new views in another pamphlet series.

Virginia was marked by many striking differences to the New England settlement. Her inhabitants were thoroughly Anglican, and her noted leading families—among others, those of Washington, Madison, Monroe, Randolph, Lee, and Jefferson—were of Cavalier ancestry. Lacking New England's "theocratic impulse," American Anglicanism proved more moderate and more theologically susceptible to liberalizing geographic, economic, and social influences. But it remained politically rigid. Exemplifying Loyalist sympathies, it reached its lowest point, naturally enough, during the Revolution. James Madison, himself an Anglican communicant, wrote a friend in 1774 that if the Church of England had prevailed in the northern colonies, subjection would have resulted for all and an American Revolution would have been highly unlikely. It is evident revolutionary ideals and zeal in Virginia were kindled by and among dissenters from the Anglican Church.

MONARCHY OR REPUBLIC   Those Congregationalist and Presbyterian clergymen who were the first to hold up the Bible as a political model for their countrymen were widely imitated by legislators and political pamphleteers during the frenetic period preceding the Constitution. And no single pamphleteer did more to combat the widespread monarchical tendencies than the much maligned but highly effective Thomas Paine. Others had discredited the British Parliament. Paine set himself to severing the one significant symbol still linking colonies and motherland—the monarchy. Thousands among the New World's settlers long since had repudiated kingship; yet other thousands still viewed it as sacred. To them its rejection seemed the rejection of God. Fully aware of this almost unconscious identification of king and God, Paine turned to Scripture to destroy both monarchical sympathies and resultant guilt feelings. He knew most Puritan descendants, despite their proclaimed worldliness and sophistication, would be most moved by scriptural sanction.

Paine expressed his antimonarchical views in *Common Sense,* basing his argument upon the Hebrew commonwealth:

> Government by kings was first introduced into the world by the Heathen, from whom the children of Israel copied the custom. It was the most prosperous invention the Devil ever set on foot for a promotion of idolatry. . . . As the exalting one man so greatly above the rest cannot be justified on the equal rights of nature, so neither can it be defended on the authority of scripture; for the will of the Almighty as declared by Gideon, and the prophet Samuel, expressly disapproves of government by kings.

Paine recounts the story, often repeated by the American rebels, of Gideon's victory over the Midianites and the manner in which the grateful Hebrews requested that Gideon and his posterity rule over them. Gideon not only declined the crown, Paine emphasizes, but he denied the people's right to offer it. He informed them instead: "The Lord shall rule over you." God's meaning cannot be misunderstood or reinterpreted, insists Paine: "That the Almighty hath here entered his protest against monarchical government is true, or the scripture is false." Paine proceeds with a detailed and critical commentary of hereditary succession, the English monarchy since the Norman Conquest, and the present English government. He concludes: "Why is the constitution of England sickly, but because monarchy hath poisoned the Republic; the Crown hath engrossed the Commons." He then states:

> In England a King hath little more to do than to make war and give away places; which, in plain terms, is to empoverish the nation and set it together by the ears. A pretty business indeed for a man to be allowed eight hundred thousand sterling a year for, and worshipped into the bargain! Of more worth is one honest man to society, and in the sight of God, than all the crowned ruffians that ever lived.

The instantaneous success of *Common Sense* meant a crushing setback for American monarchists. Its repeated emphasis of the biblical deprecation of monarchy convinced many that kingship was essentially criminal, that it invaded divine and human prerogatives.

Paine's voice was echoed by others; together these well-timed voices prepared the country for a formal separation from Britain. Paine's effectiveness did not mean all monarchical tendencies were dead. But they did become dormant, and the New England clergy and its Bible retained their influence with the Continental Congress at a time when that body was still extremely vulnerable and in need of authority.

Biblical influence took many forms. Twenty-five years before the signing of the Declaration of Independence, in 1751, Philadelphia's citizens designated one Isaac Norris to purchase and inscribe a bell to hang in the steeple of the Pennsylvania Colony's State House. Norris turned to Scripture for his inscription, choosing "Proclaim liberty throughout all the land unto all the inhabitants thereof." Thus was America's Liberty Bill stamped with a proclamation from Leviticus 25:10.

On the day the Declaration was adopted, July 4, 1776, a committee consisting of Franklin, Adams, and Jefferson was appointed to prepare a design for a seal of the new United States. The committee submitted artist Benjamin Lossing's depiction of its recommendations. For the seal's reverse side it proposed a crowned Pharaoh, sword in hand, in a speeding chariot, hotly pursuing the fleeing Israelites through the Red Sea's parted waves. On the shore, an illuminated Moses with outstretched hands causes the sea to overwhelm the Egyptians. Underneath, the motto read: "Resistance to tyrants is obedience to God." Jefferson had also suggested a portrayal of the wandering Israelites "led by a cloud by day and a pillar of fire by night."

The committee's proposed design for the seal's obverse side included a crest displaying "the Eye of Providence in a radiant Triangle whose Glory extends from the Shield and beyond the Figures." When the seal was finally adopted in 1782, only the "Eye of Providence" was retained, to signify the numerous "inter positions of providence in favour of the American cause."

The Declaration of Independence itself was both an expression of political grievances against monarchical tyranny and a justification of colonial behavior—a justification based upon those "fundamental rights of man," as Oscar Straus put it, "which were as old as the Bible," having been asserted repeatedly "from the days of Moses until the Declaration was published to the world."

Both clergy and Scripture continued to exert an influence upon the new republic's political leaders, especially upon the Constitution's framers, who were searching diligently for appropriate governmental models. The republican form of government enjoyed little prestige in the eighteenth century. Not only had the English commonwealth culminated in the return of the Stuarts, but most of the small continental republics were—like Venice—actually oligarchies, and the United Provinces of the Low Countries were declining rapidly.

During this crucial period New England's clergy, in arguing a republican form of government, continued to impress upon Congress the importance of Scripture's moral and political principles. Clergymen served as delegates in the various state conventions as these bodies evolved their own constitutional compacts. Most were ardent Federalists favoring the rapid drafting and ratification of a strong federal Constitution and the establishment of a dominant central government.

The clergy's continued political participation during and after the Revolution, understandably enough, was viewed variously. The first provincial Congress of Massachusetts officially acknowledged the public indebtedness to the ministers for championing civil and religious liberty, and asked their assistance "in avoiding the dreadful slavery with which we are now threatened." But by the century's end Jeffersonian liberals in the same state were insisting the ministers stop their attempts to govern and stick to their preaching.

New England's churchmen unquestionably were often overly zealous in political matters. But Puritanism, it should be remembered, was a Reformation phenomenon. And the Reformation represented, among other things, a return to Old Testament and early Christian democracy. Both the Hebraic and early Church writings embodied principles of liberty and rejection of absolutism.

In fact, a close look at the Hebrew commonwealth reveals many striking similarities to the American republic and helps to explain why the former was so much cited during and after the revolutionary period by political leaders and pamphleteers, as well as ministers. Some form of autonomous representative government prevailed among the Hebrews even during the Egyptian enslavement. For when Moses was sent from Midian to deliver God's message to the children of Israel, he was instructed to "go and gather the *elders* of

Israel together" and to approach Pharaoh as a representative delegation. And his first significant act after having led the Israelites through the Red Sea was to separate church, state, and military, delegating authority to those leaders chosen by the people. "Choose wise, understanding, and experienced men, according to your tribes," he told the multitude, "and I will appoint them as your heads."

The suggestion met general approval; judges were selected for merit rather than any form of hereditary distinction. In words that were to echo and reecho through seventeenth- and eighteenth-century America, Moses charged these judges to "Hear the cases between your brethren, and judge righteously between a man and his brother or the alien that is with him. You shall not be partial in judgment; you shall hear the small and the great alike; you shall not be afraid of the face of man, for the judgment is God's."

In Canaan the law was promulgated again, with the people confirming Joshua as chief executive. In time Joshua was succeeded by a series of fourteen judges, beginning with Othniel and ending with Samuel. These judges were elected and summoned to power by the people whenever the need arose. Military as well as judicial and political leaders, they served as long as the emergency persisted and then returned to their own occupation. The most notable judge in the eyes of America's Revolutionary leaders was Gideon, who, having successfully crushed the Midianite invaders, refused the people's offer of a crown.

Hebrew government, as established under Moses and perpetuated by the judges, bore a strong resemblance to the American federal system. All local affairs were under an elected tribal (or state) group, which sent elected representatives to the central governing body. As God—rather than a king—was the embodiment of the law and the source of all authority, this government has been termed both theocracy and commonwealth.

The central or national body was divided into three parts. The first consisted of the judge or chief executive, who was both chief magistrate and military commander in chief. He summoned the popular assemblies, suggested subjects for discussion, presided at the meeting, and executed all subsequent resolutions.

To balance the chief executive's power and to divide administrative responsibility, the Hebrews elected a senate, or Sanhedrin, of seventy elders. The Sanhedrin seems to have combined both a legislative and judicial function, being similar in some respects to the American Senate and Supreme Court.

The third governmental branch was the popular assembly. The scriptural text does not indicate definitely the assembly's characteristics and size, referring to it repeatedly as the "congregation" and merely differentiating between it and "all Israel."

Ironically, the Hebrew republic was not subverted by external forces or unscrupulous leaders, but by the people themselves exercising their democratic prerogative to establish a new government of their choice, which was monarchy. Thus was Saul chosen and the commonwealth terminated. Yet despite their personal loss, the Hebrews had established a historical precedent.

The Hebrew commonwealth fired the imagination of many seventeenth- and eighteenth-century historians and political theorists but none more than that of Algernon Sidney, whose *Discourses Concerning Government* served as our government founders' "chief text-book" and whose works were in the libraries of Franklin, Adams, and Jefferson, among others. Sidney concluded his analysis of the Hebrew commonwealth by praising its democratic principles:

> Having seen what government God did not ordain, it may be reasonable to examine the Nature of the Government which he did ordain; and we shall easily find that it consisted of three parts, besides the Magistrats of the several Tribes and Citys. They had a chief Magistrat, who was call'd Judg or Captain, as *Joshua, Gideon,* and others; a Council of seventy chosen men; and the General Assemblys of the People.

> The first was merely occasional. . . . The second is known by the name of the Great *Sanhedrin,* which, being instituted by *Moses* according to the command of God, continu'd till they were all save one slain by *Herod.* And the third part, which is the Assembly of the People, was so common, that none can be ignorant of it, but such as never look'd into the Scripture.

Those American leaders who did not turn directly to the Bible for intellectual inspiration were exposed to its political doctrines from a source they could not help but respect: the country's outstanding pulpit orators. One such was Dr. Ezra

Stiles, Yale College president and Ben Franklin's lifelong friend, who delivered a memorable election sermon on May 8, 1783, before the Connecticut General Assembly. Stiles traced the theory of government from the Hebrew commonwealth to his own day to prove that the "American Israel" represented the culmination of popular government and the fulfillment of biblical prophecy. He was certain the Hebrew democratic experience was prophetic of America's future prosperity and splendor.

This concern with God's role in contemporary political and civil events extended far beyond New England—although always in a different form. For despite their eminence, the Puritan clergymen obviously would have had little effect had not their repeated allusions to early Hebrew concern with political liberty evoked a significant and immediate response throughout the colonies.

Indeed, an insistence upon increased individual religious freedom long had enveloped the entire nation. For a decade Virginia had been passing laws successively broadening the citizens' religious privileges. In 1776 the Virginia Convention had adopted a bill of rights declaring "All men . . . entitled to the full and free exercise of religion, according to the dictates of conscience." Shortly afterwards, the legislature exempted dissenters from supporting the established Anglican Church or its clergy. Dissenting ministers were empowered in 1780 to perform marriages, and four years later all laws favoring the Episcopal Church were invalidated. And in 1786, while its author was in France, the Virginia legislature passed Thomas Jefferson's Statute of Religious Freedom, proclaiming that "Almighty God hath created the mind free." The standard of religious liberty established by the Virginia statute was the highest then to be found in any North American colony except Rhode Island. Other states later would attain this standard also, but usually only after bitter and prolonged opposition.

WASHINGTON AND GIDEON The Revolutionary struggle for civil and religious liberty was a difficult one. Many disillusioning experiences occurred even with military victory

in sight. The political and economic confusion during the
Revolution's closing days seemed to call for desperate measures. One movement, initiated among the military, centered
around the idea of an American monarchy—with Washington as the throne's occupant. These military leaders demanded a government that would scrap the ineffectual Articles of Confederation, revive the public credit, pay interest
on the public debt, pay the impoverished soldiers, and regain
public confidence. A strong government was needed urgently,
they argued, and for them the answer lay in an elective
monarchy.

A document embodying their views was drawn up and
presented to Washington by Colonel Nicola, a veteran officer
respected by the general. The document stated that the war
having been concluded successfully, many among the military
shared a general uneasiness at the state of current affairs and
a desire to establish a strong central government. It then
summarized the known government structures, declaring the
republican form to be the most uncertain and a constitutional
monarchy, like England's, the most secure. It offered Washington absolute political control, but concluded: "Owing to
the prejudice of the people it might not at first be prudent
to assume the title of Royalty, but if all other things were
adjusted, we believe strong arguments might be produced
for admitting the title of King."

The parallel to the offering of a crown to Gideon, the
Hebrew judge and general, is apparent, and, like Gideon,
Washington rejected the offer. But monarchical sympathies—
shared by some Federal Party leaders—were strong enough
to last through the Constitution's adoption and the Washington and Adams administrations, dying out only about the
time Jefferson was elected to the presidency.

In one form or another, then, the Declaration and Constitution writers, as well as the majority of the nation's early
political leaders, were exposed constantly to the Bible's underlying political concepts. "Perhaps it does not often occur
to readers of the Old Testament," historian Henry Field has
stated, "that there is much likeness between the Hebrew
Commonwealth and the American republic. . . . At the bottom there is one radical principle that divides a republic from
a monarchy or an aristocracy, and that is the natural equality
of men . . . which is as fully recognized in the laws of Moses
as in the Declaration of Independence."

The Declaration made clear that man-made governments

are not supreme powers unto themselves, that their actions and laws are accountable always to a still higher power. Government's function is merely to "secure" those "unalienable rights" with which their Creator has endowed each individual. Noteworthy is the Declaration's mixture of biblical and deistic influences: it holds that "the laws of nature and nature's God" constitute a supreme law binding on all human government, a law men are morally obligated to uphold and defend even against the encroachments of their own government.

Seventeenth- and eighteenth-century clergymen emphasized in their sermons the underlying unity of God, nature, and reason. They were convinced nature's laws were as truly divine as those of Scripture and exhibited as clearly God's "intelligence." Many deistic Congressional leaders were not disposed to attend church and listen to sermons. But their thorough acquaintance with England's seventeenth-century Parliamentary struggles and with eighteenth-century English literature led them to the God-nature equation.

Jefferson, for instance, expressed himself as having no doubt that nature's "laws" and "God's will" were identical. "Why should I go in search of Moses to find out what God has said to Jean Jacques Rousseau?" he asked. Was not God to be seen in the natural beauties surrounding man? "The eighteenth century did not abandon the old effort to share in the mind of God," Professor Carl Becker states. "It only went about it with greater confidence, and had at last the presumption to think that the infinite mind of God and the finite mind of man were one and the same thing." Many religious and political leaders were so offended by the Constitution's omission of God's name that they helped delay its adoption in some states. Other religious leaders, however, defended the omission. They apparently believed—as had those Sanhedrin members who had defended its omission in the Book of Esther—that God was revealed in many ways other than the word, particularly in the Constitution's ideals of liberty, justice, and equality.

When the Constitution came up for adoption in the state legislatures, it was attacked and defended on various grounds. In New York, Alexander Hamilton, James Madison, and John Jay joined together to produce a series of eighty-five persuasive essays, now known as *The Federalist Papers,* in which they urged the Constitution's ratification as a means of preserving the cherished American ideals of government and liberty. Others chose to utilize the Bible's familiar appeal, drawing analogies to the Hebrew commonwealth as the original model of popular government and commenting unfailingly upon the ultimate Hebrew error of seeking a desperate solution for social difficulties in a human monarch.

Benjamin Franklin, in a letter he headed "A Comparison of the Conduct of the Ancient Jews, and of the Anti-Federalists in the United States of America," underlined the difficulty of getting men to accept a constitution, any constitution. Even "if an angel from heaven was to bring down a constitution formed there for our use," he declares sadly, "it would nevertheless meet with violent opposition." That was Israel's experience, he points out. God himself presented to his chosen servant, Moses, before the assembled tribes, a constitution and law code. Instead of being welcomed by all, the constitution was criticized by "some discontented, restless spirits" who were moved by "various motives." From this example, Franklin concludes, "We may gather that popular opposition to a public measure is no proof of its impropriety, even though the opposition be excited and headed by men of distinction."

It was extremely ironic that the members of the Old World's three great established churches—Episcopal Lutheran, and Roman Catholic—found themselves transformed into New World dissenters. Yet if the American churches were less tolerant of human shortcomings than these older ecclesiastical bodies, their intolerance was more likely, in a surprisingly short time, to take the form of self-discipline rather than restrictive laws. Post-Reformation diversity combined with Puritan individualism and with frontier democracy to generate such numerous sects that an imposed uniformity became impossible by the early-nineteenth century. Out of this proliferation of creeds evolved a religious attitude recognizing the individual's spiritual dignity and his right of private choice.

A Protestant established church involves a contradiction. Protestantism implies an open Bible, a participating laity, and the privilege of individual judgment. This is true especially of American Protestantism, for during and after the Revolution the various state governments abolished the privileged or established churches. The Revolutionary War thus confirmed America's distinctive religious character. The Revolutionary period was marked, said Connecticut clergyman Horace

Bushnell, by "Protestantism in religion producing republicanism in government."

Three: Law

LAW
AND THE BIBLE

THE PURITAN VENTURE IN LAW Early America insisted on formulating not only its political principles according to scriptural precedent, but its legal principles as well. Its citizens often rejected English civil or common law to turn instead to the Pentateuch. They cited biblical chapter and verse in framing their criminal codes and in administering justice.

The seven hundred Puritans who disembarked at Massachusetts Bay in June, 1630, joined John Endecott's earlier and enlarged Salem contingent to form a community of over a thousand. About two hundred of these considered themselves "saints," or divinely elected leaders; their self-appointed task was to establish and maintain a cohesive religious commonwealth. From their ranks, as the flock's elders, were to be selected the clergy who would provide spiritual guidance and the magistrates who would impose God's law upon the rebellious—or even the questioning.

The Puritan elders determined to attain in the New World the Protestant ideal of a unified church and state. They were convinced that their government had to assume not only the usual civil obligations but also protection of the church by enforcement of all ecclesiastical decrees. This total preservation of orthodoxy implied suppression of domestic heresy or rebellion and rejection of English interference. Hence American Puritans soon concluded they had to be free of English ordinances and instead rely heavily upon biblical law.

The proprietory Massachusetts Bay Company's structure lent itself to their plans. It was a joint-stock company administered by a governor, deputy governor, and board of eighteen assistants. According to the king's charter, all twenty were to be selected annually by the company's stockholders or freemen. The officers, board members, and freemen constituted the General Court, which was to meet quarterly to appoint new members and establish laws for governing the land and the inhabitants within its jurisdiction. The charter's prime stipulation was that such laws not be "contrarie or repugnant" to England's laws and statutes. In addition to the General Court, the governor, deputy governor, and assistants formed an executive board, or Court of Assistants, that was to meet at least once a month.

Upon their arrival in New England the General Court and Court of Assistants were almost identical. But it soon became clear that others would have to be admitted to the status of freemen and given a voice in the General Court. The elders acted immediately to forestall this. At its first meeting in the New World, the Court of Assistants gave six of its members the powers of English justices of the peace. Two months later, in October, 1630, the General Court voted the assistants (or "magistrates," as they now were called) authority to select the governor and deputy governor, and to formulate and administer all laws they deemed necessary to the colony's well-being.

In other words, the handful of Puritan elders, acting for the entire General Court, took it upon themselves to relinquish most of the court's legal powers to an even smaller number selected from among themselves. They seem to have been little bothered that they were violating the king's charter. Yet many of these men later were to fall back repeatedly upon the charter to justify actions taken independently of the British government.

In September, 1630, the Court of Assistants announced that no one would be allowed to settle at Massachusetts Bay without its expressed permission, and some months later extended this to anyone trying to leave. A series of expulsions followed. Within six years at least twenty persons incurring the elders' displeasure had been banished. One unfortunate, Phillip Ratcliffe, was whipped, heavily fined, and had his ears removed before he was banished "for uttering mallitious & scandulous speeches against the government & the church of Salem." There was no appeal from the magistrates' decisions.

The elders had acted none too soon. By the spring of 1631 a number of colonists had attained the status of freemen and had become part of the General Court. Thereafter the General Court's membership and that of the Court of Assistants were no longer identical. Yet until 1634 approximately a dozen carefully chosen individuals controlled trade and industry by fixing prices and wages and by settling civil suits. They dispensed justice for manslaughter, theft, and fraud, and determined punishment for idleness, drunkenness, and the *reported* use of tobacco, dice, or cards.

An even more important decision made at the same spring session kept much of the colony's political and legal powers in the hands of the elders for many years. No one, it was decided, could become a freeman without meeting the rigid requirements of church membership. Since only a small part of even the more devout Puritans could meet these standards, the franchise was still seriously limited. Out of a population in 1641 of about fifteen thousand, approximately thirteen hundred men—or eight percent of the populace—could vote. Such a religious qualification for political membership was a further violation of the royal charter.

The people, however, had not voyaged to a new continent to accept the civil tyranny of fellow settlers. Whenever the magistrates pushed their authority too far—that is, beyond the limits of traditional English political and legal principles —the people, through their deputies, were quick to voice displeasure and frequently to block them. In spite of the magistrates' stubborn opposition, the number of freemen increased considerably within the first few years. In May, 1634, their selected delegates (or deputies) from the various towns appeared at the General Court and forced several significant constitutional changes. The deputies would participate thereafter in the selection and admission of freemen, election of community officers, formulation of laws, and raising of taxes and dispensing of revenues. Furthermore, the deputies were to participate in the four General Courts to be held every year.

In this, and in many other instances, New England's settlers indicated the traditional English desire for the legal security inherent in precedent, custom, and record. In fact, before leaving England the Bay Company leaders had stated their intention to impose law and order as nearly in accordance to English law as possible. But they quickly changed their minds in New England, as they realized the value of having judicial freedom of action. The leaders now argued that England's laws were unsuitable for the new colony's special conditions and were therefore invalid, and they tried hard to delay codifying any laws. But the freemen quickly expressed their fear of a small group of judges creating and

administering justice without being bound by English statute.
A lengthy tug-of-war followed, with the magistrates turning
increasingly to Scripture for legal precedent.

In the religious area the magistrates were more successful
at having their own way. Here the people generally acceded
to the magistrates' superior spiritual insights and knowledge
—particularly when these were supported by the clergy. For
their part, the magistrates considered political setbacks relatively unimportant if they alone, or with ministerial consent,
could punish religious offenders as they saw fit. To have been
denied this privilege would have jeopardized not only their
interpretation of God's divine plan but the biblical state's
success.

Again, this did not mean the magistrates could ignore
those liberal principles for which Puritans had fought in
England. Under no circumstances could the leadership use
oaths, torture, or other harsh methods to compel incriminat-
ing testimony from accused persons. Nor were mere rumors
of religious corruption adequate grounds for punishment.
Indeed, the magistrates usually wisely overlooked private and
quietly held opinions, no matter how heretical, choosing to
punish only for those publicly espoused. But if a nonbeliever
persisted in making himself obnoxious by a stubborn refusal
to relinquish harmful doctrines, the magistrates were not
inclined to be light-handed. Heresy, after all, was considered
as serious a crime as murder, representing a refusal to accept
God's decree as put forth in Scripture.

The Bay settlement was essentially a Puritan venture, and
therefore founded not only upon the king's charter but upon
the Bible's universal laws—laws that to the Puritan mind
could be extended and applied to every circumstance. This
practice had a long tradition. The Bible had exerted considerable influence upon English legal precedent since the
Middle Ages; both the medieval scholastics and later Reformation theologians viewed Scripture as the prime source of
moral, ethical, and religious law. During Mary Tudor's
Catholic reign, those English Protestants fleeing to Geneva
witnessed Calvin's civil application of biblical concepts, and
later Calvin's Scottish followers embodied in Scotland's law
the sexual restrictions of Leviticus 18.

The American Puritans had brought with them, in addition, a Congregational tradition of legalism advocating biblical authorization for every act. English Puritans and Sep-
aratists had both struggled for years to convince their coun-

trymen that Scripture's fundamental law was the surest means of realizing the divine will. In the New World the Congregational Puritans quickly established the idea that the Bible not only ordained their governmental structure and regulated its activities but provided a written and unalterable constitution. The churches, having a mere ministerial or "stewardly" power, were only to publish, execute, and enforce the holy ordinances.

Convinced of their divine mandate, the Bay elders determined to attain uniformity. For them scriptural rulings needed only to be "reinforced by the enlightened dictation of godly magistrates" to serve as the community's practical religious and legal guide. No other source was needed, they argued, nor was more than one interpretation admissible. Anyone disagreeing with this view was of necessity a heretic.

Yet the Bible was never the American Puritan's sole legal resource, for although he refused to be bound by England's statutes, he still remained a product of his rich English heritage and its intricate legal codes. In fact, to understand the early stirrings of New England law, it is necessary to dismiss several popular misconceptions.

The first is that New England law was derived solely from the Bible. Despite the Bay Colony leaders' heavy reliance upon Scripture for basic political and legal principles, they recognized quickly that it alone could not cover the colony's constantly changing social needs.

The second misconception is that English common law was imported virtually intact by the colonists. Nothing could be farther from the truth. Even had the colonists harbored the desire, they would have found it impossible. Seventeenth-century English law was a mélange of parliamentary statutes; king's courts' rulings; town, manor, and merchant customs; and the laws of numerous ecclesiastical tribunals and special commissions. Some of these rulings the colonists kept and applied, but most were totally irrelevant to New England life.

Colonial charters therefore usually authorized local authorities to formulate their own ordinances, provided the laws were *not contrary* to those of England. Thus many New England statutes were completely foreign to those of England. The only English rulings retained were those the Puritan settlers felt furthered the Bible commonwealth's ultimate goals or met immediate needs. All others were summarily rejected. Yet as English law books in time found their way across the Atlantic and a growing number of Americans went

to study at the English Inns of Court, a considerable amount
of English common law entered American legal practice. But
each statute had to make its own way.

The third misconception about the early colonial legal
system is that colonial law was essentially the same throughout the English settlements. In actuality, geographic differences and isolation, varying dates of settlement, and fluctu-
ating social conditions and ties with the mother country
caused each colony to develop a legal system peculiarly and
stubbornly its own.

American Puritan law, then, resulted from a combination
of resources, conditions, and events. The Massachusetts Code
of 1648 is an example; it represents a synthesis of Old Testament precedent and a complex English legal heritage adapted
to New England daily life. What was usable in either source
was retained, perhaps modified; what was not was rejected.
Thus the Bay Colony's legal system, which set the pattern
for all New England, resulted from both tradition and conscious design.

Though few in number, and with serious political and
social blind spots, the Puritans within twenty years laid
the foundation for more than a mere colony. By midcentury
the Bay Colony residents had hammered out a legal system
that furthered the religious goals for which it had been
founded, and encouraged a high moral and social level for
family life, a congenial atmosphere for manufacturing and
trade, and a stimulating setting for intellectual and educational advancement. Many personal and property laws far
surpassed those of contemporary England. Numerous statutes
adopted in Massachusetts by 1650 were not only soon copied
by the surrounding colonies but have provided the basis
for much modern American law.

For better or worse, the Bay colonists formulated, modified, rejected, and added those religious, political, and legal
principles from which was to evolve much of modern America. As recently as May 28, 1961, a radio newsbulletin announced the Supreme Court's decision to uphold a seventeenth-century blue law prohibiting the opening of retail establishments on Sunday.

The American Puritan's major criterion was usefulness.
He formulated his New World laws from scriptural concepts
that seemed logically applicable to the moment's needs. The
Puritan magistrate viewed both natural and biblical law as
God's primary means of imposing upon fallen man the divine

will. What divine rule to extract and apply was to be left to him and his fellow magistrates—and not to the "people" with their legislative bodies, accumulated folklaw, and written codes. Winthrop, for example, argued that the Bible's failure to list specific penalties for many crimes indicated God's wish that the magistrates, His chosen spokesmen, exercise their gifts in coping with such crimes.

All members of the general community were expected to accept the scriptural laws as interpreted and laid down by the magistrates. Even the ministers were to be held by these interpretations. A definite distinction between the church and commonwealth officers developed when shortly after their arrival in New England the ministers surrendered judicial office. They had decided that for them to serve as magistrates was to contradict God's word. However, they had no intention of abandoning their unofficial authority and influence. They not only discussed community policy among themselves, but they consulted frequently with the magistrates, to whom they assigned the choicest seats in church and to whom they regularly offered advice.

Certainly the magistrate did not hesitate to ask for ministerial advice when he felt the need for the church interpretation of God's will. But the ministers' influence was based upon respect for their divinely ordained office, their individual powers of persuasion, and their skill in interpreting the divine word.

To the magistrates fell the major task of creating on the American continent the Bible commonwealth. Clergy and laymen alike were quick to defer to the magistrate's authority. Churchmen were governed not only by Scripture but also by the elective will of their congregation. Should church or magistrates decide a minister was not conducting himself in accordance with scriptural principles (as the latter did with Roger Williams), the congregation was duty-bound to replace him.

Such occurrences were relatively rare. The ministers were the Bible's students and interpreters, and for the most part the community submissively accepted their spiritual guidance. Yet the elders soon discovered that life in America differed sharply from that in the old country. In England the Congregational leadership had been able to take for granted the majority's loyalty to biblical law; in New England the elders quickly found that strong decrees were needed to keep the rapidly increasing congregations from splintering off and introducing various heresies.

The elders also discovered that their high-handed legal procedures would be challenged at every turn. For the first twenty years the people repeatedly strove to gain a stronger voice in government and to limit the elders' powers. Seven small Puritan settlements had evolved as early as 1632, each of which the elders attempted to control by keeping a close eye and firm hand on the artisans and servants and by preventing the immigration of nonbelievers and fanatics.

But trouble came from within. In December, 1633, Roger Williams stepped forward to charge that the Indians had been unfairly treated. The king's charter, he claimed, rested on "a solemn public lie" and thus could not deprive them of their lands. As magistrates and ministers turned hurriedly in their Bibles to the Hebrew occupation of Canaan for parallels justifying the Bay Colony's existence, Williams leveled other charges. An avowed Separatist, he insisted the New England churches sever all connections with a "corrupt" Church of England. He also challenged the magistrates' authority to punish any religious infractions (such as the breaking of the Sabbath), for these constituted infractions of the religious, rather than the moral, law.

A series of bitter debates followed between Williams and the Bay Colony's civil and religious leaders. Inevitably, the General Court banished him for his "divers new and dangerous opinions against the authority of magistrates" and for defaming both magistrates and churches.

Roger Williams' fundamental crime—as the Bay elders saw it—was that he had pitted his own uncertain and untested private conscience against the leadership's collective "conscience rightly informed." In doing so he endangered the union of church and state. The elders felt the individual was entitled to his convictions only if he submitted his resultant views to their wisdom and authority.

A GROWING APPETITE FOR LIBERTY Williams's banishment did not end the magistrates' problems. They were made increasingly aware that they would have to retain political power in the face of mounting opposition from the growing number of nonbelievers migrating to the New World, and this at a time when Englishmen were becoming increasingly dissident in religion and assertive in politics. Englishmen of that era were developing a definite talent for seizing self-government.

As a growing number of freemen made the General Court an increasingly representative force, the leaders made more and more use of the Court of Assistants. The General Court managed to remain the Bay Colony's chief legislative, judicial, and administrative body, but the Court of Assistants still possessed much special authority. Its members functioned as the General Court's executive branch, with the governor and magistrates acting as the colony's administrative officers. The magistrates' judicial authority was even greater than their legislative powers. They controlled all appointments to the county courts, and they usually participated in any court case arousing their interest.

But the deputies were restless. Their admission to the General Court had whetted their appetite for increased liberties. Primarily, they wanted a law code that would fix definite penalties for specific crimes; prevailing custom allowed the individual magistrate to mete out what he considered just punishment. Magistrates and ministers strongly opposed any formal codification of the law. Not only did the magistrates wish to retain as much power as possible as long as possible, but they wished to avoid antagonizing an already hostile King Charles. The Reverend Richard Mather defended their procrastination by claiming that the magistrates could find truth clearly presented in the Bible, and to impose upon them man-made restrictions would limit their "liberty" to apply God's truth. John Winthrop more candidly pointed out that a code would force the colonists into the politically dangerous position of formulating principles contradictory to English law, while if ideas were allowed to evolve naturally, "by practice and custom . . . as in our church discipline," there would be no formal repudiation of English legal precedents.

The elders wished the New England "way" to emerge slowly and unobtrusively behind a barrage of pulpit oratory turning always on some point of Scripture. But the deputies were determined to restrict the magistrates' judicial power by means of a written constitution, a constitution embodying both the traditional English rights of the Magna Carta and common law and God's "clear and unamendable word . . .

as embodied in the Bible." In 1636 the General Court finally instructed the magistrates to draft some laws that were "agreeable" to God's word and that could serve as the commonwealth's fundamental legal code. Meanwhile the magistrates would continue to hear and decide all cases according to the established but unwritten laws, and where there was no law they would proceed "as neere the law of God" as they could.

In October, 1636, John Cotton, as a member of the committee assigned by the court to draw up such a document, presented one modeled after that "of Moses his judicials." Divided into ten chapters, Cotton's brief code prescribed the legal powers of both elders and freemen. Covering virtually all aspects of colonial life, it specifically outlawed arbitrary imprisonment and required two witnesses for conviction on either civil or criminal charges. Based primarily, though not completely, on some of the Old Testament's harsher laws, the code demanded the death penalty for idolatry, blasphemy, witchcraft, Sabbath violations, murder, adultery, incest, sodomy, bestiality, kidnaping, and for bearing false witness—as well as for being disrespectful toward magistrates and for smiting or even cursing one's parents.

Cotton's code never gained official acceptance, but it was the first attempt to provide the Bay Colony with a written legal code that could also serve as a constitution. It provided a basis for the early laws of the New Haven and Southampton colonies. More significantly, many of its suggested civil and criminal laws were incorporated in the Body of Liberties of 1641 and in the code of 1648. Another five years were to pass before the Bay Colony was to adopt its first written legal code.

These intervening years were to be marred by continual religious, political, and legal disputes. All three aspects were involved in the Anne Hutchinson trial. Described as a woman of "nimble wit and active spirit and a very voluble tongue, more bold than a man," Mrs. Hutchinson arrived in Massachusetts in 1634 and immediately began holding meetings at which she repeated and analyzed the sermons of the leading clergymen.

The authorities at first approved her zeal and dedication. They had little quarrel with her contention that the Covenant of Works had been destroyed by Adam's sin and replaced by a Covenant of Grace in which only the elect could enter. But their smiles turned to frowns at her claim that she could discern between the saved and damned. Not only did she thus usurp their prerogative, but she presumed to place some of the most respected of them among the damned. She compounded her crime by contending that the Lord's spirit sanctified and guided the elect by means of an "Inner Light," and that she herself was such a recipient and therefore in the tradition of the biblical prophets. To make matters worse, she soon attracted a sizable following among Boston's leaders, including Sir Harry Vane, the town's youthful governor.

Mrs. Hutchinson and several of her principal followers were brought to trial. To the General Court she appeared to be flouting the community's religious beliefs and entire legal procedure by placing herself above Bible and Church. Thus for her and her followers to remain in Massachusetts Bay could mean only a constant breach of the public peace. She was convicted and banished.

With her departure the advocates of total conformity were in complete control. But the issue was far from dead. Growing civil dissatisfaction among the freemen was expressed forcibly by former governor Vane before he left for England. During the controversy resulting from Mrs. Hutchinson's preachings, Vane conceded the magistrates' right to exclude undesirables from the state's borders, but only after taking action through specific law and jury trial. The state, he added, should follow the example of the churches and be guided by its charter as the churches were by Scripture. Any other course could result only in tyranny.

These views found such wide favor that the elders had to remain constantly on their guard against a popular uprising and to fall back repeatedly on their divine mandate. When some freemen objected to a 1639 General Court ruling that reduced each town's representation from three deputies to two, Winthrop fell back upon the social-contract theory:

When the people have chosen men to be their rulers, and to make their laws, and bound themselves by oath to submit thereto, now to combine together . . . in a public petition to have any order repealed . . . savors of resisting an ordinance of God . . . [and] amounts to a plain reproof of those whom God hath set over them, and putting dishonor upon them, against the tenor of the fifth commandment.

Yet for all their arbitrary authority the magistrates were

unable to withstand the freemen's continued agitation for a
written code. In 1641 there was adopted the Body of Liberties, a fairly detailed bill of rights consisting of one hundred
sections formulated under the guiding hand of Nathaniel
Ward. Committing the Bay government to recognize not only
God's law and the king's charter, the Body of Liberties required acceptance of those fundamental liberties and laws
already established by usage in the commonwealth. It was a
notable advance toward both a written code and "a commonwealth of laws and not of men." (Most of its provisions, in
modified form, were soon to find their way into the 1648
code.)

Reflecting the traditional English concern for due process
and personal liberty, the loosely organized statutes promised
equal legal protection from arbitrary arrest, impressment,
and torture for everyone within the colony, "whether Inhabitant or forreiner." Its most significant provisions, which dealt
with capital crimes, were nearly all derived from Mosaic law.
There was the added stipulation against any statute or custom
contrary to God's law.

Acceptance of the Body of Liberties indicates clearly that
when political—rather than religious or theological—questions were the direct issue between magistrates and freemen,
the latter almost unfailingly gained a concession. Having
centuries of experience with the English judicial system, they
forced elders and magistrates repeatedly to acknowledge the
terms of biblical law, the king's charter, and those laws by
which as Englishmen they had been governed. Their resultant
government, therefore, could only be one prescribed by
Scripture, required by the charter, and permitted by English
legal tradition.

The precedent of a written law code (despite its incom-
pleteness) for a New England colony having been established, another followed quickly. In the nearby Connecticut
Colony—settled only six years earlier by Massachusetts Bay
inhabitants—twelve "capital laws" were adopted in 1642.
Each carried a mandatory death penalty and a citation of
its Old Testament source. The crimes were the familiar
catalog of idolatry, witchcraft, blasphemy, murder, bestiality,
sodomy, adultery, rape, kidnapping, false witness, and rebellion. In 1650, again with a careful citing of Mosaic law, two
more statutes were added. These decreed the death penalty
for young people over sixteen who—without extreme provocation—might curse or smite their parents.

In actual fact, these small communities could hardly afford to reduce their population by a careless exertion of punitive methods. The elders felt God was satisfied merely to have such stringent laws on the books; extenuating circumstances usually were found for even the most serious lawbreakers. Furthermore, the generally applied "substitute punishments" of the stocks, whipping post, brandings, and heavy fines were deterrent enough.

Few either in Connecticut or Massachusetts doubted that these laws were a long step forward. But the Massachusetts freemen were not satisfied to have only capital punishments specified. Dissatisfied especially with the magistrates' wide discretionary powers, the freemen determined to settle for nothing short of a complete codification of all Bay Colony law.

The struggle for ultimate judicial authority began to shift in their favor. The freemen gained another major victory in 1644, when their deputies forced the reluctant elders to accept the idea of fixed penalties for specific offenses whenever possible, rather than have the latter reserve the right to vary punishment according to their own conception of the crime's seriousness. By this time the magistrates were finding it much more difficult to impose and sustain their views in the face of organized public resistance than were the ministers, who could fall back upon their vastly superior knowledge of scriptural texts and exegeses.

The ministers therefore proved invaluable allies to the magistrates. They were quick to support John Winthrop during the summer of 1644, when he defended the magistrates' discretionary powers. Winthrop argued that since the Bible generally ignored fixed penalties except for capital crimes, and since God's word served as the magistrate's major guide, there was little reason to fear arbitrary justice. The next year, when the deputies attempted to censure Winthrop for his handling of a legal matter, the clergy tipped the balance in his favor. In his acquittal speech, Winthrop flatly stated that, once granted, the magistrate's authority was not to be questioned.

Neither magistrates nor clergy valued "democracy" as we think of it today. "Democracy, I do not conceyve, that ever God did ordeyne as a fitt government eyther for church or commonwealth," wrote John Cotton. "If the people be governors, who shall be governed?" Winthrop could only agree. "A Democratie," he asserted, "is among most Civill nations, accounted the meanest & worst of all formes of Government."

John Norton could define "liberty" as the individual's right "to walk in the Faith, Worship, Doctrine and Discipline of the Gospel, according to the Order of the Gospel." These elders were determined that nothing, certainly not the popular will, should deter them from establishing that Bible commonwealth for which they had crossed an ocean and braved a wilderness.

"AN ORGY OF LEGISLATION"   Among the Puritans in England at this time ideas of religious tolerance and freedom of conscience were spreading. The Civil War had forced Congregationalists, Presbyterians, and Independents not only to join together under Cromwell's leadership but to welcome into their ranks many other Protestant sects. The resultant liberalizing spirit was felt across the Atlantic in a series of political disputes that threatened the elders' control of the Bay Colony's legislative structure and forced them to accept the inevitability of a written code.

Under persistent pressure from the freemen, joint deputy-magistrate committees had for several years been striving to revise, elaborate, and codify the various Bay Colony laws. Their combined efforts finally came to fruition in 1648 with the General Court's approval of a rather comprehensive law code known as *The Book of the General Lawes and Libertyes.* (It has been reprinted in the twentieth century as *The Laws and Liberties of Massachusetts.*) More than any other single document, this code of 1648 reveals the transformation of basic Puritan doctrines—derived from both biblical and certain English political concepts—into New England's political and legal institutions.

From their English heritage the Puritans had derived the belief that government's prime function is "to regulate man's corruption," that its divinely appointed leaders are to be obeyed unquestioningly, and that the state's welfare is much more important than the individual's. The 1648 code made this clear by stating that all those entering the Bay Colony must "tacitly submit" to this government and its "wholesome laws." The code's prefatory "Epistle" stated clearly the preeminence of God's law:

As soon as God had set up a Politicall Government among his people Israel hee gave them a body of lawes for judgement both in civil and criminal causes. These were breif and fundamental principles, yet withall so full and comprehensive as out of them clear deductions were to be drawne to particular cases in future times.

As the code's major interpreters, the magistrates sought scriptural sanction for all their decisions and actions. Hence the divine law imposed at least a limited curb upon their judicial authority. Yet they saw no reason not to draw upon other legal sources as well when the need arose, so long as the resultant laws did not contradict the Bible. Their other major source was "the traditional right and liberties of Englishmen."

The Bible and English common law's combined traditions provided the New Englander with a greater measure of political and legal stability than he otherwise would have enjoyed. Every inhabitant, regardless of his social status, stood equal before the law and could voice his opinion at public meetings. The law provided that every person in Massachusetts, whether or not a regular "Inhabitant," was to have equal justice without prejudice or delay. Thus if Massachusetts non-Puritans often suffered from strong social discrimination, even the lowliest of them were extended legal protection from economic and physical abuse.

The 1648 code contained most of the *Body of Liberties* provisions in revised and expanded forms, augmented by other laws going back to the initial settlement and some entirely new ones formulated to meet changing conditions. With relatively few further additions the code was to serve as the colony's "basic statutory law" for the rest of the century. Yet its biblical and English sources did not make it a mere mechanical refurbishing of old precepts and customs. Whatever was retained from either source was carefully reevaluated and frequently modified or expanded to fit the Bay Colony's changing civil, religious, and social ideas.

Persisting through the changing conditions and events was the influence of Mosaic law. The Puritans were as firmly convinced as ever that much of the civil and criminal law God had given ancient Israel was still binding upon them. Each of the code's capital laws specified its Old Testament source and frequently incorporated the biblical phraseology.

Like the Israelites, the Puritans considered the family the

basis of church and state. Therefore any threat to its sanctity
—such as an adulterous act—merited the death penalty.
Whereas English ecclesiastical law considered an illicit act
adulterous if either participant was married, the New England Puritans deemed it so only if the woman was married,
or even—as in Deuteronomy 22:23—merely engaged.

The 1648 code's use of its Old Testament sources is exemplified in the law prescribing punishment for a rebellious son.
Deuteronomy declares:

> If a man has a stubborn and rebellious son, who will not
> obey the voice of his father or . . . mother [they] . . .
> shall take hold of him and bring him out to the elders
> of his city. . . . Then all the men of the city shall stone
> him to death with stones; so you shall purge the evil
> from your midst; and all Israel shall hear, and fear.

The code states:

> If a man have a stubborn or REBELLIOUS SON, of suffi-
> cient years & understanding (viz) sixteen years of age,
> which will not obey the voice of his Father, or . . .
> Mother . . . [they then shall] lay hold on him & bring
> him to the Magistrates assembled in Court & testifie
> unto them, that their Son is stubborn & rebellious & will
> not obey their voice and chastisement, but lives in sun-
> dry notorious crimes, such a son shall be put to death.

The colonists attempted to mitigate the Old Testament
harshness by borrowing from English law certain qualifications. They provided lesser penalties for sexual wrongdoers
below the "age of sufficient understanding" and for rebellious
sons motivated by "extream and cruel" parental provocation.
So while preferring to rely upon Scripture whenever possible,
the Puritans were quick to disregard the death penalty for a
great many offenses.

In keeping with this approach, the Puritans made use of
the Deuteronomic proviso that the death penalty could not be
inflicted without "two or three witnesses." Again, the capital
laws were designed to prevent rather than punish crime, for
most were seldom applied, and a few were never put to use.

The Puritans also often resorted to biblical laws milder
than their English equivalents. Multiple restitution and involuntary servitude in theft cases were substituted for the English common law punishment of hanging or whipping, while

whipping sentences generally were reduced. Even servitude was imposed only when the convicted thief was unable to make restitution.

Massachusetts civil law was less bound by biblical precedent than was the criminal law, but the former still revealed a strong scriptural influence in certain areas, particularly the master-servant relationship. Deuteronomy 23:15–16 states:

> You shall not give up to his master a slave who has escaped from his master to you; he shall dwell with you, in your midst, in the place which he shall choose within one of your towns, where it pleases him best; you shall not oppress him.

To protect the master's legal rights, the Puritans added the qualifying requirement of "Tiranny and crueltie" before they extended a servant protection. Hence both the *Body of Liberties* and the code of 1648 stated that "If any servants shall flee from the Tiranny and cruelties of their masters to the howse of any freeman of the same towne, they shall be there protected and susteyned till due order be taken for their relife."

Several other colonial laws reflecting scriptural concern for the servant also added protective clauses for the master. Both Massachusetts codes echoed Exodus 21:26–27 by declaring that "If any man smite out the eye or tooth of his man-servant, or maid servant, or otherwise mayme or much disfigure him . . . he shall let them goe free from his service." Then they inserted the qualifier of the master's intent—unless the act were an accident. But the master's guilt having been established, the servant was to receive such compensation as the court thought fair.

The same approach was applied to the rule laid down in Deuteronomy 15:12–14 that at completion of seven years' service a servant was to be freed and amply provided for on his departure. The Massachusetts codes stipulated that this applied only to servants who had served diligently and faithfully; those who had proved unsatisfactory were to give "satisfaction" before gaining dismissal.

The Bible was not the sole—in many areas not even the primary—influence upon the code of 1648. There were equally striking parallels to the English Statute of Labourers. Yet the strong "substantive similarity," states legal historian G. L. Haskins, that both colonial and English legal systems "bore to biblical precept suggest that Elizabethan legislators, like those of Massachusetts, were also influenced, though to a lesser degree, by the biblical inheritance in which they both shared." The code was not only the Western world's first modern law code and the basis of Massachusetts law for decades to come, but the model for many of the other New England colonies, as well as those in New York, Delaware, and Pennsylvania.

As their American experiment's first two decades came to a close, the Puritan elders were aware that social, political, and economic events were going against them. The code of 1648 obviously could not begin to solve their growing judicial problems. After 1650 a mushrooming population and rapidly increasing commercial wealth began converting the Puritan leadership into a defensive minority that felt an overwhelming need to protect its position by "an orgy of legislation" and religious persecutions.

Cromwell's victory in England added to the leadership's arrogance, causing many leaders to feel they had little to fear from across the waters. So to the threatened death penalty for such crimes as blasphemy, parental disobedience, and denial of the Bible's validity, they now added fines for "notorious & violent heretics." Nor did they overlook less serious wrongdoings: mere "vaine swearing" cost the culprit ten shillings, while disrespect toward a minister brought a five-pound fine or a sentence to stand two hours on a lecture day on a block, with a sign bearing in capital letters "A WANTON GOSPELLER." Church-attendance laws were enforced rigidly, for hearing the Scriptures not only brought men to faith, stated the General Court, but to civil obedience and allegiance to the magistrates.

THE LONG AND TRAGIC CONFLICT The Puritan leaders were in no mood to tolerate outsiders who would introduce religious errors that could only undermine the wilderness Zion. "With eternity at stake," states historian T. J. Wertenbaker, "the Puritans were not inclined to temporize with error." They kept a constant eye upon Roger Williams' Rhode Island settlements as a potential source of dangerous heresy. In the summer of 1651, their worst fears were realized when three Baptist members of the Newport church crossed the Massachusetts border. The three went unmolested until they held religious services at which they denounced many basic Puritan doctrines. They also interrupted the Lynn meetinghouse services by refusing to remove their hats and were forcibly ejected. Brought before the General Court, the Baptists were heavily fined and banished. Two of the fines were paid, but Obadiah Holmes refused to pay, nor would he allow anyone to pay for him. Consequently he received a public whipping.

Five years later the Massachusetts elders were confronted by more serious invasions. In July, 1656, two Quaker women arrived at Boston from Barbados and immediately attacked Puritan doctrines, ministerial authority, and church covenants. The women were arrested and deported. A few days later eight more Quakers arrived from London. These too were sent back.

The General Court realized it had to take serious defensive action against this new and rapidly growing sect if it were to maintain peace. It enacted statutes leveling heavy fines against ship captains bringing Quakers to Massachusetts Bay and against anyone harboring Quaker writings or defending Quakers or their beliefs. These attempts to halt the infiltrators proved ineffective, and the laws were made harsh. Quakers became liable to ear-croppings, severe whippings, stiff jail sentences, and banishment. Those refusing to leave were to be executed. Such laws soon were prevalent throughout New England, as the Plymouth, New Haven, and Connecticut colonies followed Massachusetts. These laws were aimed not only at Quakers but at all who opposed the "true worship of God."

The Puritans were convinced that as God's chosen they had been selected to carve a new Zion from the American wilderness. For them to allow heretical beliefs could result only in a punishment similar to that suffered by the ancient Israelites. Having been thus singled out, the Puritans were not disposed to tolerate the disparate Quaker views. The particular destructiveness of Quaker doctrine, as the Puritans saw it, was similar to that of Anne Hutchinson and her followers; it lay in claiming God guides man by means of an "Inner Light" rather than by Scripture's written word. By presuming to divine guidance beyond church and clergy, Quakers revealed themselves "madmen acting according to their fran-

tic passions," declared the Reverend John Norton; thus they
had "to be restrained with chains."

The New England persecutions were defensive rather than
aggressive in nature. The Puritans did not seek converts.
They simply refused to allow heresy in the Bible commonwealth, being more anxious to expel than to destroy it. "All
Familists, Antinomians, Anabaptists and other enthusiasts
shall have free liberty to keep away from us" was the way
minister Nathaniel Ward put it. Only when dissenters refused
to leave peaceably, or insisted upon returning after expulsion,
did the Puritan leaders resort to force.

New England became the arena for a tragic religious conflict. Puritans and non-Puritans alike fought with courage
and fear, conviction and fanaticism, hope and mounting
despair. The battle was long and bloody. And the elders, realizing that time and tide were against them, lashed out with
increased stubbornness and cruelty.

Before long even some Puritan leaders could not find it in
their hearts to persist in the religious persecutions. Furthermore, influential Quakers in England were exerting pressures
through King Charles for greater tolerance. Most significantly,
an increasing number of influential New Englanders realized
the folly of punishing nonbelievers. By 1674 Quakers were
holding regular meetings in Boston, and in 1697 they erected
a meetinghouse on Brattle Street. Ironically, as their persecution lessened, the Quakers found it more difficult to attract
converts in New England. But the religious breakthrough had
occurred. The Baptists began holding regular services on an
island in Boston Harbor in 1674, and in 1686 the first Anglican minister was established in Massachusetts. Thus did the
Puritan struggle of almost three-quarters of a century—to
control completely man's religious beliefs—end in frustration
and failure. The New World was headed in another direction.

New England, however, had no monopoly of bigotry or
repressive religious laws. In Virginia, where the Church of
England was firmly established, the laws aimed at dissenters
—especially Catholics, Baptists, and Quakers—were equally
confining. Any Quaker found within the state could be jailed
without bail and the sea captain who brought him subjected
to a stiff fine. Needless to say, the publication or distribution
of Quaker printed matter was illegal.

Virginia imposed many other laws to prevent any form of
religious unorthodoxy. One early-eighteenth-century statute
literally defined the nature of true Christian belief. Not only

was it illegal to deny Old or New Testament authority, but such offenders were ineligible for public office and subject to arrest. Such restrictions, however, were increasingly inimical to the century's liberalizing spirit, and dissatisfaction with these bonds on the human spirit was spreading among enlightened Virginians.

Yet no colony was entirely free of restrictive religious statutes. Even in liberal Quaker Pennsylvania an act of 1700 subjected to fine all citizens who failed to attend Sunday church or could give no evidence of having been home reading the Scriptures.

Catholics could expect severe prejudice and restrictive legislation in almost every American colony and, in New England, even attacks from the pulpits. (To celebrate Christmas there was a criminal offense. Puritans considered it "the ill-begotten offspring of paganism and popery," and a celebrant was liable to end up at the stocks or whipping post. Not until the early-nineteenth century did Christmas become legal in New England. And it was some years after that before it became a national legal holiday.) During the early colonial period Catholics had found a haven in Maryland, where founder George Calvert had assured them religious freedom and where they had written and administered its early laws. For a time Maryland's religious liberalism rivaled that of Rhode Island. But by 1689 Protestants had attained the majority and Catholics again experienced discriminatory legislation.

As God's chosen, the Puritans looked upon this life as mere preparation for the next. They were convinced they had within their grasp at least the possibility of heaven's eternal pleasures, provided they did not fall victim to Satan's ever-present temptations. Their fears for man's behavior and fate were embodied in the stern Calvinist code. And both ecclesiastical and civil leaders took it upon themselves to enforce its stringent morality upon all. This meant a rigid adherence to the law as interpreted by the magistrates. The entire community had to ferret out and eliminate sin in every conceivable form.

Hence every Puritan was engaged in the "holy watching" of his neighbor's spiritual and moral welfare. Each reported directly to the community's most powerful enforcement official, the minister, whose adverse account usually resulted in an appearance by the wrongdoer before an unfavorably disposed magistrate. To overlook a friend's misdeeds was to do him harm, for correction alone led to spiritual improvement or regeneration.

Magistrates and ministers constituted a formidable team. Between them they dominated Puritan society. Neither Bible nor clergy could be confined to "religious matters," for religion permeated all New England life. Whenever the freemen opposed the magistrates, the ministers—armed with their scriptural texts—stepped in to argue down the opposition. The magistrates reciprocated by a rigid enforcement of religious uniformity. If they occasionally experienced differences of opinion, both groups realized the colony's peaceful existence was too important to allow serious frictions to develop.

While the magistrates and ministers did not pass laws officially prohibiting levity, they considered laughter and gaiety inappropriate for God's chosen engaged in daily combat with Satan for possession of their souls. Some joy of the occasion was permitted at weddings, but without "riotous or immodest irregularities." Those leaving the meetinghouse following the midweek lectures were not to adjourn to the tavern, nor were harvest huskings to degenerate into merrymaking occasions.

These views underlay the deep Puritan aversion for the maypole. William Bradford has reported the elders' shocked horror at learning that Thomas Morton and his high-spirited followers at Mount Wollaston (Merrymount, the present site of Quincy, Massachusetts) had erected a maypole. They frolicked about it "many days together," Bradford wrote, "inviting the Indian women for their consorts, dancing and frisking together like so many fairies or furies," and introducing into the New World "the beastly practices of the mad Bacchanalians." In an episode that has become part of our national folklore, an armed Bay Colony contingent, under the humorless John Endecott, soon arrived to destroy the pole and warn the celebrants.

The Puritans declared illegal all forms of gambling, especially dice and cards. For according to Scripture the ancients had frequently resorted to "lots" to determine God's will, and consequently it was sacrilege to use them for common sport. Even shuffleboard and bowling—if played at public houses— were prohibited, as they not only frittered away God's time but encouraged the "waste of wine and beer."

The elders were not opposed to moderate drinking and issued numerous licenses for the sale of wine, beer, and even "stronger waters." But they detested drunkenness. They passed a law in 1639 prohibiting the "abominable" pagan practice of drinking toasts. This was obviously a carry-over from the times when heathens made drink offerings to demons, declared Cotton Mather; no worthy Christian, he insisted, desired to retain rapport with the dark powers.

Legislation was fairly easy; enforcement was not. Four decades later the synod of 1679 was still lamenting that the "heathenish and idolatrous practice of health-drinking is too frequent." Certainly this failure to stamp out drunkenness was not due to a lack of zeal either on the part of the elders or their official informers, the tithing men. These were individuals appointed to supervise the moral behavior of ten neighboring families and to report to the magistrate any neglect of the Sabbath or private worship, as well as intemperance, profanity, or even idleness. Any youth caught sledding, swimming, or any adult merely enjoying himself when he could be better employed, could expect either a warning to mend his ways or actual punishment.

Life appears to have been anything but gay for the young New Englander. He was beset by community restrictions, and he had to accept unquestioningly the weight of parental authority. An angry parent could haul his son before a magistrate authorized to impose upon a disobedient young person a sentence of ten stripes for each offense.

The only New Englanders having a more difficult time than the young male were his mother and sisters. As "daughters of the temptress Eve," women were looked upon as Satan's prime instrument for evil and were treated accordingly. The Puritan elders had adultery much on their minds. They were given to lamenting the "hainous breaches of the Seventh Commandment," which, as they saw it, was traceable to such "immodest apparel" as revealed "naked necks and arms" and—as unlikely as it appears for seventeenth-century New England—"naked breasts." Woe befell the woman, therefore, who appeared in public revealing more than face and hands. Short-sleeved, low-necked gowns ending above the ankles were not only "wicked" but illegal, and a 1650 law actually prohibited "short sleeves, whereby the nakedness of the arm may be discovered."

Even the well-covered woman was not beyond censure or punishment if her attire was considered too expensive, affected, or simply beyond her social station. Such indulgence was a clear indication of overweening pride. This applied also to men. Much bothered by the "new and immodest fashions," the General Court of 1634 forbade garments "with any lace on it, silver, gold or thread . . . also all cutworks, embroidered or needlework caps, bands and rails . . . all gold and silver girdles, hatbands, belts, ruffs, beaver hats." For such "superfluities" served "little use or benefit, but to the nourishment of pride." It was foolish for sinful man to "garb, in garish attire," declared poet-clergyman Urian Oakes, "that body of clay that is going to the dust and the worms."

> Hath God brought us into a wilderness and caused us to dwell alone and separated us for a peculiar people to himself, that we should imitate the nations in these vanities? . . . When persons spend more time in trimming their bodies than their souls . . . you may say of them . . . that they are like the cinnamon tree, nothing good but the bark.

The magistrates found curbing human vanity no easy task. Nathaniel Ward undoubtedly expressed the sentiment of many Boston elders when he wrote in 1645 that he could not understand how—at a time when God was prone to shake both the heavens and earth—any woman could don such "exotic garb" as to resemble "a bar-goose, an ill-shaped shell fish." No wonder, he added, "they wear drails on the hinder parts of their heads: having nothing, it seems, in the forepart but a few squirrel's brains."

The Puritans were discovering that while New England's first trial-tested generation had been able to control their natural instincts and drives, their children lacked equal incentive. Parental hardships and dangers were mere hearsay. What need to deprive the flesh and spirit amidst America's plenty? A God bountiful enough to provide the American abundance was hardly as fearsome as the elders claimed.

By 1679 Boston's churches were so disturbed by the laxity of public morals and behavior that their representatives met to determine what evils had provoked God to mete out punishments on New England. The difficulties with the Indians, as well as widespread sickness and various misfortunes, were taken as signs of God's anger. The committee's final report recalled in dramatic terms the Puritan fathers' high principles: The fathers' crossing of the Atlantic had re-created Abraham's journey from Ur and the Egyptian exodus; with God's guidance they had cleared a wilderness and defeated the heathen inhabitants. But the sons lacked their fathers' high purposes. They had fallen prey to the weaknesses of the flesh and aroused God's anger. Few had remained righteous.

This report of 1679 was submitted to the General Court, then published and circulated as the *Necessity of Reformation*. It constitutes a confession that the standards of "sainthood" upon which the Puritan founders had based their Bible commonwealth were impossible to attain.

WITCHES ON TRIAL   Easily the saddest episode of the American Puritan experience was the Salem (now Danvers) witch trials during 1691–1692. Today it is easy to dismiss the entire episode as the major instance of Puritan ignorance and cruelty. Yet such a view ignores the historical context in which these events occurred and does not help to explain how so learned and sophisticated a society as that of seventeenth-century Massachusetts Bay could have been moved to such barbarous acts.

The existence of witches had been almost universally accepted for centuries before Salem's tragic events. The "invisible world" was as real as the visible one for even "enlightened" minds. No one could be certain as to what hovered just beyond man's vision. Most shared Cotton Mather's certainty that the air was permeated by active legions of Satan's demonic followers. A vengeful Satan and his cohorts, they believed, waged a relentless campaign to thwart God's design for mankind. To achieve their ends, Satan and his followers often made themselves visible by entering and possessing the victim, or by taking on his shape. Both Catholic and Protestant Europe through the centuries had put to death large numbers of witches.

New England's Puritans were particularly sensitive to the possibility of the Satanic presence. What more likely stronghold for these demonic powers than the bleak North American wilderness, with its savage barbarians and their unholy medicine men whose heathen rites undoubtedly were pleasing to Satan? As no one could be absolutely certain he had been elected for grace, every man, woman, and child was a potential victim. Further, the Old Testament made clear that God

frequently chastised an entire people for the deeds of the few.
Therefore, all had to be carefully watched. Moral and spiritual vigilance could not be relaxed.

With this background, a series of late-seventeenth-century
events made the colonists acutely witch conscious. A group
of New England clergymen in 1681 unknowingly prepared
the way for the subsequent tragedies. To combat a growing
rationalistic attitude toward religion, these divines began collecting and publishing "supernatural" evidence. They were
interested particularly in

> divine judgments, tempests, floods, earthquakes, thunders as are unusual, strange apparitions, or what ever
> else shall happen that is prodigious, witchcrafts, diabolical possessions, remarkable judgments upon noted sinners, eminent deliverances and answers to prayer.

Increase Mather completed and published his compilation of
these wondrous things in 1684 under the title *An Essay for
the Recording of Illustrious Providences*. Read with wide-eyed interest throughout New England, it soon planted the
seeds of later hysteria. Fate conspired to lend Mather's book
considerable assistance. In the same year James II revoked
the Bay Colony Charter and sent a hated royal governor. In
1688 the French and Indians launched a new series of attacks
on the frontier villages, and in Boston the four children of a
mason named Goodwin began throwing "extraordinary and
prenatural" fits.

The ministers decided that Satan's first evil instrument was
a demented laundress whose senile muttering was interpreted
as a confession and who was hanged with dispatch. Cotton
Mather took a personal hand by moving three of the Goodwin children into his home for prayer, fasting, and close
observation. The attention bestowed on these young people
makes it surprising that it took three years for a fresh outbreak—this time in the home of the Reverend Samuel Parris
of Salem Village. Filled with tales of witches and magic by
two West Indian slaves—John Indian and his wife, Tituba—
Parris' nine-year-old daughter and eleven-year-old niece began complaining of being pricked, choked, bitten, and
pinched by invisible hands and visible apparitions.

The clergy again stepped in with prayer, fasting, and the
hope that God might "rebuke" Satan. The General Court

ordered a general fast. Soon approximately forty people were suffering "horrible torments by evil spirits." A deluge of symptoms, accusations, and investigations followed. Long-standing family feuds, bitter social and political rivalries, and personal jealousies erupted amidst charges and counter-charges.

The clergy acted swiftly. Led by the two Mathers, a dozen ministers drew up a paper recommending rapid and vigorous prosecution of those who had "rendered themselves ob-noxious, according to the direction given in the Laws of God, and the wholesome statutes of the English nation, for the detection of witchcraft." The ministers did add the warning that prosecution should proceed with "very critical and ex-quisite caution" and that conviction should be based on more than mere hearsay, wild accusation, or claims of spectral affliction. But the warning was lost in the subsequent hysteria.

A special court was set up and a series of hasty trials fol-lowed. In the summer of 1692 nineteen men and women and two dogs were convicted and hanged for witchcraft. Giles Corey, a courageous eighty-year-old who refused to plead either guilty or not guilty to the indictment, was pressed to death under increasing weights of stone in accordance with British common law. Fifty-five people confessed to being witches, and about a hundred more found themselves in jail awaiting trial.

The hangings served to dissipate the mob hysteria. By early fall voices were heard urging an end to the executions. Doubts as to the entire proceedings were raised, as some of the colony's "unblamable" persons (relatives and friends of the judges and ministers) were being accused. Obviously something was wrong. In October, Sir William Phips, the recently returned English governor, dismissed the special court of oyer and terminer that had conducted the trials. The "witchcraft" delusion had run its course.

Naturally belief in witchcraft did not immediately cease. There were several other confessions. But in May the gov-ernor signed a general pardon. A "period of penitence" followed. The General Court proclaimed a fast day in 1697, and Judge Samuel Sewall, the famed diarist, made his per-sonal peace with God by standing in church to hear read aloud his confession of error for his part in the tragic pro-ceedings. During the following decade several of those who had served on the trial juries also sought public pardon, as did many others variously involved. And the General Court gave official stamp to the communal guilt in 1711 by reversing all bills of attainder against the executed victims. The Salem witch trial episode had come to a belated close.

THE NEED FOR A CONSTITUTION   The trials were tangible proof that the lofty values of the fathers had somehow been lost sight of, that the letter had replaced the spirit of the law. As Professor Wertenbaker points out, the Puritan code's "very rigidity . . . eventually tended to undermine morality. It did harm in not discriminating sufficiently between petty misdemeanors and serious crime. When the gathering of firewood on the Sabbath was punished with the same severity as adultery or theft, adultery and theft lost some of their flagrancy." The clergy constantly bewailed the frequency with which laws were broken. Apparently strict punishments did little to prevent numerous Sabbath infractions. The synod of 1679 lamented that many New Englanders persisted in walking or traveling, or in otherwise pursuing their "servile callings and employments" on the Lord's Day—all of which violated the Fourth Commandment.

A series of new laws in 1716 and again in 1727 governing Sabbath conduct were added to the already prohibitive list. A *Boston News-Letter* notice in 1748 warned that justices would patrol the city's streets to arrest anyone walking or standing about or breaking the Sabbath laws in any other way. One city ordinance, dating back to 1701, prohibited making a coffin or digging a grave on the Sabbath; it also declared interment unlawful from Saturday sundown to Monday morning, as funerals profaned the holy day by attracting crowds of idle servants and children.

Ministers continued to condemn the profanity, card-playing, long hair, wigs, and excessive drinking of their parishioners, but they saw a special sign of New England's spiritual decay in the growing popularity of the time-wasting and immoral practice of dancing. So bothersome was dancing in Boston by 1684 that the ministers published a pamphlet entitled *An Arrow against Profane and Promiscuous Dancing, drawn out of the Quiver of the Scriptures*. This having little effect, they hauled a newly arrived dancing master, one Francis Stepney, into court for holding "mixt dances," and on "lecture-day." Stepney's activities were quashed easily, but love of the dance was another matter. The minuet was soon a great favorite among the city's wealthy merchants, and by 1723 dancing schools were advertising their services in the newspapers despite bitter ministerial opposition.

To the Puritan elders the cause of the younger generation's lack of moral zeal was clear. There were families, they declared, that did not pray together constantly and many households in which the Scriptures were not read daily. And hard as it was to believe, some homes even lacked Bibles. Such indulgent, permissive parents had only themselves to blame that New England was blessed with but few "hopeful buds" among the new generation.

Economic and social forces also were at work frustrating the moral and religious goals of the Puritan fathers; an inevitable part of the New World's living conditions, these forces broke down the Puritan state's isolation. To dominate the community, it was not only necessary for elders, magistrates, and ministers to enjoy political sovereignty, but for the people to be concentrated in town, within the leadership's easy reach. It was necessary also that the wealth be so evenly distributed that no secular group could attain a position challenging the religious authority. For these reasons the founders had established the small agricultural village or town as the Bible commonwealth's central social unit. But expanding population and economic opportunity soon wrought great changes. Many newcomers turned to commerce rather than agriculture, and shipbuilding and fishing soon thrived all along New England's coast. Fishing became the region's prime industry and fish its chief commodity. The new industries brought a new way of life as villages quickly developed into thriving cities.

There were other changes too. Each new generation developed its own wants and needs. The second- and third-generation New Englanders who continued to till the soil were anxious to move from their fathers' lands and develop their own. New areas outside the villages were cleared, and the individual farm replaced the common field. These "native" New Englanders were joined by hordes of European immigrants, for the dream of owning his own land brought many an impoverished agricultural worker or tenant farmer to the New World. Land hunger eventually pushed waves of pioneers to the Pacific Coast and brought about the disintegration of the Puritan state.

Grasping the dangers implicit in the steady movement from village to farm, the Bay Colony founders tried to thwart the economic trend by passing laws. As early as September, 1635, and again in 1636, the General Court decreed that no future dwelling within its jurisdiction could be built without permission more than a half mile from the meetinghouse. But the resultant pressures by those forced to travel to farm their lands caused the order to be rescinded in 1640. Before long, it wasn't possible for ministers and elders to check up on their parishioners and punish them for every minor violation. And the considerable distances and bad roads made it relatively easy to explain away absences at Sabbath services.

Expansion and development of new territories gave rise to new communities, schools, churches, covenants, and town meetings. Disruption of the old unity was hastened also by the rapid influx of new arrivals. Successful farmers, merchants, or artisans needed apprentices, workers, and servants for their homes. At first, attempts were made to draw sharp divisions between the old and new settlers, especially in the ownership of land. But despite the passage of various restrictive property laws, the newcomers were able increasingly to take root in the New England soil and hasten the end of the old Puritan state.

The Puritans, who believed wholeheartedly in their mission and who had sacrificed and endured much to fulfill it, vigorously combated all attempts to weaken their Bible state. Driven in time to desperation by unmistakable signs of defeat, they resorted to intolerance and cruelty. Yet they left a rich social heritage that did much to shape American legal history throughout the Colonial and Revolutionary periods.

To the modern eye, Puritan social theory seems far removed from twentieth-century legal and governmental concepts. Yet a good many of its underlying assumptions and resultant patterns embodied political ideas that have persisted in American thought. Town-meeting government, popular elections, a bicameral council, and the conception of a social covenant between governor and governed are Puritan contributions to American life. These, and others, were derived primarily from their veneration of Scripture as the embodiment of God's will and plan. Despite the superficially antireligious tone of much eighteenth-century rationalistic philosophy, these germinal ideas flourished throughout the century and greatly influenced political and legal theorists during the American republic's formative years.

Most enlightened eighteenth-century intellectual and political leaders in America were determined to profit by the seventeenth century's achievements and mistakes. They were thoroughly convinced that religious beliefs were the individual's private and inviolate right. These men were not cynics. They believed wholeheartedly in man's natural decency and ability to produce lasting and noble social traditions. But they were also highly realistic students of history, keenly aware of the need to protect mankind's basic goodness from its recurrent tyrannical and bigoted urges. They wanted enlightened but durable political structures and laws—ones that could not be changed or ignored easily by a minority leadership so hungry for power and scornful of natural rights that it became contemptuous of obligations to the individual.

A written constitution was the obvious solution. But in formulating such a constitution, these planners were careful to expose the government's authority to continual scrutiny and regulation. They saw to it that no official, however important, was beyond the law. They established several governmental branches to prevent those enacting laws from enforcing them, and to prevent those who enforced them from serving as their interpreters. These checks and balances restricted efficiency to a degree, but this disadvantage was easily overbalanced by the obvious advantages to individual freedom. This became especially true when subsequent economic and military problems extended federal authority far beyond the point envisioned by the planners.

The Constitution's writers therefore fashioned a political structure in which human error would occur primarily in the open and its effects contained or remedied. They did not intend to place government in the control of a few wise leaders who then would take unchallenged political action. History had revealed the folly of such an approach. A free people's constitution, they realized, required clearly defined governmental standards and obligations. Above all, most planners agreed, government should not take upon itself the authority to determine the religious beliefs of its citizens, nor to favor one church above the other. America, henceforth, was to have no state church.

This conviction did not indicate a lack of interest in or respect for spiritual belief—quite the contrary. These men simply were keenly aware of the bias and persecution that

had occurred in every American colony in which church
leaders had been in a position to legislate against nonbelievers. To avoid such recurrences (and a power struggle
among the now proliferating denominations), it clearly was
necessary to guarantee freedom of religious action to everyone, especially to those who chose not to believe. For the
planners had little doubt that were the state granted the right
to compel worship, it soon would determine the type of
worship.

These views have caused the mistaken but frequent charge
that America's revolutionary leaders were agnostics, if not
atheists. Actually, the more they probed and analyzed the
universe's wonders, the more concerned they became with
a First Cause. They did insist their speculation be unham-
pered by the limitations of denominational beliefs. Rather
than quarrel with man's basic spiritual needs, they wished to
give them free play. But most were convinced that all religions ought to recognize man's broadening philosophical and
scientific horizons.

Because they looked upon the God-man relationship as a
deeply personal matter, they opposed all laws imposing any
one interpretation of man's place in the universe, or that
compelled worship or church attendance. (Several states had
such laws.) Nor did they look with favor upon statutes bestowing special privileges upon the clergy.

Not all the Revolutionary leaders acknowledged a formal
faith, although most had been raised in a strong religious
tradition. Even those reacting against rigorous Calvinistic
childhoods still adhered to basic religious concepts. Indeed,
their obsession with man's rights resulted from the conviction
that independent religious belief was a moral necessity. For
man's "natural laws" and "natural rights" were "God-given."
Having been so endowed by his Creator, man was certainly
capable of governing his own affairs, provided a proper legal
framework had been established.

Yet if there was considerable unity in the Revolutionary
leaders' general attitude toward religion, their individual
creeds ranged from Samual Adams's Puritanism to Thomas
Paine's skeptical deism. Some came in for sharp criticism
for their liberalism from contemporary and later orthodox
critics. George Washington has been described as having
lacked any formal belief; Thomas Jefferson frequently has
been cited as an actual foe of organized religion, while

Thomas Paine was referred to by Theodore Roosevelt as a "filthy little atheist."

More accurately, these men were deistic sons of the Enlightenment. Their recorded views on religious subjects reveal each had very pronounced religious convictions. They were frequently critical of past or existing religious institutions, but their reasons tended to be political rather than theological. They opposed especially those churches that demanded freedom for themselves but sought to deny it to others. Thomas Paine directed much energy to proving God's existence and "universal design." Thomas Jefferson strove anxiously to separate religious beliefs from any form of state support, believing any such political involvement resulted only in injustice and discrimination. His quarrel was not with religion but with monopoly and political power hiding behind religion. Faith was at its best, he held, when relieved of the burden of imposing enforced belief. Convinced that God and nature were one, Jefferson felt that increased scientific knowledge only enhanced the enlightened individual's respect for God.

But the prime concern of Jefferson and the others was to define clearly the respective relationships of government and individual to the church. These hardheaded pragmatists were fully aware of both the deeply personal nature of the religious experience and a historical record of religious turmoil. They were determined that the individual be protected equally from an authoritarian government and his own religious zeal.

Much modern controversy about the founding fathers' religious beliefs centers upon their intentions toward the federal government's role in education. Advocates and opponents of federal aid to education support their respective views by quoting from the Constitution and the private papers of the Continental Congress members. This argument usually hinges on two basic points. The first is that the Constitution's First Amendment states Congress shall pass "no law respecting an establishment of religion," thus denying Congress the right to establish an official state church.

The second is that the Constitution does not specifically forbid the federal government from engaging in activities not related to the establishment of a state church. However, modern Supreme Court decisions have upheld the principle that virtually any federal action supporting religion violates the First Amendment. Opponents of this position contend the Constitution itself offers clear proof that had its authors (who

had clearly indicated their opposition to an American established church) been equally opposed to any other federal
participation in religious activities, they would have said so.

These issues are again being debated and undoubtedly shall
continue to be for some time to come. But there can be little
dispute as to the First Amendment's two basic points: that
the government cannot place its official seal upon any specific
church and that it must remain impartial in its relationships
with all religious groups. In any event, the individual American emerges with the right to the freest form of religious
expression in man's history.

THE STRUGGLE FOR RELIGIOUS FREEDOM Today
every American takes for granted religious freedom. But its
attainment was fought for from the beginning of the American experiment by a few tough-skinned religious idealists.
Not until the eighteenth century were their numbers increased
to the point where their ideas could prevail. And yet, despite
the strongly entrenched position of certain powerful churches
(the Congregational churches in New England and the Anglican in Virginia), the division of church and state was
inevitable in America.

Roger Williams and William Penn, among others, planted
early the seeds of "separation." This "separation-of-church-
and-state" concept (in Jefferson's phrase) is undoubtedly one
of America's greatest single contributions to human thought.
A society in which the secular state has no jurisdiction over
man's relationship to his God, in which religious organizations are unrecognized by the law—except as voluntary and
private associations—is literally without historical precedent.

Only a handful of scattered dreamers had envisioned a
society in which it would be considered morally wrong for a
civil ruler to impose his religious beliefs on the people, or for
the church to dominate secular affairs. Roger Williams was
probably first in the New World to express this idea when he
pointed out that God had placed the Ten Commandments on
two tablets. On one were those laws prescribing man's relation to God, on the other were those dealing with man's
relations to man. Thus had God indicated clearly, stated

Williams, that the God-man relationship was within the divine jurisdiction, while that of man to man was matter for human tribunals.

The freedom-of-religion idea first found its way into the various state constitutions and then into the federal Constitution. But, as Henry Steele Commager points out, "It is one thing to establish the general principle; another to apply it and carry it to its logical conclusions." The eighteenth century in America brought many disruptive forces: an expanding, socially leveling frontier and the increased nationalism resulting from the War for Independence. It brought also the secularism of the French Revolution and Enlightenment, and its deistic influence upon leading American intellectuals. One major result of this intellectual ferment was the emergence of numerous and varied dissenting sects that attracted many of the religiously inclined. Yet it was well into the nineteenth century (1833 to be exact) before the Congregational churches were completely divorced from the state of Massachusetts.

Complete religious liberty on a national basis was even slower, for it was not until the twentieth century that legal discriminations against Catholics, Jews, deists, and nonbelievers were finally eliminated. At that, both religious tolerance and separation of church and state resulted more from practical necessity than philosophical principle. Time and experience were needed to prove conclusively that in a society based upon a tradition of nonconformity and filled with individuals of various religious, linguistic, and racial backgrounds, "religious freedom was the only workable policy."

Official religious intolerance and persecution in America now are history, but social, educational, and professional discrimination for religious and racial reasons still are very much with us. To decree liberty and tolerance, then, is but an initial step; to enforce these decrees is a continuing struggle.

Today even the most civil-rights-minded Americans are divided over where the line is to be drawn between "authority and conscience." How far can the state go to enforce its judicial decisions regarding religious practices? The Supreme Court—despite the disclaimers of Jews and Seventh-day Adventists—has recently upheld the state ordinances distinguishing Sunday from weekdays. Many states not only still require some religious form of affirmation but penalize blasphemy. (In a unanimous decision, in June, 1961, the United

States Supreme Court ruled unconstitutional Maryland's constitutional requirement that every state officeholder declare his belief in God's existence.) And the thorny question of federal aid to education is made even more so by the related one of whether the receipt of tax funds by parochial schools constitutes a violation of the separation principle. The general public has remained divided on these issues, but then so have our best judicial minds.

The legal and emotional difficulties involved in the question of religious freedom are to be seen not only in early New England's statutes and experiences but in those of the other colonies as well. Even in the comparatively liberal Maryland Colony, founded as a haven for Catholics, tolerance was extended only to those "professing to believe in Jesus Christ."

William Penn was of a distinct, if notable, minority in 1670 when he insisted that for men to restrain or persecute those exercising liberty of conscience was "to impeach the honor of God." For "no man is so accountable to his fellow-creatures," he argued, "as to be imposed upon . . . for any matter of conscience whatever." Yet when drafting his *Frame of Government* in 1682 Penn could insist that all council members and magistrates be "such as profess faith in Jesus Christ," and he promised unqualified freedom only to those acknowledging "the one Almighty and Eternal God to be the Creator, Upholder and Ruler of the World." Shortly thereafter a Pennsylvania law required officers and voters to declare their belief in Christ. This meant that while Jews or non-Christian theists could live in Pennsylvania they could not vote or hold office. Deists and atheists could not even enter. So in the seventeenth century only Rhode Island allowed what a twentieth-century American would consider complete religious freedom.

However, Penn, like Roger Williams before him, was far ahead of his time. Not until the eighteenth century were there heard such voices as those of Thomas Jefferson, James Madison, and George Mason arguing for "freedom of conscience" in the modern sense. Even during the Revolution religious freedom was at best a form of limited tolerance. The Maryland Constitution of 1776 extended "religious liberty" only to those "professing the Christian religion" and empowered the legislature to "lay a general and equal tax, for the support of the Christian religion," upon all inhabitants.

Thomas Jefferson and James Madison led the fight in the

new nation to make religious freedom mean something more than mere tolerance. Raised as Anglicans, both were disturbed that theirs was the established church in every colony from Maryland south, recognizing such a situation as not conducive to religious or political liberty.

One could be sentenced to death in early-seventeenth-century Virginia for criticizing the Trinity or any other Christian article of faith, and until the Revolution any Christian denying the Trinity could lose legal custody of his children. Supported by taxation and special assessments, the Anglican clergy alone could perform marriages or officiate at baptisms. And although they represented the minority belief in many places, the Anglicans were able to limit the religious and secular activities of all other sects. Hardly surprising then that Jefferson and Madison shared the increasingly popular view that any church-state connection was morally wrong.

During the Revolutionary period Presbyterians and Baptists, assisted by Quakers and Mennonites, led the fight in Virginia for greater religious freedom and church-state separation. Members of these sects had migrated to western Virginia in numbers sufficient to exceed the Anglican population and were soon clamoring to abolish taxes supporting the Church of England. They argued that the magistrates' jurisdiction should not be "extended to the salvation of souls."

Shortly before the First Amendment's adoption, Presbyterian church leaders expressed their opposition to taxation for religious purposes by declaring religion too personal and its right of exercise unalienable to be "resigned to the will of society at large . . . much less to the Legislature—which derives its authority wholly from the consent of the people." At the First Amendment's adoption John Leland, Virginia's Baptist spokesman, argued that "government has no more to do with religious opinions of man than with the principles of mathematics."

These religious spokesmen must have been taken aback to have their views succinctly expressed by a deist like Tom Paine, who wrote in *Common Sense*: "As to religion, I hold it to be the indispensable duty of government to protect all conscientious professors thereof, and I know of no other business which government hath to do therewith."

On June 12, 1776, James Madison and fellow Episcopalian George Mason introduced to the Virginia Convention Mason's bill of rights advocating the "free exercise of religion."

Much more vital issues were involved than merely abolishing a tax-supported church. Still in effect was a common law making heresy a capital offense punishable by burning. Also on the statute books was a 1705 law declaring that anyone raised as a Christian who denied the existence of God, the Trinity, the truth of Christianity, and the Bible's divine authority, or insisted there existed more than the one God, was ineligible to hold civil, military, or ecclesiastical office; he could receive no gift or legacy, nor act as a guardian or executor. And he was eligible for a three-year prison term. Admittedly the law was gathering dust, but there existed always the danger of its being used.

The Church of England's formal disestablishment in America began on January 1, 1777, with a law suspending payment of tithes. The liberals, however, would settle for nothing short of complete severance of church and state. With this goal in mind, Jefferson drafted in 1777 his Virginia Statute of Religious Liberty, possibly "the most famous single document in the history of religious freedom in America." Two years later, during his tenure as Virginia's governor, Jefferson presented it to the General Assembly and began what he was to describe as "the severest contest in which I have ever been engaged."

The battle was a long one. In 1784, with Jefferson in France, his Virginia Statute was championed by Madison, Mason, and John Taylor, among others. Madison that year produced his famous state paper addressed to the Virginia General Assembly, A Memorial and Remonstrance on the Religious Rights of Man. His particular target was a proposed bill to provide tax funds for religious teaching.

Pointing to history, Madison argued that wherever "ecclesiastical establishments" had shaped civil society they had upheld political tyranny; in no instance had they protected the people's liberties. A truly just government, he held, should protect a citizen's religious rights with the same zeal it applied to his person and property. It should neither invade a sect's equal rights nor allow any sect to infringe those of another. Any government should realize, he concluded, that all attempts to impose by legal sanction acts disagreeable to great numbers of citizens only weakens the laws in general and slackens all social bonds. Four years later Madison's ideas were embodied in the First Amendment.

Having successfully defeated the religious-teaching bill, Madison, Mason, and Taylor reintroduced into the General

Assembly Jefferson's Virginia Statute of Religious Liberty, and in 1786 they finally saw it enacted into law. A man's civil rights should have no more dependence on his religious views, Jefferson here declared, than on his views in physics or geometry. To bar any man from public office for a religious opinion was to deny him his natural rights; to allow the civil magistrate to restrain individual expression was to destroy all religious freedom. All should profess their religious opinions without restraint, molestation, or loss of "civil capacities."

At the Philadelphia Convention the next year, Madison, Mason, and others of similar persuasion followed up their Virginia victory by excluding from the federal Constitution any reference to God. They wished it to be a completely secular document. The only religious reference they allowed was the negative one prohibiting any religious test for federal office, although they were fully aware they were making "Jews, Turks and infidels" eligible for the presidency. They considered unnecessary any other guarantee of religious liberty, since the federal government would have no legal jurisdiction in any religious matter.

Within four years this logic revealed its inadequacy; there was obvious need for an amendment specifically barring government involvement in religion and assuring religion's free exercise. Upon his return from France in 1789 Jefferson joined in the fight for the bill of rights, with its First Amendment providing that "Congress shall make no law respecting an establishment of religion, or prohibiting the free exercise thereof." With the bill's passage, Jefferson felt free to declare the Constitution now was "unquestionably the wisest yet presented to man." He would later leave instructions that his monument should state only that "Here was Buried/ Thomas Jefferson/ Author of the Declaration/ of American Independence,/ of the Statute of Virginia/ for Religious Freedom,/ and Father of the University of Virginia."

Jefferson and Madison's pride in their accomplishment is understandable. Yet the fight to end the legislating of the mind was far from over. But if slow, progress has been steady. The Anglican Church was disestablished in Pennsylvania, Delaware, and New Jersey as early as 1776, in New York and North Carolina by 1777. In 1789 Georgia followed suit, and in 1790 South Carolina. In almost every instance opposition to increased religious freedom was bitter. Immediately following Vermont's passage of a religious-liberty bill, the *Dartmouth Gazette* (November 18, 1807) labeled it a striking example "of the pernicious and direful, the infernal consequences to which the leveling spirit of democracy must inevitably tend." For the *Gazette* the act's sole object was to eradicate "every moral, virtuous and religious principle from the human heart."

In Connecticut the Congregational churches were tax-supported until the state constitution's adoption in 1818. To that point marriages performed by ministers of other denominations (Episcopalians excepted) were illegal, and Unitarianism was considered a felony. Not until 1833 were the final links between church and state severed in Massachusetts. And then only the vociferous, prolonged, and combined efforts of Episcopalians, Baptists, and Quakers removed the laws requiring all state inhabitants to support with taxes the Congregational churches.

The nation's views on religious expression have changed greatly since the days of the Bible commonwealth. Modern America is now as secular as it is religious. A tax-supported church (as in England) seems to most Americans "an indefensible anachronism," and Jefferson and Madison's major religious principles are part of federal and state legal codes. Few Americans question the need to keep separate church and state—although what constitutes "separation" frequently proves a difficult problem.

Yet the struggle for complete religious understanding continues. The various influences set in motion by the Protestant Reformation—especially those expressed in terms of scriptural and English common law—helped shape an American nation deeply respectful of both Holy Writ and written Constitution, yet a nation comprised of highly vocal interpreters of Bible and Constitution.

The result is an America that is "pluralistic" in religion. And both the secular- and religious-minded cannot but be grateful for the freedom this term implies.

Four: Education

RELIGION, THE BIBLE, AND THE SCHOOLS

CAMBRIDGE-TRAINED PURITANS SET AN EXAMPLE
Mankind has for many centuries looked to its wise men to provide the means, or knowledge, both for placating the supernatural and solving most of its social problems. But no nation has developed a stronger belief in education's magical powers than has America. Certainly no other country's educational history reflects more clearly the steady evolution of its social institutions, and the impact on them of its religious beliefs and practices. Nor has any other people striven harder to develop a school system that would not infringe upon individual freedom or church autonomy. America's educational roots go deep into European cultural history, but its schools have changed and developed many concepts peculiar to the American context.

The Puritan inhabitants of early America intended their schools to prepare the young to walk in God's way. They had no doubt that individual salvation was achieved by directly approaching God, without the encumbrances of church ritual or structure. For them the individual's most effective means of absorbing God's word was to read it for himself. A Puritan's spiritual salvation (or damnation) depended then to a considerable extent on his ability to read. The Reformation had produced this radical idea of universal education; Puritan colonists carried it to the New World.

English Puritans had inherited a rich national tradition of religious education. Indeed, England's grammar schools and universities (particularly Cambridge) provided the stimuli and guides for New England's school system and curricula. Theology, in both its ecclesiastical and philosophical aspects, was the English universities' central academic interest from the Middle Ages to the eighteenth century. For until well into the seventeenth century an English university's prime purpose was to supply clergymen for the Anglican Church. Consequently, all fellowship holders and most of those working toward degrees were planning religious careers. All other disciplines were considered secondary, or ignored entirely.

Science, medicine, law, scholarship, and creative literature were pursued outside the universities. The single academic exception at both Oxford and Cambridge was Hebrew learning, in which such outstanding English Orientalists as Thomas Bilson, Nicholas Fuller, John Lightfoot, Edward Pococke, Miles Smith, and Abraham Wheelock ranked with the best of continental scholars. When scholars were required to translate from the Hebrew Old Testament and Apocrypha in preparing the King James Bible, thirty-two were gathered with little difficulty.

The Reformation emphasis upon learning stimulated the founding of grammar schools in England, and a great many were established under Edward VI and Elizabeth. By the seventeenth century apparently a capable youth could prepare himself for the university at any one of 360 neighborhood grammar schools scattered throughout England.

Some schools were controlled by municipalities, but most were regulated by private corporations, university colleges, or boards of trustees. Almost every town of consequence could boast an endowed grammar school, with London alone having eleven. Most schools required entrance fees and incidental expenses, but they also offered scholarships covering total tuition and board for needy students, while some public and private schools were absolutely free.

Whatever their means of support, all English schools trained boys for the Church of England. The schoolmasters usually were churchmen, and religion was integral to the curriculum. The church was increasingly aware of the importance of biblical linguistics, and established such classically oriented grammar schools as St. Paul's, Christ's Hospital, Westminster, and Merchant Taylors, where most English schoolboys had ample opportunity to learn Hebrew.

The York School charter of January, 1546–47, stipulated that the master was to "have understandinge in the Hebrew, Greek, and Latin tongues," and most of the other grammar schools (and the universities) seem to have taken up Hebrew study soon after this date. By the seventeenth century

Hebrew was an accepted part of the grammar-school curriculum.

Charles Hoole, master of the free school at Rotherham in Yorkshire, has left a detailed account of early-seventeenth-century teaching methods in the grammar schools; he reports that the English Bible served as the pupils' initial textbook, being studied for its language as well as content. In the fourth form Hoole himself replaced the English with a Latin version, and in the sixth with texts in Greek and Hebrew.

Having mastered the rudiments, the student was expected to translate various Pentateuch portions from English and Latin into Hebrew. He then proceeded to translate Psalms, Proverbs, Ecclesiastes, and Job, in that order, and to pen orations, verses, and epistles in Hebrew. In a Latin exercise addressed to his father, the Puritan poet John Milton extols his parent for encouraging him to follow up his Roman and Greek studies with "Palestine's prophetic songs divine." It is not clear at what age Milton acquired his knowledge of Hebrew, but he later stated that this language should be absorbed before the student completes grammar school so that the Scriptures might be read in their original tongue; he then adds, rather offhandedly, "whereto it would be no impossibility to add the Chaldee, and the Syriac dialect."

Hebrew and Greek gained impetus at this time from the demands of theological controversy raging between Protestant and Roman Catholic scholars. The period from 1588 to 1609 was the greatest in Jesuit scholarship, and the English Puritans, who had depended solely on their Bibles—and often on the English versions alone—soon found themselves no match for Jesuit debaters commanding a rich tradition of biblical research and ecclesiastical history. As the seventeenth century unfolded, English Protestant disputants hastily immersed themselves in Latin, Greek, and Hebrew in order to hold their own. They familiarized themselves not only with patristic and Byzantine Greek but with the Greek of the New Testament. And they soon found it necessary to extend their Hebraic studies from the text of the Hebrew Canon to all the related tongues of the Semitic language group.

The increasing academic importance of Hebrew is reflected in a 1605 funeral sermon by Thomas Playfere, at that time Cambridge's most distinguished pulpit orator. Describing Hebrew as the "ancientest, the shortest, the plainest of all languages," he emphasizes its general importance to religious scholarship. A minister may be forgiven his inability to read the rabbinic writings, declares Playfere, yet unless he has a sound grasp of his scriptural text in the original Hebrew "he is compted but a maimed, or as it were but halfe a divine, especially in this learned age."

The England in which Milton grew up was marked by religious zeal and theological concern. People crowded the churches, listening avidly to sermons that today would seem incredibly long. It was a time of memorable preachers. Lancelot Andrewes, John Donne, Joseph Hall, James Ussher, Thomas Fuller, and Jeremy Taylor were only a few of the eloquent pulpit voices. The twentieth-century American may find it difficult to grasp the sermon's importance, but in addition to its religious function the seventeenth-century sermon served those needs now satisfied to a degree by the various mass media.

The English nation had become imbued with the vision of a theocracy on earth. A 1644 Parliamentary ordinance required all ministerial candidates to read the Hebrew and Greek Testaments. At least 10,000 clergymen (and countless lay preachers) spread throughout England the findings of biblical scholars. Biblical learning was no longer the preoccupation of clerics and scholars alone. The Bible had become the core of the Protestant movement; it provided the average Englishman with the means of receiving God's word directly and materially influenced his thinking. And the average, or middle-class, Englishman tended to be Puritan.

But English Puritans had not fared well since 1570, when John Cartwright, their great theorist and spokesman, lost his chair in divinity at Cambridge. Things took an even worse turn in 1603 when James Stuart came to the throne. Resenting Puritanism's "antimonarchical" tendencies, James encouraged the ouster of Puritans from government and academic posts. In 1629 social harassment was replaced by actual persecution, and the Puritan exodus was launched.

The emigrant leaders were university-trained clergymen or grammar-school-educated gentry and merchants. Together these men formed an intellectual ruling class whose standards were accepted by the Massachusetts Bay, New Haven, Connecticut, and even Rhode Island communities and perpetuated in Harvard College.

The University of Cambridge had trained many outstanding Puritan theologians and was the New Englander's accepted intellectual guide and standard. The overriding concern at Cambridge (as at Oxford and Dublin) had been with the struggle between those who would restore to the Anglican Church as much of the medieval church as possible and those who would rid it of whatever lacked scriptural sanction. Many sympathizers with the first view migrated to the Virginia and Maryland colonies.

The New Englanders planned a fresh approach to ethics and morality, church and state, family and school, one that would enable them to attain a new City of God. Hence every congregation needed a learned minister to expound Scripture properly, and every member required sufficient education to follow the exposition. Also, young and old required enough ability to read the capital laws. The American Puritans were determined that the intellectual level to which they had become accustomed in England would not be lowered in the New World, whatever the hardships and peculiar demands of their new life.

Within the Bay Colony's first decade, the Puritans established North America's first public school system and college —and the first printing press outside Mexico. The press was operating in Cambridge by 1639. It originally produced sermons and tracts, but soon was turning out works of history, biography, and poetry. These works formed the intellectual base for colonial thought, and much of this thought has left its mark upon American thought.

The Puritans had preceded even the printing press with the "first flower of their wilderness"—Harvard College. Historians point to Harvard's appearance in 1636, a mere six years after that of the first sizable Puritan contingent, as concrete proof of Puritan concern for education. The wisdom and sturdiness with which the Puritans built is borne out by Harvard's influence upon so many later American colleges and universities and on the country's general intellectual life.

The Massachusetts General Court voted the college into existence in October, 1636, and appropriated £400 for the purpose. Indian hostilities and the Anne Hutchinson episode delayed the project for over a year. But by the summer of 1638 the Pequot Indians had been subdued, the Antinomians outvoted, and Mrs. Hutchinson dispatched. Six magistrates and six ministers then were appointed as a Board of Overseers, a one-acre Cambridge campus—with house—purchased, a professor appointed, and a freshman class organized. That September, on the death of Cambridge graduate John Harvard, the college inherited his four-hundred-book library and half his modest estate. The college then became Harvard College, and the country's first institution of higher learning was launched.

The new school was beset by difficulties. Harvard's major chronicler, Samuel Eliot Morison, states that for many "in the radical fringe of the puritan movement . . . hostility to universities and to learned ministers was an article of faith. Sincere fanatics called the universities 'stews of Anti-Christ,' 'houses of lies,' that 'stink before God with the most loathsome abomination.' "

But during the next decade the college overcame all external opposition and internal difficulties to develop an academic structure and curriculum patterned after, and rivaling, those of the English universities.

The Puritan community's zealous efforts in Harvard's behalf was due only in part to its understandable desire for an educated ministry. Certainly a religious spirit permeated the college. Yet, as Professor Morison points out, both community and college, while fully aware of their spiritual obligations, had no intention of stifling intellectual inquiry. Dissatisfied with Protestant theology's narrow confines, most New Englanders advocated the broadest type of higher education. It was to this end that Harvard College was dedicated. Indeed, by assuming the power to grant degrees, Harvard may be credited, as A. W. Lowell was to put it, with America's "first declaration of independence, in that it declared and settled for the colonies the principles of freedom of education from control by Church and State in the mother country."

The Puritans were not overly concerned with democratic procedures, and undemocratic practices developed from time to time at Harvard, Yale, and the other colonial colleges. Some historians have exaggerated such shortcomings. More significantly, boys of ability, whatever their social or economic status, usually found scholarships or jobs available.

Harvard having established the precedent, such schools as Yale, Amherst, Mount Holyoke, and New York University soon were started by early settlers determined also to give their young people adequate training for the future.

Neither Harvard nor its immediate academic successors in New England, although religiously oriented, were theological seminaries; only half of Harvard's seventeenth-century graduates became ministers. And only upon receipt of his bachelor of arts could a student actually begin his theological studies. Undergraduates, whatever their vocational goals, were required to take a classical course similar to that given to their elders at Cambridge. Instruction was in Latin (as were most of the textbooks) and centered upon six of the medieval Seven Arts and the Three Philosophies—as well as upon Greek, Hebrew, and Ancient History.

The Puritans thus provided their young with a well-rounded classical education. Yet they little doubted that a sound academic program had two principal ends: knowledge of God through increased awareness of his word, and a strong orientation toward proper conduct or action. Every student, therefore, was expected to analyze the Bible in Hebrew and Greek, to be familiar with some of Protestant-ism's basic works, and to explicate the numerous sermons to which he was exposed.

HEBREW AND GREEK NEEDED   Hebrew and Greek were obvious prerequisites for a proper reading of the Old and New Testaments.

The Puritans' strong identification with the children of Israel had engendered a veneration for the Hebrew tongue; further, they believed that the Old Testament was all the more valid when rendered in the original Hebrew rather than in translation. Many prominent early New Englanders were ardent Hebraists. Among them were ministers Richard Mather, John Eliot, and Thomas Welde; these men translated the Psalms from Hebrew into English, submitting their results to Harvard president John Dunster for final revision. The fruit of their efforts was the famous *Bay Psalm Book,* the first book published in the American colonies. There were other Hebraists among the Puritans. Increase Mather delivered Hebrew discourses, and his son, Cotton, produced a treatise on Hebrew punctuation. John Udall translated Peter Martinius' Hebrew grammar and compiled a Hebrew dictionary, *The Key of the Holy Tongue.* John Davenport saw to it that Hebrew was included in the New Haven Colony's first public-school curriculum.

Harvard students received a thorough grounding in Semitic studies; they took Hebrew, Syriac, and Aramaic one day a week for their entire four years. Nor did they lack adequate instruction or materials. Harvard presidents John Dunster and Charles Chauncy were sound Hebraists, and the Harvard Library possessed an excellent array of Targums (Aramaic translations or paraphrases of the Old Testament), Talmuds, and rabbinical writings. Proof as to the efficiency of the Hebraic instruction is offered by the many baccalaureate theses devoted to the fine points of Hebrew grammar and syntax. But the Harvard students' principal Hebrew text remained the Old Testament.

A proper reading of the New Testament required adequate Greek preparation, and sometimes Hebrew and Greek instruction started prior to college entrance. Both the Boston Latin School and the free school in St. Andrew's parish (after 1695) offered Hebrew and Greek, and other New England grammar schools also may have done so. One 1655 Harvard entrance requirement expected the new student to have some knowledge of Greek grammar, and the same year the college inaugurated a custom requiring sophomores, juniors, and seniors, as part of morning prayer, to render a verse of Old Testament Hebrew into Greek.

Not until 1782 were students—and then only in special cases—allowed to substitute French for Hebrew study, and until 1817 every Harvard commencement exercise contained a Hebrew oration.

Harvard set the pattern for American private colleges throughout the colonial period. Their presidents were almost always clergymen—as were at least half of every trustees board. And religious instruction and chapel attendance were required. Harvard's founders had been determined not to leave behind an illiterate ministry; similarly, Yale's founders declared their zeal to uphold and propogate Protestantism by "a succession of Learned and Orthodox men." Like their Harvard predecessors, the Yale trustees were not interested merely in a divinity school; they wished to create a center where young people could be instructed in the arts and sciences and where they might be prepared for employment both in church and government.

Yale also placed strong emphasis upon Hebrew study and its original seal depicted an open Bible bearing the Hebrew inscription *Urim Vetumim* (Light and Truth). In deference to those beginning students who might not yet have had Hebrew, the authorities added the Latin translation, *Lux et*

Veritas. Yale has remained a thriving center for Hebraic and Judaic studies.

The later independent colleges in New England and the Middle colonies all revealed the Harvard-Yale influence. Princeton, Brown, King's College (Columbia), Queen's College (Rutgers), and Dartmouth emphasized a broad classical education as preparation primarily for later theological study and only secondarily for public service. King's College, for example, was dedicated to teaching "principles of Christianity and Morality generally agreed upon." Samuel Johnson, its first president, authored *An English and Hebrew Grammer, Being the First Short Rudiments of Those Two Languages Taught Together, to Which is Added a Synopsis of all the Parts of Learning.* He considered Hebrew "essential to a Gentleman's education," expected all King's College tutors to be well versed in it, and taught its fundamentals to his children and grandchildren.

Dartmouth, established just prior to the Revolution, had the double assignment of training missionaries to the Indians and of supplying the region's numerous new churches and congregations with a learned and orthodox ministry. Included among its faculty were such Hebrew scholars as John Smith and Benjamin Hale. Rutgers, Princeton, and Brown also made Hebrew part of their curricula.

Farther south, William and Mary and the Philadelphia Academy (University of Pennsylvania) had less ministerial control and were more concerned than their northern neighbors with preparing students for practical and public careers. Yet even they could boast a distinguished tradition of Hebraic studies.

Most of the schools mentioned have offered Hebrew uninterruptedly since their inception.

ARMOR AGAINST SATAN   American higher education prior to the twentieth century, even under the best conditions, affected a relatively small proportion of the national populace. Certainly this held true throughout the colonial period. More encompassing were the elementary and grammar schools. These public schools proved the chief means of forming America's cultural patterns and of transmitting them to succeeding generations. Historically, educating an entire population at public expense, as a civil right under direct state rather than church auspices, was unknown until tried in seventeenth-century Massachusetts. With a few scattered exceptions in Renaissance Italy, Europe (from Rome's fall until the seventeenth century) accepted church dominance of all social, moral, and intellectual institutions. Education, in particular, was viewed as one of the church's natural means of perpetuating its concepts and discipline.

Upon his arrival in New England the Puritan had little thought of a free secular education for children of all classes. Yet he was trapped by his own religious philosophy. To the Puritan mind illiteracy was synonymous with heresy. Many New England communities began hiring teachers before any law required it. And more often than not the community had to bear most of the expense. Boston started the practice in 1635, Charleston followed the next year, and in the next decade or so the towns of Dorchester, Dedham, Cambridge, New Haven, Hartford, and Roxbury followed suit. Teaching standards varied with the abilities and inclinations of the available schoolmasters.

By 1642 it was obvious that, left to their own conscience, many New England parents neglected their children's education. The concerned leaders passed the Massachusetts Act of 1642, making parents responsible for elementary education. In fact, the law required parents not only to keep their children constantly and properly employed but to teach them and the indentured servants "to read the english tongue, and knowledge of the Capital laws: upon penaltie of twentie shillings for each neglect therein. Also that all masters of families doe once a week (at the Least) catechize their children and servants in the grounds and principles of Religion."

New England education clearly was not the result of a grass-roots movement. An educated and autocratic leadership handed down to the people the needs and ideas for formal learning in the form of laws. A century passed before the leadership convinced the people of the value of a tax-supported education, and a second century elapsed before this concept spread beyond New England.

The average New Englander was far from rich. He often needed his children's labor on the farm or fishing boat. But his leaders gave him little opportunity to forget his moral and religious obligation to provide the young with an education. There are those, thundered Harvard's president Charles Chauncy in a 1655 commencement sermon, who would prefer to overlook such an obligation; these recalcitrants are not even "troubled with strict sabbaths" but wish only to "follow their worldly business and have their children . . . drudge for them at plough, or hough, or such like servil imployments, that themselves may be eased."

New England educators before the eighteenth century made little attempt either to secularize or democratize their school system. Except for Rhode Island's inhabitants, New Englanders had little use for democracy in general. It seemed to them to have no logical connection to education, which was essentially the most obvious and direct means of approaching God. Yet they made education easily available and relatively inexpensive for those male students willing to work and capable of absorbing Latin grammar. However, the Puritans showed little concern for the education of girls beyond the ability to read their Bibles and catechisms, and even less for boys who failed to cope with Latin, the language of instruction.

Although New England had sharply demarcated social and economic classes, the Puritan caste system was not nearly as rigid as it often has been described. Many, arriving as unskilled laborers or servants, by initiative and ability considerably improved their social and economic status. A man could choose almost any occupation, and the continual immigrant influx produced an elaborate apprentice system and ever-increasing trade opportunities.

As in most communities, wealth was perhaps New England's major social determinant—that is, wealth and the proper religious outlook. But education followed close behind. An ex-laborer of increased affluence could see his children take advantage of the village grammar school and Harvard's educational opportunities and then marry into the most respected older families. Twentieth-century America's highly mobile social patterns actually were evolving in the autocratic and authoritarian Bible commonwealth.

Thus it seems especially ironic that Rhode Island—the most democratic, liberal, and individualistic of New England communities—should have proved the educational laggard. The other colonies quickly copied Massachusetts Bay's compulsory common- and grammar-schools act of 1647. By 1672 all of New England—except Rhode Island—could boast a compulsory education system. Only toward the end of the seventeenth century were even private schools established at Newport—and then merely for children of the more well-to-do, and only one Rhode Island youth is known to have entered college before the eighteenth century. Not until the eighteenth century was half over did Rhode Island develop an intellectual life worthy of her founders' penetrating and original minds.

Twentieth-century commentators have had difficulty reconciling the Puritans' approach to education with the convenient stereotype of grim, dogmatic religious fanatics. So it is with mingled surprise and admiration that a staff writer for a popular national magazine recently declared that "What the Puritans actually invented was the universal, compulsory, tax-supported educational system, the prototype in all important respects of what was to become the public school." To be completely accurate, it should be recognized that by 1600 England had free grammar schools that served as models for their American counterparts. Yet it remains true that the Puritans not only introduced such schools to the New World but placed them under community rather than church control and tried, whenever possible, to appoint lay schoolmasters. The Puritan contribution to modern public education was not a small one.

The inhabitants of all the colonies were moved by various social, political, and intellectual motives. But for the New Englander religion was never far from the surface. To be ignorant was to invite heresy and error. Conversely, to know the capital laws was to be aware of God's most important dictums. The printed codes always cited a capital law's scriptural source to enhance its importance, and the laws were required to be published so that every commonwealth inhabitant would be familiar with them. If, after warnings by the town selectmen (who tested or "catechized" the children periodically), parents neglected the education of children (or of servants), the children could be removed from their custody.

The Massachusetts Act of 1647 is held to be the earliest general education law of modern times, as it made education, for the first time, a "public responsibility." Every Massachusetts town having fifty families was to hire a schoolmaster, whose wages would be paid either by parents or town, as each community decided. Reading instruction was to be available to all who qualified, regardless of ability to pay.

No one was to be denied an elementary education because of his economic status. Towns having a hundred families were required to establish a grammar school, with schoolmasters capable of preparing students for the university.

In the famous preamble to the 1647 act the New Englander left little doubt as to his belief that education was a means of enhancing religious health, "It being one chief project of that old deluder, Satan, to keep men from the knowledge of Scriptures, as in former times keeping them in an unknown tongue."

Morison warns against overlooking the strategy involved in affixing a religious sanction to a social obligation so that reluctant inhabitants would be willing to accept the financial burden of education. There is no denying the validity of his observation. Yet it is clear this legislative basis for America's public education stemmed from the Puritan conviction that the needs of church and commonwealth were interrelated.

The ministers never allowed their congregations to forget the need not merely to read but to read Scripture, and not occasionally or once a week, but daily. The Bible emphasized that children were God's special concern. Woe, therefore, unto the parent on Judgment Day, warned the Puritan ministers, who failed properly to prepare a child to meet his Maker. More than one shivering New Englander must have been moved to action by Cotton Mather's chilling admonition that should a child lack either spiritual knowledge or wisdom because of parental negligence, that parent could expect a terrible punishment indeed on the Day of Judgment.

The Puritan approach to education—especially as exemplified in the Massachusetts Act of 1647—bore many similarities to that of the ancient Hebrews, with whom they identified so closely. Both peoples viewed education as a means to develop in man a sense of his obligation to uphold divine law.

Hebraic ceremonies and festivals attempted to convey these values to the young. Children's lives were to be "a continual learning," and Hebrew parents were admonished to impress upon their children the truth of God's principles by constant use of appropriate words and signs.

Like the Puritans, the Hebrews in their early history were little concerned with teaching the student to do more than read. Hebrew literature had been created during the ninth to seventh centuries B.C. by the priests and prophets, and while some parts took a written form before the Babylonian exile, most continued to be transmitted orally from generation to generation. The Hebrews established no formal schools during the preexilic period, as priests and prophets directed their legal interpretations at adults. As in New England, the Hebrew father (and, to a lesser degree, the mother) had the responsibility of training the child in God's law and the communal traditions. This approach prevailed until the first century B.C.

In exile, the Hebrews became aware their literature needed codifying. Slowly the oral lore was written down and divided into books of Law, Prophets, and Writings. The teacher's mantle passed from the prophets, who had articulated the literature, to the scribes (*soferim*), who were mostly from the priestly caste, or Levites, and who transcribed and commented on the now-sacred books. The scribes soon became known as the "expounders" of the law and constituted the first organized teaching body in Jewish history.

At first the scribes directed their free public and synagogue lectures at the fathers, who in turn continued to instruct the young. But by the first century B.C. it had become apparent to Jerusalem's religious authorities (as it was later to New England's elders) that many fathers were inadequate teachers and that fatherless children were deprived of educational opportunities. One of history's earliest known compulsory school laws was introduced early in the first century A.D. by Rabbi Simeon ben Shetah, president of the Sanhedrin, who decreed that Jerusalem's children no longer be taught at home but in public schools established for the purpose. And about the middle of the first century A.D., Joshua ben Gamla, the high priest, ordered elementary schools established in every Palestinian town. In A.D. 232 the patriarch Judah II felt compelled to punish several congregations for failing to provide adequate teaching facilities. "A community that neglects to establish schools for children is bound to perish," he warned.

Cotton Mather seems to have had a somewhat similar thought in mind when he wrote, more than fourteen and one-half centuries later:

The reader knows that in every town among Jews, there was a *school*, whereat children were taught the reading of the *law*; and if there were any town destitute of a *school,* the men of place did stand excommunicate, until one were erected; besides and beyond which they had *midrashoth,* or *divinity-schools,* in which they expounded the law to their disciples. Whether the churches of *New England* have been duly careful or not about *their* other *schools,* they have not been altogether careless about their *midrashoth*; and it is well for them that they have not.

Other similarities are evident between Hebrew and Puritan education practices. Both peoples felt an elementary education for girls was sufficient, and both imposed strict social discipline. The bearded rabbis would have nodded in agreement at Cotton Mather's famous epigram, "Better whipt, than Damn'd."

And the rabbis would have been pleased that the Puritans too regarded the rod as a necessary but last resort, to be used only after every form of gentler persuasion had failed. He could never bring himself to strike a child, Mather admitted, except when the latter was guilty of some extreme obstinancy or wrongdoing. While Proverbs repeatedly encouraged "the rod of discipline," it also emphasized that "A rebuke goes deeper into a man of understanding than a hundred blows into a fool." The Hebrew teacher was enjoined, therefore, to avoid coercion, to attempt to win his pupils' affections, and to be as patient as possible with slow learners. If a whipping was called for, he was to employ a small strap instead of a stick.

Certainly the hardworking agricultural Puritans could accept the Hebrew view that intellectual learning without knowledge of a trade represented an impractical and incomplete education. For despite his son's compulsory attendance at elementary school, the Hebrew father was expected to teach his son a practical vocation. "He who does not teach his son a trade," warned the Talmud, "virtually teaches him to steal."

Both Hebrews and Puritans viewed children as ignorant of the knowledge and fear of God and therefore vulnerable to Satan's blandishments. But everyone was born with the capacity for absorbing knowledge, and the parent who failed to insure his child's acquisition of religious instruction was remiss in fulfilling the covenant. With either people, ignorance of God's law did not mitigate the spiritual crime for child or parent.

For the Puritan, certainly, childish innocence in no way lessened the burden of evil man naturally inherited as a son of sinful Adam. His naïveté merely prevented the child from restraining his evil tendencies. The vital thing was to begin religious instruction as soon as possible; only in earliest childhood could training transform an evil nature into a moral one. Any other period was too late, as Satan began his assaults upon the infant. The parent was required by law to teach his child, at least once a week, from a "catechism" book, which summarized Puritan doctrines in question-and-answer form. This steady religious diet was somewhat counterbalanced when the child began formal school, where the approach (if not the goal) tended to be more secular.

Before age five the child might attend a reading school, where he would be expected to master the rudiments of reading, perhaps from a copy of John Cotton's *Milk for Babes, Drawn Out of the Breasts of both Testaments Chiefly for the Spirituall Nourishment of Boston Babes in either England*. School laws required merely a reading ability; thus only upon indicating some special competence in reading his primer or Bible did a student move on to learn ciphering and writing from a writing master or in a writing school. From the writing school he went (at about age seven or eight) to a grammar school. Here he was exposed to the classics and proved his capacity (or lack of it) for Harvard College by coping with Latin and Greek. He could expect a seven-year classical curriculum, generally similar to that of the Elizabethan grammar schools, with little concern for modern history or science.

RISE OF THE SECULAR SCHOOL   Neither in grammar school nor at Harvard were the classics so presented as to conflict with or cast doubt upon religious belief. The Puritans had no intention of producing skeptics, and there is little indication that seventeenth-century studies resulted in any. Reading and writing were learned from texts brimming with religious precepts. The most famous of these, Benjamin Harris' *The New England Primer* (c. 1683), began its alphabet instruction with "In Adam's Fall/We Sinned all."

New England's educational attitudes and development differed sharply from those of the Southern colonies. Social growth and geography contributed significantly to these differences. New England's populace concentrated first in the small agricultural villages that evolved steadily into a well-integrated cluster of seaport and river communities. Village schools were relatively easy to establish and support. Virginia settlement was more dispersed, with individual plantations, separated by bad roads, serving as the social and economic unit. With Jamestown literally the only village before 1700, it becomes clear that in seventeenth-century Virginia any organized approach to education simply was not feasible. (This also became increasingly true in eighteenth-century New England, as an expanding population spread to outlying farms and replaced the increasingly distant village schoolhouse with the itinerant schoolmaster.)

Virginia's basic colonizing principle was simply to extend English civil and religious practices. The Anglican aristocracy had little desire to develop an original or even independent educational system. Its clergy saw scant value in universal education or literacy. Neither church nor government developed a sense of obligation to educate the people.

Virginia's growth pattern and leadership had far-reaching effects on its education. Destined to play a highly important intellectual and political role in eighteenth-century American history, Virginia made no significant early contribution to the evolution of the nation's public schools. The wealthy tidewater aristocracy provided its children with tutors and later sent them abroad or to New England or to the exclusive College of William and Mary, established in 1693. Those public schools that did come slowly into existence were started by the parish or by individual clergymen. Here religion naturally played a more significant role. Tutors and teachers were expected to be devout and thoroughly conversant with Scriptures, and textbooks were heavily laden with religious matter.

Religion also influenced the educational processes of such Middle colonies as New York, New Jersey, and Pennsylvania. Like that of Virginia, but for a different reason, these colonial governments did not assist in educating the young. Virginia was a cohesive English settlement; the inhabitants of the Middle colonies represented a variety of cultures and religious persuasions. Their views of the Bible differed, and so did the languages in which they read it. There was little

chance of their agreeing on how it should be taught. Hence
their schools were started and supported by the various
churches and educational societies, and government at best
was expected not to interfere.

In time—as succeeding generations moved westward—
the idea spread that education was a community rather than
a church responsibility. Religious and classical studies
throughout the colonies were strongly affected, undergoing
severe academic shrinkage during the post-revolutionary period. The specific reasons for this shrinkage are many and
varied, but most are related to the founding fathers' separation of church and state and the resultant de-emphasis of
religious teaching in tax-supported schools.

The republic's formation introduced vast changes in America's educational structure. But an earlier first step had been
the New England town hall's replacement of the meetinghouse as the community's administrative center. All the town
business—including school matters—were discussed in the
town halls; the taxes decided upon to meet school expenses
now were civil rather than church funds.

Town authorities began early in the eighteenth century to
take from the ministers the power to "certificate" the schoolmasters, and despite the reluctance of many schools to discard ministerial control, the minister's role was reduced by
the century's close merely to accompanying civil officials
on their school visits. Church schools had become in effect
state schools. By the time the founding fathers started formulating the national and state governments, few states cared
to quarrel with this New England principle that, as state
institutions, schools should be controlled by the state.

A gradual but steady secularizing process had been put in
motion, one very much a part of the eighteenth century's
rationalist pattern of general religious de-emphasis. By midcentury most of America's intellectual leaders had embraced
skepticism and deism. By 1776 only one American in ten
was affiliated officially with a church organization.

Religion in America still exerted an important influence
upon many areas of American life. But this influence was
more general and diffuse than in the past and had a different
coloration. Along the frontier the dissenting Baptists and
Methodists had developed strong social voices. And both
deists and these nonconformist sects were determined that
history's many religious tragedies should not be repeated here.
Their alliance guaranteed the enactment of the First Amend-

ment, which severed any and every possible tie between government and a religious organization.

The new nation's leaders devoted themselves increasingly to protecting from one another the various, and often competing, religious sects. They sought also to protect the non-believers from the more militantly religious and to place the federal government beyond the possibility of religious domination. To guarantee freedom of worship (or nonworship) to all, and to prevent any one religion from becoming "established" as government-sanctioned, the Constitution's drafters evolved the principle of church-state separation. Education, having been so closely associated with religion, was also dissociated from the federal structure; it was delegated to the authority of the various state legislatures as part of the "other powers" not restricted by the Constitution to Congress.

The eighteenth-century humanists dominating the Continental Congress could see that the entire American democratic experiment depended on a vastly expanded educational base, and they were quick to champion "universal" education. "A popular government without popular information or the means of acquiring it," wrote James Madison, "is but a prologue to a farce or a tragedy." Certainly if they were to prove the Declaration of Independence's assertion that "all men are created equal," they would have to extend the franchise considerably, for when Washington became president only one in seven "free adult males" could vote. The humanists were convinced only an educated people could understand its political rights and responsibilities or sustain a democratic republic in which all had a voice.

"If the condition of man is to be progressively ameliorated," stated Thomas Jefferson, spokesman for so much of the century's humanistic thought, "education is to be the chief instrument in effecting it." He and his fellow humanists were certain that properly allied with reason there was little universal education could not accomplish: "Enlighten the people generally, and tyranny and oppression of body and mind will vanish like evil spirits at the dawn of day."

A national system of public education obviously was needed to prepare Americans for voting. The founding fathers' approach to education was predominantly secular. They believed education to be the concern solely of civic authorities and that public funds should not be used for sectarian teachings. Jefferson characteristically made a pioneer attempt in that direction when, amid the Revolutionary turbulence of 1779, he presented to the Virginia Assembly his "Bill for the More General Diffusion of Knowledge." This was a plan for a tax-supported public-school system embodying all levels of education through the university level. It was designed to educate free for three years all young people "endowed with genius and virtue . . . without regard to wealth, birth or other accidental condition or circumstance." Jefferson proposed that education was to be devoid of all "religious reading, instruction, or exercise" that was in any way "inconsistent with the tenets of any religious sect or denomination." This qualification just about eliminated any form of religious teaching.

In 1784 James Madison led a successful fight in the Virginia General Assembly against "A Bill Establishing a Provision for Teachers of the Christian Religion." Madison's eloquent statement of views, *A Memorial and Remonstrance on the Religious Rights of Man*, was the first noteworthy attempt to block completely the use of tax funds to support religious teachers; it undoubtedly influenced the First Amendment's actual phrasing.

By 1787 Jefferson saw some of his earlier ideas materialize when Congress passed the Northwest Ordinance, which became the legal and administrative code for the Middle West's sparsely settled public lands. In addition to freedom of worship and trial by jury, the territorial government was authorized to promote "schools and the means of education," with one-mile-square sections throughout the vast area set aside to support educational activities. The resources from these special grants in time paid for numerous educational installations, from schoolhouses to state universities.

Events were moving much too rapidly for some of the nation's leaders. These men could not conceive of schools completely divorced from religious instruction. They hadn't insisted upon educational provisions in the Constitution only because they had expected the traditional teaching modes to continue. Dr. Benjamin Rush is an example; this noted physician, educator, political leader, and signer of the Declaration of Independence championed Bible study in all public schools. His *A Defense of the Use of the Bible as a School Book* argued that the Bible not only emphasized those democratic principles toward which all Americans were striving (the equality of men and a code of proper laws and moral values), but provided the only adequate basis for a satisfactory education.

The Bible continued in wide use as a public-school reader. Catechizing remained a popular practice, and many textbooks retained their strongly religious character. At the same time many schools simply did not bother to end sectarian teachings. In general, however, the Congressional intellectual climate, reflected by the First Amendment, gradually asserted itself. A new pattern emerged when the New Hampshire (1792) and Connecticut (1818) constitutions specified that public funds were to be used only for public schools. (Even when Congregational ministers in these states retained local supervision of community schools, no religious sect could share the tax moneys.) Other states were quick to follow. From 1844 on, existing state constitutions steadily were altered to prohibit the use of tax funds for denominational purposes of any kind, and those states entering the Union were careful to include such laws.

"TO FOLLOW THE TRUTH"   As the nineteenth century progressed most political leaders committed themselves to church-state separation, and the colonial period's religious approaches to education gave way to rationalism's secular ones. American education's prime concern became the pragmatic and utilitarian one of preparing all for "a useful and happy life," of making each American an effectively functioning member of an increasingly commercial, scientific, and industrial society.

America was being transformed rapidly by the socially leveling forces of the western frontier and the growing eastern industrial centers. European immigrants streaming into the cities needed instruction in English and the American social process, while the newly settled Midwestern states needed innumerable new schools. Perhaps the most important educational need was created by the steady elimination of property qualifications for the right to vote.

Technical, scientific, and professional curricula were in demand. Much less concern was expressed for the "mental discipline" of Hebrew, Greek, Latin, and the other classical studies. Established colleges looked less frequently to religious organizations and more to wealthy merchants and manufacturers for financial assistance. The schools they added were in science, engineering, medicine, and law.

The nineteenth century also saw an increasing number of states become university sponsors. State universities developed quickly after the Revolution and introduced radical curricular changes. The first few—the universities of Georgia (1784) and North Carolina (1789)—did continue some traditional academic-religious practices. These encouraged the leadership of Protestant ministers and laymen, taught Christian philosophy, and required Sunday-worship attendance. But it was a time of change for tax-supported schools.

The Revolution's social and political ideas officially entered the academic world in 1819 with the University of Virginia. No sectarian group was to have a voice in the school's teachings, nor were any sectarian views to be favored. "This institution will be based on the illimitable freedom of the human mind," wrote Jefferson (its "spiritual" father) to an English acquaintance. "For here we are not afraid to follow truth wherever it may lead, nor to tolerate any error so long as reason is left free to combat it." Later the state universities of Michigan (1837) and Wisconsin (1849) followed Virginia's example in rigidly enforcing the church-state separation principle. They abolished compulsory daily and Sunday services, broadened the conventional college curriculum, and developed professional schools. And they were careful not to acquire denominational ties.

Organized religion refused to lie dormant. In reaction to these secularizing social and intellectual forces, an evangelistic fervor engulfed American churches during the first half of the nineteenth century. Orthodox churches and evangelistic sects began establishing denominational colleges that would not only propagate faith but would combat deism, liberalism, and "French radicalism." The Baptist Convention of 1820, for instance, adopted the slogan, "every state its own Baptist college," and Methodists, Congregationalists, and Presbyterians followed suit. The Catholic Church also established three colleges during these years. These denominational colleges, however, experienced a high mortality rate.

Throughout the nineteenth century neither public nor private colleges continued the former emphasis on Semitic studies. When taught, the Scriptures were translated into English and relegated to "Bible as Literature" courses within the English literature department. Greek virtually disappeared from the undergraduate program. Both Hebrew and

Greek were reserved for specialists and relegated to graduate departments in Semitic or Oriental languages, or theology, or to seminaries.

Increased secularization also ended the custom of selecting ministers to be college presidents, many of whom had been highly competent scholars. In 1840, clergymen or trained churchmen occupied the presidencies of virtually every important American college; in 1940, clergymen-presidents were virtually nonexistent, but they have been making a limited reappearance during the past two decades.

Although the state universities are nonreligious, most of them today offer elective courses in comparative religions, history of religion, and the Bible as literature. Some state universities even hold chapel services on a strictly voluntary basis, and one (the University of South Carolina) is governed by a charter proviso that its president must be neither atheist nor infidel.

In the twentieth century's troubled first decades some universities discontinued their few remaining Hebrew and Semitics courses or departments. But in recent years an upsurge in Semitic languages in general—and in Hebraic and Jewish linguistics and philosophy in particular—has been evident in a number of colleges and universities. A reawakened interest in religious ideas, the emergence of outstanding theologians of all faiths, the creation of modern Israel, and the finding of the Dead Sea scrolls may be contributing factors.

In the past few decades several state universities have established undergraduate and graduate programs in religion. In 1925 the University of Iowa took the first step with an interdenominational program leading to the doctorate. (Private subscription covered faculty salaries, with the university providing physical facilities and administrative expenses.) Since then other state universities, such as Michigan, Hawaii, and Oregon, have developed somewhat similar programs. And numerous state universities have established and financed chairs of religion.

A DEMOCRATIC PATTERN EMERGES   The colleges and universities generally had an easier time shifting from a religious to a secular basis than did the public schools. As secular considerations increasingly replaced religious ones, those formulating and controlling school curricula were no longer churchmen. The church elders, who had dominated not only the community's thought but its political and social concepts as well, gave way to leaders who depended upon gaining the public's financial support for nonreligious reasons.

The entire community or "state," not merely those sharing specific religious dogmas, was now involved in every public school. Everyone was expected to help finance schools, whether or not he was the parent of schoolchildren and whatever his social, political, or religious views. And no sectarian teaching or favoritism could be allowed in schools dependent for finances upon the varied total community.

This reorientation process took time, progressing much more rapidly in some states than in others. By the time of the Civil War American schools born of seventeenth-century Protestant factionalism had evolved into the modern, tax-supported, secular, and democratic public-school system. "There was hardly any uniformity from one state or even one city to another," writes Robert Coughlan in *Life,* "but from primary schools to state universities, somewhere in the Union all the essential parts had been invented."

So radical a transformation, however, was not without wide and bitter opposition. Some attacked the public schools as "socialistic"; others claimed it would make the masses dissatisfied and their children unwilling to work with their hands. Many resented paying for the education of children other than their own, while some were opposed to "free" education. But the fiercest opposition, not surprisingly, came from the various religious groups. For the devout the shock of American education being no longer religious had not yet worn off.

In the midst of this educational turbulence Horace Mann made his contribution. Massachusetts established the country's first state board of education in 1837, with Mann, a lawyer by training, as its secretary. Mann was a public-education enthusiast, and under his leadership Massachusetts developed within twelve years a highly efficient public-school system. He studied European school philosophies for usable ideas as he set to building teachers' colleges and school libraries, improving teachers' salaries, lengthening school terms, and establishing an education journal. In 1842 he saw Massachusetts pass a compulsory-education law. Mann's organizational skill made the Massachusetts school system a model for communities throughout the country; it also brought down upon him the wrath of Protestantism's dissenting sects. This time the religious spokesmen were not fighting secularism in the schools but Mann's advocacy of a nonsectarian Bible-religion as part of America's public education.

Mann was far from hostile to religion; in fact, he was thoroughly convinced that a proper education involved moral and ethical, as well as technical and scientific, knowledge. And the most significant moral values, he felt, were those contained in the Bible and therefore shared by all Christianity. He believed, however, that sectarianism was wrongheaded and shortsighted. Hence he held that the Bible, as Protestantism's "common denominator," should become an integral part of school life. Teachers were to read aloud those sections encouraging morally uplifting behavior, but they were to refrain from sectarian interpretation or comment, for their students represented all denominations.

Horace Mann's approach seemed a happy compromise to a difficult problem. Certainly most of New England, where the dissenting sects had broken the Congregationalist monopoly, appeared satisfied to accept Mann's "pan-Protestant" attitude. Mann's ideas also found favor with most of the Protestant groups in the Middle Atlantic states and along the frontier, where Calvinism had never become as firmly entrenched as in New England.

Other groups, however, within and without Protestantism, viewed Mann's approach as a breach of the First Amendment's rigid separation of church and state. During this period Massachusetts gradually withdrew support from sectarian colleges, insisting that those she incorporated apply no religious test either to faculty or students.

Nothing, it appeared, could halt the growth of nonsectarian public education or the steady decline of church-sponsored private schools.

Then a new element entered in American life: large-scale Catholic immigration. During the Revolutionary period there had been probably no more than 25,000 Catholics in America; by 1850 there were more than a million and a half. And Mann's insistence that the schools allow the Bible to "speak for itself" held for Catholics little appeal; they did not want their children exposed to the Protestant Bible in any form.

Arriving in great numbers from Ireland and the Catholic parts of Germany in mid-nineteenth century (and later from southern and eastern Europe), Catholics found the American public schools in turbulent transition from Protestantism to secularism. Protestants and secularists alike were tense and suspicious—and increasingly hostile to the rapidly growing non-Protestant aggregation. For their part the Catholics could see little difference between the various Protestant sects and resented the exposure of their children in the public schools to even the mildest Protestant exercises. Catholic parents resorted to the courts to challenge Bible instruction in the classroom. But the courts decided repeatedly that school authorities possessed the legal right to require all students to read the Bible. They also ruled that the King James Version generally was recognized to be "non-sectarian."

Anti-Catholic feeling began to crystallize as early as the 1840's when New York City Catholics, under Bishop John Hughes's leadership, made their first serious attempt to get a proportionate share of the city school funds. Their parochial schools had received at least partial support from the public funds in New York City (prior to 1824) and in Lowell, Massachusetts (1835–52). But times and the emotional climate were changing. When their request was denied, the Catholics appealed to the New York state legislature.

The legislature decided the only practical arrangement was the complete divorce of public education and religious organizations, and in 1842 passed an act specifically stopping any form of public financial assistance for sectarian schools. Each sect now had to conduct denominational instruction at its own expense. Undaunted by this and subsequent defeats, Catholics throughout the country continued their court battles.

Widespread fear and anger resulted in a wave of anti-Catholic riots, accusations, and political agitation. In June, 1843, the extremist American Republic party was formed in New York with a program aimed at denying Catholics and the foreign-born the right to vote or hold "executive, legislative, judicial or diplomatic" office, at preventing the union of church and state, and at keeping the King James Bible in the schools.

During May and June of the following year, violence burst out in Philadelphia between Catholics and American Republic Association members. The state militia was able to restore order only after about twenty persons were killed and a hundred injured. The various "nativist" groups joined together in July, 1845, as the Native American Party. In 1849 the Native Americans formed a clandestine anti-Catholic organization called the Order of the Star-Spangled Banner; its members used the password "I don't know," and the movement soon became popularly known as the "Know-Nothing" party. By 1854 the party was a significant political force, but internal dissension over the slavery issue caused its disruption following the 1856 election.

Frightened by the turbulence resulting from the Catholic campaign to share in New York's school funds, the other state legislatures determined to prevent similar incidents; most passed legislation making it illegal to give public funds to any school teaching or practicing a sectarian doctrine. By the close of the nineteenth century few states still could offer financial assistance to denominational schools, even if they so chose. In brief, when confronted with the alternatives of sharing public funds with Catholic parochial schools or eliminating the Bible and all other religious instruction from the public schools, the Protestant majority chose the latter. Subsequent attempts by Catholics to receive public funds were denied them, and Catholics, despite overwhelming financial problems, set to developing their own schools.

Although the public schools are now almost completely secular, some religious traces remain, principally in the rural South. For example, many states prohibiting sectarian textbooks in the public school still have the daily reading—without comment—of a few Bible verses, recitation of a non-denominational prayer (despite the Supreme Court), or a classroom placard bearing the Ten Commandments. A few southern and eastern states require Bible-reading. This type of religious activity in the schools seems to have increased in recent years.

Many groups (religious and secular) object to any Bible in the public classroom as a possible "opening wedge"; other bitter controversies center merely upon selecting a translation acceptable alike to Protestant, Catholic, and Jew. The Supreme Court has stated repeatedly that a federal question is not involved in state laws requiring public-school Bible-reading and has refused to rule in such cases. Those states allowing the Bible in the public classroom usually stipulate it be read "without written note or oral comment."

There is a significant difference between the Catholic reaction to American secular education and that of the later-immigrating Jews of eastern Europe. By the time Jews flocked to America during the two decades preceding and the two following the turn of the twentieth century, school secularization was an accomplished fact. Judaism's biblical orientation had created a thousand-year-plus tradition of establishing schools for the young whenever possible. With their emergence from Europe's ghettos during the Napoleonic era, the Jews had absorbed—with pathetic eagerness—Western literature, science, and culture. But the majority of new Jewish-Americans were emigrees from Czarist Russia and Poland, where few were allowed to attend the government schools. Those who did suffered bigotry and persecution and had to accept exposure to Christian ritual and teachings.

In America the Jewish immigrant discovered the government schools not only insisted on his children's attendance but treated them as equals. The Jewish newcomer could find little to criticize in such acceptance and equality, and to this day Jewish-Americans are among the strongest supporters of the public schools. Most religious Jews prefer to have their children receive sectarian instruction in an after-hours or Sunday school. Those who wish a more intensive Jewish education for their young send them to parochial schools. Yet few Jewish voices are ever heard demanding public funds for Jewish parochial schools, and usually Jewish citizens are among the first to criticize or combat any attempt to reintroduce religious elements into public instruction.

Catholics, on the other hand, unable to accept such a principle, have increased their support of released-time experiments in recent years. Today the overwhelming majority of students in released-time programs are Catholic. The released-time approach—actually a Protestant experiment of pre-World War I vintage—gives the Catholic Church a means of providing religious instruction to those of its children who attend public schools. An increasing number of Protestants, while still opposing any form of state aid to parochial schools, share the Catholic view that the public schools would profit from released- and dismissed-time programs.

The legal battles over religion in the classroom continue unabated. Often they appear more political than legal, and at times they take the form of a controversy between public and private schools. Separation advocates claim that the secular public schools, encompassing as they do children from the entire American social spectrum, serve as a unifying and democratizing social force. They argue that private schools—most of which are parochial—tend through their sectarian sympathies and concepts to promote "divisiveness."

If most critics of private education (religious or secular) do not favor actually outlawing private schools, they still are quick to point out their social shortcomings. These critics are fond of quoting Thomas Jefferson's statement that "by bringing the sects together, and mixing them with the mass of other students, we shall soften their asperities, liberalize and neutralize their prejudices and make the general religion a religion of peace, reason, and morality." An American Federation of Teachers resolution of 1947 echoed Jefferson's statement by asserting that "the interests of the democratic community are best served where children of all component groups of American society are enrolled in a common public school." In 1957 the National Education Association expressed similar sentiments: "In the give and take of growing up together, public school children have learned the real meaning of brotherhood; they have become friends with children of all faiths. Only a common school can serve this great end."

The public-school advocates charge the parochial schools with isolating children from the great American "educational melting pot" during those impressionable years when adult behavior patterns are formed. "The greater the proportion of our youth who fail to attend our public-schools and who receive their education elsewhere," James Bryant Conant has stated, "the greater the threat to our democratic unity." These critics also feel the religious schools should be satisfied to be regarded by the government as tax-exempt institutions.

Many Americans, however, are ardent champions of the private school. Ernest van den Haag, professor of social philosophy at New York University, recently has written: "Private education is often thought undemocratic. However, in the ordinary sense of the word, there is nothing undemocratic about private, or democratic about public, schools. England—a democracy—has many private schools; the Soviet Union—a dictatorship—has public education exclusively." Father John Courtney Murray, among the most articulate of contemporary Catholic writers in America, has argued that any unity resulting from compulsory secularism is of little value. America's basic concern, he emphasizes, should not be for a "standard 'democratic' mass" but for "the equality of *differences.*"

These issues, seemingly innate to religious and secular education, pose difficult questions for twentieth-century America. The nation's religious leaders and educators are divided as to how, when, and if religious teachings should be integrated into the tax-supported schools and colleges. Opinions vary greatly within each group. Many churchmen favor the inclusion of such teachings in public institutions; others are adamantly opposed. Conversely, many secular educators reject any form of religious instruction, while others favor it—at least in the form of a "common core" of "spiritual values."

Yet all groups, secular and religious alike, can claim a significant part of our educational tradition. And, as in the past, any answers they may evolve undoubtedly will be partial rather than total, temporary rather than permanent, and interrelated rather than separate. Yet this too is very much a part of the American democratic tradition.

Five: Medicine

GOD, THE PHYSICIAN, AND HYGIENE

ILLNESS AS A DIVINE PUNISHMENT   The legacy of medical knowledge bequeathed by the Bible and its related writings obviously is not exclusively America's. But as she has shared with the rest of the civilized world the wisdom and experience gained by the early Hebrew priests, talmudic rabbis, and Christian fathers, a survey of the Judeo-Christian influence upon Western medicine and hygiene becomes relevant here.

In biblical law man's body and spirit belonged to God and were therefore one. All that befell man emanated from a God who announced, "I kill and I make alive; I wound and I heal; and there is none that can deliver out of my hand." (Deuteronomy 32:39.) As he could serve God adequately only when sound in body and mind, man's health became a religious obligation and bodily neglect a sin.

Disease was a sign of punishment. It indicated individual, family, or clan guilt, as well as human frailty and divine displeasure. Such diverse historical spokesmen as Augustine, Boccaccio, and Luther accepted without question any physical misfortune as proof of God's anger.

The American Puritan had no doubt that illness revealed God's chastising hand. Cotton Mather explained a New England epidemic as a scourge "which the just Judgment of God has reserved for our late Ages." And a mere century ago, in both unhygienic Europe and the United States, considerable prayer was expended in an attempt to discover how a sufferer or his family had incurred God's wrath. That filth and squalor might be the cause of disease seldom occurred to anyone. Even today not only epidemics but hurricanes, earthquakes, and tidal waves are described legally as "acts of God."

Hardly surprising then that when ill, the ancient Hebrew turned not to the physician, of whom there was no lack, but to the priest. As God's "executor," the priest could reinforce a simple physical remedy with prayer, fasting, and sacrifice; also, he usually exacted a pledge of rigid adherence to God's law. "If thou wilt diligently hearken to the voice of the Lord thy God, and wilt do that which is right in his eyes, and wilt give ear to his commandments, and keep all his statutes," the Hebrew was told, "I will put none of these diseases upon thee, which I have put upon the Egyptians; for I am the Lord that healeth thee."

Illness seen as divine punishment became redemptive. Contrite man was to accept his punishment with courage and forbearance and reject mere human assistance. Hence a suffering Job could castigate unsympathetic friends as "worthless physicians," and Jeremiah could taunt Egypt with her defeat by Nebuchadnezzar, declaring, "In vain you have used many medicines; there is no healing for you."

This conviction that medical care without prayer indicated a lack of spiritual faith is seen in the Apocrypha. Tobit states he went to the physicians for his troubled eyes, "but they helped me not." Only a miracle cured him. And the early Christians combated the popularity of magic and occult practices by turning from empirical medicine to the early Judaic concept of no salvation without faith, nor medication without prayer. James advises:

> Is any one among you suffering? Let him pray. . . . Is any among you sick? Let him call for the elders of the church, and let them pray over him, anointing him with oil in the name of the Lord; and the prayer of faith will save the sick man, and the Lord will raise him up; and if he has committed sins, he will be forgiven (James 5:13–15).

The Talmud later reveals a complete reversal of the Jewish attitude toward the physician during the Alexandrian and medieval periods. But this initial biblical suspicion of medical treatment caused Hebrew medicine to be a preventive, rather than healing, art. It made treatment of the sick less important than disease prevention through hygiene and sanitation. For a clean body gave obvious proof of a pure soul. Detailed regulations for ritual purity and general hygiene were carefully codified and later recorded in Exodus, Leviticus, Numbers and 2 Samuel. Modified by time, these rules were passed on to Christianity.

The priestly code of hygiene was not parochial, having evolved slowly through contact with various surrounding cultures. Indeed, the priests were more than willing to share their knowledge with their neighbors. This priestly willingness to convey their findings to others was approved by later talmudists and medieval Jewish commentators.

It is in preventive medicine that Hebraic medico-religious practices exerted their major influence upon later European civilization. This influence was the more significant in that it did not pass down through the rabbinical writings alone, but also through the early Church fathers, who knew and absorbed many early Judaic ideas. Even the much publicized Essenes apparently were transmitters of Jewish hygienic practices. Certainly history attests to the subsequent effectiveness of these ritual laws, for amid the most intense medieval misery and privation, Jews retained remarkably high standards of health, hygiene, and communal sanitation.

The ancient Hebrews are now recognized as having evolved the "science of public health." Their health laws, writes science historian D. T. Atkinson, "formed the basis of sanitation in the more advanced countries of the world for over two thousand years." No people, he continues,

> before or since, has left us such a wealth of laws relative to hygiene and sanitation as the Hebrews. These important laws, coming down through the ages, are still in use to a marked degree in every country in the world sufficiently enlightened to observe them. One has but to read the book of Leviticus carefully and thoughtfully to conclude that the admonitions of Moses contained therein are, in fact, the groundwork of most of today's sanitary laws. As one closes the book, he must, regardless of his spiritual leanings, feel that the wisdom therein expressed regarding the rules to protect health are superior to any which then existed in the world and that to this day they have been little improved upon.

Examples are plentiful. Deuteronomy presents not only a careful dietetic program but also rules for military hygiene so practical they are still followed by modern field troops.

Numbers declares "unclean" for seven days anyone touching a corpse or merely stepping into the tent in which it lies. Leviticus establishes a complete hygienic regimen centering upon unclean objects, as well as upon prevention of contagious diseases.

Leviticus also describes explicitly the Hebrew manner of coping with the dreaded scourge of leprosy. So accurate are the Bible's leprosy descriptions that modern commentators consider them to be unrivaled for the next seventeen hundred years. Some insist modern medical literature contains more confusion in the symptomatology of leprosy's various types than is to be found in the biblical narrative.

The Hebrews apparently realized that leprosy was conveyed by continued contact and that systematic isolation was needed. The priest carefully inspected the leper, searching the skin for discolorations and checking for raised or depressed lesions and signs of previous skin disease; he noted also any ulcers and changes in hair color. As subsequent changes required continued observation, he isolated the patient for an initial seven-day period; thus was introduced the vitally important practice of social "quarantine."

The isolation procedure was fixed, strict, and thorough. The patient's clothes—and often his house—were destroyed; his upper lip was covered, and when contact with others was imminent, he was obliged to cry out as he approached, "Unclean, unclean." Regardless of social rank, he was required to live apart as long as the disease persisted. King Azariah, for instance, was "a leper to the day of his death, and he dwelt in a separate house," a house that may well represent the earliest foreshadowing of the modern hospital. Only the priest could declare a leper "clean" and return him to society.

Leprosy was only one of many skin disorders mentioned in the Bible. Causing greater concern and numerous moral injunctions was the occurrence of venereal disease. The "issue," or "Zob," receiving attention in Numbers 5:2 and Leviticus 15 has been identified by Preuss as gonorrhea. Those infected were isolated immediately so as not to "defile the camp." Every object touched by or in contact with the sufferer was declared "unclean"; anyone coming into contact with the sick or their objects was required to wash his clothes and bathe. The patient was instructed to wait until the discharge had stopped, then "count for himself seven days for his cleansing, and wash his clothes . . . then he shall bathe his body in running water, and shall be clean."

This biblical emphasizing of personal cleanliness has moved noted medical historian Karl Sudhoff to claim that mankind is indebted to Semitism for two of its greatest hygienic ideas: a weekly day of rest and direct prophylaxis of disease. Even the highly developed Greek medicine, "despite its theory of natural causation," he adds, "was blind to the fact of contagion, or direct transmission of disease." It remained for Mosaic law to give society

> the idea of the imperative necessity of isolating those afflicted with a chronic contagious disease; in addition, the purification measures recommended in Leviticus for infested houses constitute the armament of modern prevention of epidemic diseases. . . . The whole concept of the transmission of serious diseases by social intercourse with the afflicted and of the consequent isolation of the diseased, became property of the West by the religious route. . . . In this tenacious fight of centuries, the methods of which were borrowed from the Mosaic Code, the Occident triumphed over leprosy. Guided by this intellectual torch, it accomplished the first great feat in direct prophylaxis.

The Hebrews naturally had medical problems other than diseases. The inevitable needs of obstetrics, gynecology, and pediatrics receive considerable scriptural attention: conception, pregnancy, difficult labor, delivery, and care of mother and infant are mentioned.

Throughout the Old Testament, no matter what illness is mentioned, a reference to bathing usually follows. While obviously originated for religious purposes, bathing served to interrelate the spiritual and physical, becoming an integral and persistent part of Jewish communal life. Added to the general concern with disease, hygiene, and sanitation, there are further references to pharmacists, medicinal remedies, cosmetics, dietetics, and legal medicine.

Both dietetics and legal medicine merit a comment. Rules of compensation for injury were carefully formulated, and such factors as cost of treatment, loss of wages, suffering, permanent disability, and embarrassment were considered. Punishment was added for *intentional* injury. Exodus 21:18–19 states:

When men quarrel and one strikes the other with a stone or with his fist and the man does not die but keeps his bed, then if the man rises again and walks abroad with his staff, he that struck him shall be clear; only he shall pay for the loss of his time, and shall have him thoroughly healed.

It is probably no exaggeration to claim that these stipulations mark the beginnings of medical jurisprudence.

The biblical dietary laws are of particular interest. Medical authorities recently have stressed the damaging biological effects of the animal fat constituent cholesterol, believing its excessive consumption hastens hardening of the arteries (cardiovascular) diseases.

Interestingly enough, both Bible and Talmud warn against consumption of fat. The Bible is especially adamant, stating flatly that "all fat is the Lord's"; therefore, "it shall be a perpetual statute throughout your generations, in all your dwelling places that you eat neither fat nor blood." And repeated instructions are given for the removal and sacrificial burning of the fat tissues.

In time, however, it became apparent to the most orthodox Jew that a complete fat-free diet was impractical and unnecessary. And talmudic writers began a slight reinterpretation of the strict biblical admonitions. They decided only an animal's "heavy and congealed fat," which is not interwoven with the meat and is easily removed, was forbidden. The fluid fat (oils) and the fat closely interwoven and a part of muscular tissue were accepted as nourishing and beneficial. Centuries later the medieval philosopher-physician Maimonides was to add the common-sense advice that "fat injures and fatigues the body, disturbs the functions and slows up its movement; therefore . . . stout and obese persons should . . . walk more."

Modern medical men quarrel little with these and many other biblical and talmudic dictums. The emphasis in Daniel 1:12–16 upon the importance of a daily intake of vegetables has caused historian J. A. Tobey to declare that the ancient Hebrew dietary and hygienic rules "were thoroughly sound, so completely so, in fact, that many of them are not only observed today, but are full of modern wisdom and sanity."

Anatomy, however, was another matter. Here biblical knowledge was limited, for dissection was forbidden, being viewed as a dishonor to the dead—a belief the Hebrews shared with the Egyptians, Greeks, and later Arabs. Information was based solely upon animal organs, external study of the body, and observation following injuries and severe wounds. Thus, except for circumcision and bloodletting, there was little concern with surgery. Wounds, however, were dressed with wine and balsam oil, and sometimes sutured, while broken bones were set and covered with roller bandage. Ezekiel 30:21 describes the procedure: "Son of man, I have broken the arm of Pharaoh king of Egypt; and lo, it has not been bound up, to heal it by binding it with a bandage, so that it may become strong to wield the sword."

Apparently some emergency first-aid treatment, particularly mouth-to-mouth resuscitation, was used—to judge from an experience attributed both to Elijah and Elisha. Each is credited with having revived a child by breathing into his mouth.

Both Old and New Testaments refer to various forms of mental derangement. The pathetic Saul suffers from persistent mental depression, while Nebuchadnezzar's mental affliction causes him to be "driven from among men" and to eat grass "like an ox." There is also concern with dreams as "visions of the head" and with such malfunctions of the nervous system as epilepsy, hysteria, paralysis, and sciatica.

"HONOR A PHYSICIAN"   The status of Judaic medical practice and the physician changed radically during the talmudic period. Disease and illness were still viewed as divine visitations, but the permissibility of human intervention was increasingly asserted. Scriptural sanction for the human physician was sought. New meaning was given to the passage in Samuel in which the "spirit of God" is viewed as responsible only for joy and good fortune, while the lesser "spirit from God" caused illness and misfortune. The rabbis decided the phrase in Exodus 21:19 demanding that an individual injuring another "shall have him thoroughly healed" also meant that man could take a more active role in treating illness. With other similar reinterpretations Judaic suspicion of medicine and physician steadily gave way to a new

view, one clearly expressed in the Apocryphal book of Ecclesiasticus:

Honour a physician. . . . For the Lord hath created him.
For of the Most High cometh healing.
And he shall receive honour of the king.
The skill of the physician shall lift up his head:
And in the sight of great men he shall be in admiration.
The Lord hath created medicines out of the earth;
And he that is wise will not abhor them. . . .
Of such doth the apothecary make a confection;
And of his works there is no end;
And from him is peace over all the earth.

Centuries later enlightened Christian schoolmen were to cite this passage as evidence of God's approval of human healing and as proof that such action was "not contrary to the Catholic faith." The Talmud strongly reflects this complete reversal. For God had stated, emphasized the rabbis, that "I am the Lord your healer."

The Jewish physician's prestige rose steadily from the days of the *tannaim* ("teachers"). Beginning with Rabbi Mar Samuel (165–257), there developed a strong tradition of combining the professions of rabbi and physician. Contributing to this partnership was the scriptural precedent of priestly involvement in health matters. However, an important additional factor was the view expressed in the Talmud's *Wisdom of the Fathers* that the study or teaching of God's law should not be used to earn a livelihood. Thus every rabbi was faced with the necessity of sustaining himself and his family by means of a secular occupation. Medicine became an obvious favorite, allowing him not only to convey God's word but also to alleviate suffering. Medicine was the only dignified occupation independent of the state available, for Jews were excluded from educated society and public office. Hence the rabbis became devoted to science very early and remained so for many centuries.

The most notable exemplar of this dual tradition was Rabbi Moses ben Maimon (1135–1204). Usually referred to as Maimonides, this scholar, philosopher, and scientist overcame medieval bigotry and numerous social obstacles to become court physician to Saladin, the all-powerful ruler of the Moslem world. A great Aristotelian scholar, Maimonides infused Jewish culture with both Greek and Arabic science and philosophy. His *The Guide for the Perplexed* stressed again the closeness of medicine and religion; his *Tractatus de Regimine Sanitatis*, designed for Saladin's private use, and *The Preservation of Youth*, compiled for Saladin's son, Sultan Al Afdal, contained much on personal hygiene, diet, and health practices. Based upon deep intellect, great common sense, and wide experience, many of his observations retain their pertinence. Maimonides seems to have been keenly aware, for instance, that sound diagnosis and therapy depend upon the interaction of mind and body.

The Jewish physician gained religious and social acceptance during the talmudic and medieval period denied him in the biblical era. And he was expected to meet high ethical standards. Every physician was required to be licensed for practice by the local Jewish judicial council. Less qualified practitioners were graded as bloodletters, midwives, or circumcisers. In time every Jewish community was instructed to have at least one physician, and it was not considered wise to live where one was lacking.

Ironically, the general excellence of medieval Jewish physicians was reinforced by the strict and jealous surveillance to which the outside community constantly subjected them. This external pressure gave added meaning to the talmudic warning that "a physician who treated without examination brought harm," while the physicians themselves cautioned one another not to use any cure whose effectiveness they could not prove with scientific reasons. The Greek and Roman view that physicians had the right to kill was rejected completely, and the physician's liability in case of error or malpractice was carefully regulated. Both Bible and Talmud law stop short of the Code of Hammurabi's requirement that an unsuccessful physician suffer death, or at least the loss of his fingers.

While expressing intense scorn for the quack and charlatan, the rabbis had only admiration and respect for the "faithful physician," a term they also applied reverently to God. They considered it proper for a deserving physician to be compensated for his services, and they insisted that a physician who took nothing was worth nothing. Yet equally concerned that no hardship be inflicted on the patient, they decided that patients should place whatever amount each thought proper in the doctor's office moneybox, adding that the poor not only were not required to pay but might even expect a gift from the physician.

Neither wealth nor position, the rabbis emphasized, was as

important as compassion in treating the sick. This concept became so firmly ingrained in the Jewish ethical tradition that in the thirteenth-century Rabbi Judah of Ratisbon, in his *Sefer Hasidim,* declares:

> If a rich man and a poor man be sick and thou seest all the world going to see the rich man, go thou to the poor one, even though he be ignorant and unlettered.

And the Midrash, the ancient homiletical Torah commentary, admonishes the physician always to treat a patient with sympathy and forbearance:

> Even when the physician sees that death is approaching, he still says to the patient, "Eat this and abstain from that, drink this and not that," but he does not say "Your end is near."

It rebukes the prophet Isaiah for bluntly telling King Hezekiah that he was soon to die.

The Talmud viewed God's laws as designed to further rather than to limit human life; hence almost any ordinance could be ignored to protect individual well-being. Conversely, anyone neglecting his health, practicing asceticism without reason, or refusing a cure for fear of breaching a law was a sinner and could be forced to submit, for such a refusal was a "piety of madness."

The new esteem enjoyed by the medical profession was the partial result of vastly increased medical knowledge. Much of this added knowledge was in pathology, as the natural result of traditional Jewish concern with the ritual fitness of animal flesh. The rabbis established rules, based upon Leviticus, forbidding the consumption of diseased meat. All slaughtered animals were carefully examined for changes in the color, position, consistency, and structure of organs; bones, muscles, and glands were not only scrutinized closely but histologically and topographically described.

In direct contrast to the Bible, the Talmud contains a good deal of anatomical and surgical knowledge—enough to merit a full-length study. But even a brief review reveals its amazing range and depth at a time when most of Western civilization was given to superstition, magic, and alchemy. By the early Middle Ages, when other trained surgeons were virtually nonexistent in Europe, Jewish physicians trained in

Arabia were not only performing surgery and dissection, but specializing in it exclusively.

Not only were Jewish physicians operating for stones in the bladder, performing Caesarian sections and amputations, and inserting artificial teeth (patients could have them in gold, silver, or wood), but they also were coping with fractures, rabies, pleurisy, and jaundice. While neither Hippocrates, Galen, nor Western medieval medical literature mentioned hemophilia, the Babylonian talmudists described it more than two thousand years ago. Discovering circumcision often caused excessive loss of blood and death, the rabbis decided the victims had inherited a propensity toward bleeding. Apparently the rabbis not only realized that the bleeding was caused by a lack of blood viscosity, which interfered with the protective clotting, but that women—although not bleeders themselves—transmitted the disease to their sons.

Adding to the biblical list of human diseases, the Talmud identifies and recommends treatment for others of the mouth, throat, lungs, heart, and stomach, as well as for hemorrhoids, intestinal worms, and biliary disturbances.

The rabbis seem to have attained a surprising degree of biological sophistication. They state that "there are many germs and insects that are dangerous to health, as well as minute organisms existing everywhere in abundance; if man could see them all he could not exist." At a time when the venerated Hippocrates and his disciples were evolving their famous theory that disease was merely the result of an imbalance in the body's "four humors" (blood, phlegm, yellow bile, and black bile), the talmudists were insisting that disease symptoms are outward manifestations of internal tissue and organ changes—a view very close to the twentieth-century one. The talmudists were literally alone in their awareness that disease causes structural changes in the body.

Some 1,500 years ago they also developed a method of determining the total amount of blood in the body, comparing the color of the body's blood, when mixed with a measured amount of water, with samples of blood and water in known rates. A similar method was reintroduced in the mid-nineteenth century. From the blood's color the rabbis learned to determine the source of bleeding and the condition of the lungs. They also made repeated efforts to determine the exact number of bones in the human body, but apparently they couldn't agree whether the exact figure should be 248 or 252. And while Greek physicians looked upon a trachea injury or spleen removal as fatal, the rabbis, in accordance with modern medical practice, considered both as relatively minor occurrences.

It is worth noting that with the exception of a few minor sects Judaism rejected the healing powers of religious shrines and saints' relics. Having once accepted the social importance of increased medical knowledge, the talmudists never again permitted a confusion between their faith in God's healing powers and their confidence in the physician or his medical science.

Christianity retained a negative view of medicine and the human physician for centuries after Judaism had rejected it. For the early fathers held the human body to be an "impure and worthless, if not despicable," barrier between the individual and his redemption. To ignore its "vile" corporeal needs, to transcend the physical, was to approach more closely the world of the spirit. For St. Jerome, in the fourth century, "the purity of the body and its garments meant the impurity of the soul."

Nevertheless, the church made a significant contribution to the history of medical care by introducing an entirely new attitude toward the sick, an attitude taking concrete form in the historical development of the hospital.

A primitive approach probably lies in the Mosaic provisos for isolating the diseased in "houses of separation" devoted entirely to the ill. In time this idea became entwined with the traditional Hebraic emphasis upon hospitality for the stranger, particularly the sick traveler who could not be cared for in his own home. By talmudic times there had developed in every Jewish community the custom of reserving portions of homes for sick transients. Hence the same Jerome who could dismiss all corporeal needs as degrading could praise the Roman lady Fabiola for founding a hospital, pointing out that in so doing she was actually imitating Jewish custom.

The hospital's roots may rest in the Old Testament and Talmud, but the hospital itself attained its growth and shape in Christian practice. Heretofore the destitute sick—outside of Judaism—had received little charitable aid and less personal care. But as Christianity became Rome's official religion, the spread of scriptural doctrines radically changed the significance of disease and the social position of the ill. The sick Christian was no longer a sinful, inferior being to be chastised and abandoned by his fellows. To succor him became a Christian duty essential to the soul's growth. Christians were expected to attend, nurse, and pray for him, and church officials to anoint him with oil "in the name of the Lord."

This new concern for the sick introduced the charity hospital into Christian Europe.

From the fourth century on, hospitals were erected for charitable rather than economic or military reasons, with the monastaries soon becoming active in their management. St. Benedict of Nursia was among the first to impress upon his monks the need to care for the ill. Founder of the Benedictine order, he established in 529 a monastery on Monte Cassino that quickly became a famed center for collecting, copying, and preserving ancient manuscripts, including those dealing with medicine.

Yet the church's attitude toward medical practice remained contradictory. Some monastic orders were not as medically enlightened or as tolerant as the Benedictines, and conflicting medical views developed. The powerful Bernard of Clairvaux, founder of the Cistercians, ordered his monks not to practice medicine, and instructed them not to touch physic when they themselves were ill. "To buy drugs, to consult physicians, to take medicine," he asserted, "befits not religion." Hence Christian medicine throughout the Middle Ages remained primarily "faith healing."

The church for a time even accepted Bernard's view that medical practice was unsuitable for the clergy. During the twelfth and thirteenth centuries alone eight church councils passed prohibitive edicts, claiming that concern for matters physical detracted from the spiritual, that medical fees constituted a worldly intrusion into holy orders, and that many aspects of sick care offended modesty. Surgery came in for special condemnation. The Fourth Lateran Council (1215), for instance, stressed that priests were not to engage in any activity endangering life. The council's point was well taken, for medieval surgery was extremely hazardous even under the best conditions. Unfortunately, this official stand not only resulted in stopping churchmen (Europe's only learned Christian group) from practicing medicine, but made suspect the entire medical profession.

For the medieval Christian, then, as for the very early Hebrew, God's spirit and the prayer of the faithful, rather than medical knowledge, provided the good man with the "gifts of healing." The church's attitude changed with time, but considerable reinterpretation and reorientation were required to justify the physician and to reconcile Christian faith with medical practice.

THE "ANGELIC CONJUNCTION"   Inevitably, medieval European medicine remained in non-Christian hands. Discounting the "vagrant quack" and "stationary humbugs," medieval medicine was practiced primarily by Jewish physicians trained in Arabia and Alexandria. Not directly bound by church law, they helped disseminate medical knowledge throughout Europe. The University of Montpellier, perhaps Europe's oldest university, counted among its founders in 1025 a group of Spanish-Jewish doctors. And the school of Salerno, chartered by Frederick II in 1231 as Christian Europe's first full-fledged medical school, represented an amalgamation of Greek, Latin, Arabic, and Hebrew medical influences.

Hardly surprising then that in an age when medicine often was considered akin to magic, the Jew's medical eminence made him the more suspect. The Jewish experience with bubonic plague during the Middle Ages provides a classic example. Judaic contact with the plague goes back to biblical times. Modern scholars point out that the "mice" described in 1 Samuel 5 and 6 as ravaging the land and afflicting the Philistine with "tumors" were undoubtedly rats and that the disease was bubonic plague, which is spread by rat's fleas. This early contact proved important, for when the plague scourged Europe as the Black Death, the Jews were better prepared to deal with it than was any other group.

The Arab world welcomed both Greek and Hebrew cultures, each of which included a great deal of medical and hygienic knowledge. The medical writings of Hippocrates and Galen had been translated into Arabic, and in Europe this language was known principally to the Jews. They retranslated these works into Latin and Hebrew. Many of the outstanding physicians in the Moslem world, such as the famed Maimonides, were Jews. These contributed much to the literature of sanitation; Maimonides' *Tractatus de Regimine Sanitatis,* for instance, still is highly rated.

Islam's militant surge introduced a highly advanced form of sanitary science into Moslem Europe. Spanish cities, therefore, could boast of clean, paved streets at a time when Londoners and Parisians were still littering their streets with refuse. For outside the ghettos sewerage was unknown in medieval Christian Europe. Historian Atkinson vividly describes general conditions at the time of the plague.

> By the Christians the plague was considered a visitation of Providence and was allowed to run its deadly course unchecked by sanitary measures. Sewerage at this time was a thing unknown among the gentiles. The people were crowded together, and refuse was thrown in the streets. The example of a great number of consecrated men, living in sackcloth and ashes, was emulated by the poorer classes whose dwellings were unspeakably filthy. Erasmus tells us that at this time the floors of gentile homes were made of rushes and were strewn with an ancient collection of "beer, grease, fragments, and everything nasty." The plague being carried by rats, no condition could have been more conducive to its spread than was afforded by this general uncleanliness.

In the ghettos, however, Torah and Talmud sanitation laws were put into immediate effect. Cleanup movements were instituted and all refuse burned, causing the rats to gravitate in search of food. Stricken Jews were carefully isolated, and wells and water buckets were kept covered. Whether the Jews were aware that rats were disease carriers is problematical, but evidently they recognized the connection between dirt and disease. As a result, while anywhere from one-fourth to one-third of Europe's Christian populace died (estimates range from twenty-five to sixty million deaths in flare-ups from 1348 to 1720), Jewish losses were held to about five percent.

Jewish success against the Black Plague amid medieval ignorance and superstition had predictably tragic results. Stories soon spread that Jews had caused the plague by poisoning wells. How else explain their seeming immunity? Hysterical mobs, seeking quick and convenient solutions to the plague, were soon roaming the streets and countrysides. Jewish massacres, usually in the form of funeral pyres, flared throughout Europe. Confessions of guilt were wrung by torture from many Jews—and from any Christian protesting this means of combatting disease.

Among those tortured and burned was Balavignus, Strasburg's great Jewish physician, who had led the fight against the plague armed with biblical and talmudic medical knowledge. Luckily his work in sanitation did not end on his funeral pyre. Johann Peter Frank, an eighteenth-century Bavarian Jew, embodied many of Balavignus' findings in his own major work on public hygiene, *A Complete System of Medical Polity,* in which he analyzed in detail man's physical and social environment.

Scholar, writer, and teacher, Frank directed health and medical practices for the rulers of five countries. He developed elaborate plans for correct sewerage and water supply that did much to eliminate the great European plagues. He also treated patients, reorganized hospitals, taught students, and instructed monarchs how to protect their subjects' health. Frank's reputation evidently reached Napoleon, who made an unsuccessful attempt to lure him to Paris.

Frank was imbued with the biblical tradition's stringent health regulations. Thus when he saw a powerful health movement develop in his own time, he urged strong regulatory state health laws:

> The internal security of the State is the aim of the general science of police. A very important part thereof is the science that teaches us to handle methodically the health of human beings living in society. . . . Consequently we must promote the welfare of the population by means which will enable persons cheerfully and for lengthy periods to enjoy the advantages which society can offer them. . . . Medical police, therefore, like the science of police in general, is a defensive art . . . a doctrine whereby human beings . . . can be protected against the evil consequences of crowding too thickly upon the ground. . . . How strange it is that this science which day by day grows more essential to our race, should still be so little cultivated.

But Frank was keenly aware also of police-power limitations. His prime concern was not strong central authority but human welfare. He therefore strove to have health legislation enforced only through lawful state organs:

> An intelligent police does not interfere with the privacy of the home. If the police, this ruler of people, lets itself be misused for spying, it degenerates and becomes the

tyrant of human societies, and it disturbs the public order which it is called upon to protect.

Like the biblical prophets and talmudic jurists before him, Frank clearly felt that man's physical well-being could best be safeguarded by intelligently applied laws. Our modern public-health laws indicate the logical practicality of this approach in a complex society.

Significantly, most of the early American concern with medical problems was expressed by clergymen serving the colonists as physicians, a combination Cotton Mather referred to as the "Angelic-Conjunction." The frequency of the colonial minister-physician was attributable to the same causes responsible for the earlier rabbi-physician: the religious profession alone did not provide an adequate livelihood. Medicine also enabled clergymen to combine their scientific and moral concerns. They not only viewed science and religion as harmonious but as mutually beneficial. Seventeenth-century American medicine, furthermore, lacked a "professional focus." There were no medical schools, licensing bodies, general hospitals, or scientific organizations. Medical literature, interest, or knowledge were meager at best.

Clergymen inherited the physician's function by virtual default. These men were imbued with the biblical tradition's medical ethics. Edward Stafford, writing from London in 1643 to Governor John Winthrop of Massachusetts, repeatedly echoes talmudic sentiments:

> No man can with a good conscience take a fee or reward before ye partie receive benefit apparent: and then he is not to demand anything, but what God shall putt into the heart of the partie to give him, for it comes from God. A man is not to neglect that partie, to whom he hath once administered, but to visit him at least once a day, and to medle with no more, than he can well attend. In so doing he shall discharge a good conscience before God and Man.

Thomas Thacker, the Old South Church of Boston's first minister and an Arabic and Hebraic scholar, relied upon scriptural precedent in writing the first medical treatise printed in the American colonies, *A Brief Rule to Guide the Common People of New-England How To Order Themselves and Theirs in the Small Pocks, or Measles* (1677). His emphasis is upon the community's moral obligation to quarantine smallpox victims.

Undoubtedly the most influential figure in early eighteenth-century Massachusetts was clergyman Cotton Mather, dubbed by several modern commentators the "first significant figure in American medicine." Motivated almost equally by theology and medicine, Mather filled his sermons with medical imagery, referring repeatedly to Christ as the "great" or "glorious" physician. He stressed the traditional relationship of disease and sin, insisting "Sickness is in Fact the whip of God for the sins of man." Every sinner, he declares in a sermon entitled *The Great Physician,* is disease-ridden: "He has the Palsey of an unsteady Mind; He has the Feavour of Unchastity. . . . He has the Cancer of Envy; He has the Tympany of Pride." Hitting his stride, Mather tells his probably squirming listeners they constitute "a Congregation of Sick Souls: Where am I preaching, Sirs, but in an Hospital?"

An unquestioning Calvinist, Mather was thoroughly imbued with the Old Testament view that illness represents divine punishment for evil and that all evil stems from original sin. Illness and disease, therefore, serve God as a prime means of punishing the wicked, individually or as a group. The youngest ailing child was not excluded:

> Think; of the grievous Effects of Sin! This wretched Infant has not arrived unto years of sense enough to sin after the similitude of the transgression committed by Adam. Nevertheless the Transgression of Adam . . . has involved this Infant in the guilt of it. And the poison of the old serpent, which infected Adam when he fell into Transgression by hearkening to the Tempter, has corrupted all mankind, and is a seed unto such disease as this Infant is now laboring under. Lord, what are we, and what our children but a Generation of Vipers?

Mather's repeated reminder to the sick that their sufferings resulted from sins against God clearly was a pre-Christian concept; he had rejected the New Testament view of sickness as a sign of *grace* for the Old Testament belief of its *disgrace.* Smallpox victims had every reason, he insisted, to look upon themselves as loathsome creatures. And despite his medical sophistication, Mather was convinced sickness often could be alleviated solely by prayer, "the Universal Medicine." Incurables, however, were to recognize and accept a wrathful God's righteous justice. Mather was not above seizing upon personal illness to frighten the victim into piety, nor of warning others that their particular physical constitutions made them highly vulnerable to demonic possession and insanity.

Yet this same Puritan has been credited with having ushered in modern preventive medicine. A curious mixture of zealot and scientist, Mather could devote himself with equal assurance to hunting witches or to providing "refresher" training for medical practitioners and medicines for the needy. His *The Angel of Bethesda* is easily the most complete compilation of colonial medical knowledge. In it he reveals a surprising awareness of the "psychosomatic" interrelationship of mental and physical ills. But his approach remains essentially religious. The physician should, he states,

> with all possible Ingenuity of Conversation, find out, what Matter of Anxiety there may have been upon the Mind of the Patient. . . . Having discovered the Burden, lett him use all the Ways he can devise, to take it off. Offer him such Thoughts as may be the best Anodynes for his distressed Mind; especially . . . the Ways to a Composure upon Religious Principles.

Mather's religious beliefs did not blind him to the need for medical progress. He saw no reason why science—rightly applied—should interfere with true faith. It was Cotton and Increase Mather and their fellow clergymen who defended Dr. Zabdiel Boyleston's "scandalous" smallpox inoculations against the medical profession's attacks. From about 1716 on, Mather had been reading with interest foreign reports of the "oriental folk practice of inoculation." When smallpox was introduced into Boston by a ship from the West Indies, in April, 1721, he immediately wrote several polite letters to the city's physicians suggesting they begin inoculating the residents. He succeeded only in evoking their hostility for his "meddling." Boyleston was the lone exception; he agreed, and within three weeks he had inoculated ten people and brought down upon his and Mather's head charges of offending against God and man.

Dr. William Douglass led the opposition. The only possessor of the M.D. degree in Boston, Douglass declared, in the *Boston Gazette* (July 17), that inoculation not only was medically dangerous but an interference with God's "Providence." Two weeks later the Mathers and four of their clerical colleagues used the *Gazette* to point out they, too, placed "a humble trust in our Great preserver," considering themselves to be in complete "Subjection to His All-wide Providence." Subsequent events were to prove science—and God—on the clergy's side; even Douglass came to favor inoculation.

The much-maligned Cotton Mather must have contemplated himself finally with warm satisfaction; he had won posterity a major medical victory. More than any other early American, he personified that "complete medico-theological synthesis" so emphasized in the Bible. And he was not one to overlook so considerable a self-achievement.

Another medically sophisticated churchman was Methodism's founder, John Wesley, who was almost as concerned with physical matters as he was with those of the spirit. Like Mather, he admonished his followers to consult only physicians of accepted piety. While in America and ministering to the Indians in Georgia, he put to use many of the Bible's hygenic practices, stressing cleanliness as "next to Godliness." And in his *Primitive Physick: or an Easy and Natural Method of Curing Most Diseases,* he emphasized the importance of both mental and physical hygiene. Stafford, Thacker, Mather, and Wesley represent the many clergymen who early in America's history strove to apply God's word to man's physical and social well-being.

Not all the religiously oriented, then or now, in America or abroad, were won over completely to progressive medical procedure. The battle for social enlightenment is a continual one in all areas of thought. The Bible and its related writings have proved the source of many advanced medical concepts, but they have been used with equal fervor by medicine's opponents. A much-cited illustration is provided by the nineteenth-century dispute over anesthesia. The Bible, as usual, was quoted by both opponents and defenders. As the dispute narrowed down to the use of anesthesia in childbirth, the attackers quoted Genesis 3:16, "To the woman he said, I will greatly multiply your pain in childbearing; in pain you shall bring forth children." The defenders replied in kind. Dr. James Y. Simpson, a noted Scottish professor in obstetrics, turned calmly to Genesis 2:21, "So the Lord God caused a deep sleep to fall upon the man, and while he slept took one of his ribs and closed up its place with flesh."

The Bible's advocacy of communal sanitation and isolation of the diseased can be traced in many modern quarantine and other public health laws preventing the spread of contagion.

Nathan Isaacs, late professor of business law at Harvard, has written:

> In an American case upholding the constitutionality of a Public Health Act, the court said: "Measures to prevent the spread of dangerous diseases and to provide for the isolation and segregation of those diseased are practically as old as history . . . The law of Moses segregated the lepers, and their forced cry of 'Unclean! Unclean!' was the forerunner of the modern warning placard" (Rock v. Carney, Michigan Reports, 280). The deep concern of Jewish law for the stranger, the afflicted, the widow and the orphan, its humanitarian measures reaching to the ox that treadeth the corn and to the mother-bird, its concern for the labourer toiling in the vineyards, the hired man awaiting his reward, the poor debtors—all this has given inspiration as well as aid and comfort to reformers even when their proposed Bills copied none of the phraseology of the Bible.

Today most of the world's more progressive areas are almost completely free from the great plagues of the past. Improved sanitation has been the key factor. Many people at different times in history have sensed this need for greater personal and communal cleanliness. But those in the West obviously owe a debt to the Scriptures and to those wise enough to apply the biblical teachings as they related to their own times and needs.

Six: Literature

AMERICAN LITERATURE AND THE RELIGIOUS TRADITION

COLONIAL WRITING   Early American life merely extended European thought and customs. Its ideas and forms, its religion, philosophy, and science, its politics, manners, and dress were Old World borrowings. The colonists immediately began modifying the familiar to fit their new environment, but the old ideas still were a long time disappearing. Colonial literature, especially its religious themes, embodied a lengthy and varied European intellectual heritage.

The Bible had entered English literature at its very Anglo-Saxon beginnings. The early English poets Caedmon and Cynewulf and their respective "schools," as well as a number of little known and anonymous versifiers, devoted themselves to poetic versions of biblical books, characters, and events. Old English and early Middle English writings from the eighth to thirteenth centuries were filled with metrical versions of Genesis, Exodus, Daniel, Psalms, and the Gospels; they also contained poetic tales of Adam and Eve, Judith, Christ and Satan, and the Apostles. Augmenting these were numerous metrical recastings of assorted creeds, prayers, homilies, proverbs, saints' lives, and religious folktales. Even the *Old English Annals,* begun under King Alfred (844-899) and conveying much of what is known of English history from the ninth to twelfth centuries, were modeled after the Hebrew Chronicles and prefaced by the Ten Commandments and other portions of Mosaic law.

By the time the seventeenth-century Dissenters departed for the New World, they possessed a literary heritage enriched from its start by the Judeo-Christian tradition. Post-Reformation England was attempting valiantly to absorb and fuse the

Scriptures, Greek classics, medieval religion, and Renaissance and Reformation ideologies.

Religious matters involved everyone. Rich and poor, lettered and ignorant alike, took deep personal interest in current theological questions. Central to all religious issues was the Bible. The seventeenth century's religious atmosphere had been created and liberalized by the Italian Renaissance. Manifesting itself in many ways, the Renaissance's most significant development for religion was its introduction of printing into Europe. Johann Gutenberg's Latin Bible, published about 1456, was the first of approximately one hundred Spanish, Italian, French, Dutch, German, and Bohemian editions during the late-fifteenth century. But perhaps the greatest boon to Renaissance biblical scholarship was the 1488 printing of the Old Testament in the original Hebrew.

By mid-sixteenth century, Renaissance humanism was bringing to England a good deal of Greek—or seemingly Greek—learning. But Hellenistic knowledge long since had fused with Persian and Arabian metaphysics and medieval Christian and Jewish cabalistic mysticism. English humanism. was characterized, therefore, not only by Greek study but by an intense interest in its allied Semitic tongues. The interest was due to such continental scholars as Pico della Mirandola, Jacob Loans, Johann Reuchlin, and a notable group of other Semitic authorities. This new Semitic learning enabled Martin Luther, familiar with Hebrew and Greek, to influence contemporary theological thought by translating the Bible from its original tongues.

This religious element within the Renaissance proved increasingly significant for the English mind. By mid-sixteenth century, Greek and Semitic linguistic study was enhanced by a growing Protestant concern for Scripture. English Protestant exiles returning from Geneva, Frankfort, and Strasbourg, upon Mary Tudor's death, were convinced of the need for a society based upon the Bible's intellectual and moral discipline. In 1611 this conviction culminated in the printing of the King James Bible.

The roots of this translation go back to 1500 at least and the planting of the Protestant attitude in England. Elizabeth's reign alone saw at least one hundred and thirty distinct Bible and Testament printings, with the Geneva Bible (1560) by far the most popular "household" edition. Easy to handle because of its small size, this version had no less than ninety printings. Apparently enough Bibles were printed during the

Elizabethan period to supply every English Protestant family desiring a copy.

The average Englishman's direct contact with the Bible not only influenced his thinking but helped fashion his language. He was little touched by Greek and Latin; these lost much of their appeal in translation, and their classical writings reached only the intelligentsia. Hebrew, however, lent itself to English translation with amazing ease, having much in common with those Anglo-Saxon linguistic elements still retained in the English of 1600. Both Hebrew and Anglo-Saxon are "elemental" and "simple," F. E. Gaebelein points out:

> The Old Testament imagery derives its strength from nature and the primitive emotions. Physical activity is at the root of most Hebrew words . . . and Anglo-Saxon partakes of the same characteristics; it has a real affinity for the Hebrew. The fact that the English of the Elizabethan period was nearer to the Anglo-Saxon than the English of today takes on, therefore, a significance for those who are seeking to explain the literary supremacy of the King James Bible.

In translating both Testaments, William Tyndale aimed at the intelligent and increasingly aggressive middle class. Adopting a direct, concise style equally distant from the pedantic and colloquial, he fashioned a pragmatic, homely, and native idiom. Tyndale's prose served as a model for succeeding English Bible translators and for scientific theorists from Bacon to the Royal Society's members.

Following Tyndale's example, Bible translators fashioned for literature a vigorous and concrete vernacular having few abstract and learned words. And though their vocabularies were relatively modest, the various English Bibles provided Elizabethan and Jacobean writers with a rich vein of imagery and phraseology. They provided also almost the only literature easily accessible to ordinary Englishmen. Such vigorous polemical writers as John Milton found the new idiom's hard, biting terms and familiar images perfect for their special needs. And the rapidly developing printing press enabled them to reach the growing reading public. Thus the scholar and nation's language levels met.

English Renaissance poetry also reflected a biblical influence. Many sixteenth-century poetic experimenters—Wyatt, Surrey, Gascoigne, Sidney, and Chapman among them—experienced, as Israel Baroway puts it, an "aesthetic compulsion . . . to shape the mystifying rhythms and the exotic imagery of Biblical poetry into familiar Renaissance patterns." By midcentury, metrical versions of the Psalms were widely used. Prominent literary spokesmen—Thomas Lodge, Barnaby Googe, and Sir John Harrington—used "Divine Poetry" to defend all poetry against its detractors. Many Elizabethan dramatists also utilized scriptural materials. Plays dealing with King David were particularly popular. There were stage productions, too, of Solomon and Sheba, Abraham and Lot, and "heaster & asheweros," as well as a series of dramas centering on the unhappy Jephthah—including a popular Bartholomew Fair puppet play entitled *Jephtha's Rash Vow*.

Dramatized biblical tales persisted throughout the Elizabethan period. Their characters appeared in masques and pageants as well as plays. With the rise of the middle class, however, Puritanism's voice grew more powerful and the intellectual climate more sober. Opposed to all stage dramas, the Puritans objected particularly to the theater's use of scriptural themes. As a result, during the decades after Elizabeth's death, the Bible virtually disappeared from the English stage, while the theater itself was soon patronized only by a progressively smaller court group.

Yet the England of Shakespeare's youth and productivity was permeated by biblical thought and phrase. It was an England in which the Renaissance spirit, slowly but irrevocably, gave way to the Puritan view of life and God. Shakespeare himself was much at home with biblical imagery and allusions, and more than twelve hundred biblical references have been found in his writings.

As a group, Elizabethan poets and dramatists were neither atheistic nor amoral in their writings. Indeed, their interest in and reverence for the Bible helped prepare the intellectual climate for their more sober-minded Jacobean literary successors. Even so Puritan a poet as John Milton found in their writings precedent for his own use of the Bible.

Milton ranked the Psalms—as well as Job and the Song of Songs—above the epics of Homer, Virgil, and Tasso and the tragedies of Sophocles and Euripides. Conceding considerable good might be derived from the best of pagan philosophers, he argues these had caught but a partial glimpse of the truth. Thus there was some falsehood in even the greatest of their works. In referring to the Hebrew prophets he states, "In them is plainest taught, and easiest learnt,/What makes a nation happy, and keeps it so,/What ruins kingdoms and lays cities flat."

Those Puritans who journeyed to the New World discerned no clear line between literature and religion. For that matter, during the century these "great, grim, earnest men" shaped New England life they were much too busy to write—or even read—imaginative or "polite" literature. They were determined to plant in the wilderness a commonwealth dedicated to God's word. They had discovered quickly that establishing such a commonwealth meant not only adjusting themselves to difficult climatic, physical, and social conditions, but placating or combating the Indians every step of the way. They learned also that to sustain the faithful, convince the skeptics, and enlighten the benighted, they would have to rely upon the spoken and written word. The result was a vast body of prayers, sermons, tracts, journals, and histories—all reflecting a heavy sense of the eternal fires awaiting most of Adam's sinful sons.

So it was that for the first one hundred and fifty years American literature was practical rather than aesthetic. It was devoted not to worldly love or natural beauty but to biblical piety and orthodoxy, and the time's political and social needs. Such scattered exceptions as Anne Bradstreet's "Contemplations" or Benjamin Franklin's *Busybody Papers* were to be found; Jonathan Edwards' *Personal Narrative* and John Woolman's *Journal* revealed both excellent literary style and deep religious conviction. But not until the Revolutionary period did a body of planters, merchants, and professional men develop an intellectual climate hospitable to literature and the fine arts. Actually, not until Philip Freneau and William Cullen Bryant's nature poetry and Washington Irving's prose sketches did American writing veer from the purely theological and political.

The New Englanders were determined to keep public record of all that befell their Bible commonwealth. Writing in clear, vigorous, careful prose, much of it modeled upon the Geneva and King James Bibles, they produced a steady stream of histories, chronicles, and autobiographies, all emphasizing that the Puritan exodus was in keeping with the divine plan. These writings often centered upon secular experiences, but they always ended with the argument that God's providential hand had shaped the outcome.

This insistence upon God's interest is central to such early

historical accounts of the American settlement as William
Bradford's *History of Plymouth Plantation,* John Winthrop's
Journal, Thomas Morton's *New English Canaan,* and William
Wood's *New England's Prospect.* The first New England nar-
rative, however, was the anonymous *A True Relation,* a
chronicle of the Plymouth Colony's birth year.

A True Relation—in spite of its many fine qualities—has
been overshadowed by Bradford's famous *History of Plymouth Plantation.* Writing in the two decades between 1630-
1650, Bradford avoided the melodramatic posturings of Renaissance exploration literature and the fire and brimstone of
traditional Puritan writings. He employed a spare, lucid style
reminiscent of the biblical Hebrew he admired. His account
of the Pilgrims' difficulties in England, Holland, aboard the
Mayflower, and during the first years at Plymouth has shaped
and brightened America's national folklore. Out of his sober
and unpretentious prose, the innate drama emerges of a
heroic community's struggle for survival against overwhelming odds.

The more aggressive, numerous, and prosperous Puritans
at nearby Massachusetts Bay did not produce a chronicler of
Bradford's literary stature. But they did have historians who
could match him in zeal or surpass him in scholarship and
worldly experience. Their chronicler was the Bay Colony's
first governor, John Winthrop, whose personal diary, or
Journal, presented the first detailed record of all New England
life from 1630 to 1648. So complete was the *Journal* that its
first editor, Noah Webster, retitled it *The History of New
England.*

John Winthrop was a dedicated civil servant, not a man of
letters. His place in American literature is based entirely upon
his candid revelation of the orthodox Puritan mind in action.
His is a crabbed and awkward prose style, and American
thought moved away from many of his basic values, but his
Journal's documentary importance remains high. Winthrop's
justification of the Puritan "Way" was paralleled by Edward
Johnson's *Wonder-Working Providences of Sion's Saviour in
New England* (1654). Carpenter, farmer, and civic official,
Johnson, like Winthrop, attempted to convince his readers
that New England's leadership was carrying out God's intent
and that all that had befallen them was in keeping with the
divine plan.

Time and the English temperament and tradition were
working against these leaders. English Puritans, fed on a long

tradition of dissent, had brought with them to New England not only strong Calvinist tendencies but also only slightly less potent independent, or nonconformist, inclinations. And a significant split developed within Puritanism during the seventeenth century, a split best seen in the different lives and writings of John Winthrop and Roger Williams. Whereas Winthrop and Johnson expose to history the orthodox Puritan mind, Roger Williams presents posterity with a glimpse into the mind of the unorthodox, or highly liberal, Puritan.

Williams' thought is epitomized in a pamphlet series resulting from a verbal battle over religious tolerance that he waged with orthodoxy's champion, John Cotton. On a trip to England, Williams encountered Cotton's tract *A Letter of Mr. John Cotton to Mr. Williams* (1643), which defended Massachusetts Bay for banishing Williams and advocated enforcement of religious uniformity. Williams countered with *Queries of Highest Consideration,* urging total separation of church and state. Still not satisfied, Williams published the following summer *The Bloudy Tenent of Persecution for Cause of Conscience* (1644), declaring all civil authority to rest with the people, who have the right to dissolve their government whenever they choose.

A disturbed English Parliament ordered the book burned; Williams, wisely, had published it anonymously. Cotton countered with two impassioned defenses of the New England way. Then aiming directly at Williams, he published during the following two years *The Bloudy Tenent Washed and Made White in the Bloud of the Lambe* and *A Reply to Mr. Williams.*

But the last word has proved to be Williams'. He forwarded ideas that a century and a half later appear in the Constitution and bill of rights. A champion of separatism, Williams rejected completely the "divine right" theory that God establishes a state by direct fiat and that its officials— royal, appointed, or elected—are therefore His stewards on earth and merit unquestioning obedience. Advocating instead the social compact, Williams insisted the state results from a continuous civil agreement, or contract, among its members, who merely delegate authority to their leaders; therefore governmental sovereignty lies ultimately and always in the citizenry. He regarded every state as the product of the social will, and its government merely a social instrument of communal expression. To Williams the people were always superior to the law.

Williams was by nature a mystic. He relied unquestioningly upon the "Inner Light" resulting from individual communion with God and personal interpretation of Scripture. Any attempt to coerce the individual to think a certain way was not only a crime against man but God. That any government—a mere social instrument—should exert such pressure was to Williams an abrogation of civil and religious law. Williams saw very little need for church organizations, ministers, creeds, or rituals. If others wished such things, he was content they should have them (even the Quakers, whom he greatly disliked). But only intellectual persuasion, never coercion, he felt, should be used to alter another's opinion. If business enterprises could maintain both competition and friendship, so could the various religious and secular groups: "It is the will and command of God, that . . . a *permission* of the most *Paganish, Jewish, Turkish,* or Antichristian *consciences* and *worships,* be granted to *all* men in all *Nations* and *Countries:* and they are only to be *fought* against with . . . the *sword* of *God's spirit,* the *Word* of *God.*"

To insure that Rhode Island's court of last resort would be the people, or their elected representatives, Williams saw to it that the government received only the power necessary to guarantee justice for all. No authority was to be passed on as a perpetual gift. And he never overcame the fear that a written constitution could become in time too inflexible to protect individual freedoms under changing conditions.

Williams was far ahead of his time, and like social and religious nonconformists everywhere he paid a heavy price for his prophetic vision. Yet a hundred and forty years later his political beliefs became the Revolution's rallying cries, and a half-century after that Emerson and the transcendentalists were expressing similar religious ideas. Like Winthrop, Williams was no literary stylist. His place in American literature derives from his originality, liberality, and farsightedness. Williams utilized Scripture to fortify his logic and was guided by its letter and spirit. But he learned little from its simple, concise prose. Loaded with strained similes and overweight puns, his "antique" sentences contrast strikingly with his daringly original ideas. In Roger Williams, Puritan nonconformity attempted to answer the basic questions of the church-state relationship—and the individual's proper relationship to each.

The answers provided by Williams—and other independents, such as Anne Hutchinson, John Wise, and the Quaker

John Woolman—are in many ways closer to modern American values than those provided by their more orthodox contemporaries. In the long run both orthodox and rebel thinkers shaped the early forms of American thought and writings, as both groups zealously described God's sustained interest in them.

Their zeal was passed on to the first native-born New England generation. The new generation produced its own versions of God's interest in its affairs, as indicated in the title of the first such work, Nathaniel Morton's *New Englands Memoriall; or A Brief Relation of the Most Memorable and Remarkable Passages of the Providence of God, manifested to the Planters of New-England in America; with special Reference to the First Colony thereof, Called New Plymouth* (1669). An official publication of the Plymouth Colony, the authorities had it printed on the college press at Cambridge, paying the grumbling printer with twenty pounds of corn and a barrel of beef. Morton was Governor Bradford's nephew; his inclusion of key segments of his uncle's history introduced the "Pilgrim tradition" into American folklore. Bradford's noble chronicle was not to be published for almost another two centuries.

A new note was introduced into New England historical writing in 1675 with the outbreak of King Philip's war. Spurred by English interest in Indians, American writers quickly turned out a series of brief war narratives. Creating most excitement was Edward Wharton's *New Englands Present Sufferings under their Cruel Neighbouring Indians.* A New England Quaker, Wharton—to the dismay of his Puritan neighbors—blamed the war not on the Indians but on the Puritans: God was merely exacting a due price for Quaker persecutions.

Some Puritan leaders also viewed the war as divine punishment, but these worthies were undecided as to whether God was displeased with the younger generation because of its "moral lapses," or with the magistrates for being too easy on the Quakers and other heretics. Therefore they countered with their own interpretations of the Indian war. Of these, only Cotton Mather's *Arma Virosque Cano* (1695) reveals any literary distinction.

The best writing resulting from King Philip's war was a different type of narrative, Mary Rowlandson's famous account of her captivity. In simple, clear, almost unemotional prose this little-educated frontier minister's wife described the savage slaughter of her village. Mrs. Rowlandson's low-keyed re-creation of her experiences caught public fancy upon its initial 1682 publication. Its title reveals again the New England need to acknowledge publicly the divine hand in all temporal matters: *The Sovereignty and Goodness of God . . . . being a Narrative of the Captivity and Restauration of Mrs. Rowlandson . . . . Written by Her Own Hand for Her private Use, and now made Publick at the earnest Desire of Some Friends*. It has been much reprinted down to the present, both in America and England.

Mrs. Rowlandson's success launched the Indian captivity narrative as a new branch of prose literature. Most of these efforts repeated in titles and texts the authors' gratitude to God for mercifully allowing them to remain alive to tell their stories. "Oh that we could praise the Lord for his great goodness towards us!" exclaims one of them, Captain Thomas Wheeler. The good captain's sentiments were echoed by all the writers of what historian Samuel Eliot Morison terms "the Wonder-working Providence school of thought." In style, tone, content, these fast-paced, unadorned autobiographical accounts of captivity experiences contrast sharply with those of New England's self-conscious, self-appointed historians.

At this time when New England's Puritans were carving out a new society, their coreligionists in old England were not only reading but writing imaginative literature. Ballad sheets were hawked in the streets, and all English grammar-school boys penned required Latin verses. But the colonists had problems more serious than writing poetry, drama, or fiction. They had difficulty enough merely getting through the day. Yet American Puritan writing was not entirely lacking in the imaginative, creative, or sensitive. In stressing man's temporary earthly status, it was not only direct, earnest, and purposeful, but frequently moving and exciting. And although these early Americans considered poetry a "minor craft," they still produced a strenuously sincere and sizable body of maxims, epitaphs, broadsides, and historical ballads.

PURITAN POETRY Admittedly, most American Puritan poetry is bad. The poet's primary concern was neither muse nor critic but farmer, merchant, and fisherman. He saw his task as moving "the hearts and minds of men to righteousness," not pleasing the sophisticated aesthete. Yet if New England could produce Michael Wigglesworth's theological doggerel and the awkward syntax and rhythms of the *Bay Psalm* translators, it brought forth also Anne Bradstreet's adequate metrics and Edward Taylor's moving metaphysical conceits.

The Puritan did not fail to appreciate poetry's aesthetic or spiritual effects. "There is somewhat of Heaven in Holy Poetry," declared Richard Baxter. "It charmeth souls into loving harmony and concord." The Puritan realized poetry was the most likely means of expressing his veneration and awe of God. Kenneth Murdock writes:

> There is no more striking instance in history of the constant need of the religious mind for some sort of poetic expression than the Puritan's quest for poetry. . . . For all the Puritan's confidence in his theology there was in his life and in his relation to God plenty of 'mystery and darkness,' and poetry was no mere luxury for him. It was a necessity, as it must always be for profoundly religious men, and his persistent quest of it testifies both to the depth of his feeling and the greatness of his needs.

Colonial poetry flowed from various modes of life and thought. Mrs. Bradstreet could express herself in lyrical, even amorous, terms. Physician Benjamin Tompson, the first native-born colonial poet, fashioned an epic on King Philip's war. But religion easily dominated the content and intent of early New England verse. Finding the Psalms especially inspiring, the Puritans used them for battle songs as well as public worship.

The first of the two Bay Psalm Books (the first book printed in America, in 1640) aimed at providing New England with a hymnal that would be a highly literal metrical version of the Psalms. Among the important clergymen chosen to convert the scripture Hebrew into seventeenth-century verse were Thomas Welde, John Eliot, and Richard Mather. Their final version has made literary history. Its awkward construction, garbled syntax, flat style, uninspired rhetoric, uneven cadences, and false rhymes have remained unequaled in American poetry. The twenty-third Psalm's famous opening lines:

> The Lord is my shepherd; I shall not want.
> He maketh me to lie down in green pastures:
>   he leadeth me beside the still waters.
> He restoreth my soul: he leadeth me in the
>   paths of righteousness for his name's sake.

emerged here as:

> The Lord to mee a shepheard is,
>   want therefore shall not I.
> Hee in the folds of tender-grasse,
>   doeth cause mee downe to lie;
> To waters calme me gently leads
>   Restore my soule doth hee.
> He doth in paths of righteousness:
>   for his names sake leade mee.

The translators were aware their verses left much to be desired artistically. But their avowed goal was a literal rendition suitable for accompaniment by the few melodies the Puritan considered appropriate for services. John Cotton (not Richard Mather as has been generally believed) stated the translators' case in his preface to the completed work:

> If, therefore the verses are not alwayes so smooth and elegant as some may desire or expect; let them consider that God's Altar needs not our polishings; for wee have respected rather a plaine translation, then to smooth our verses with the sweetness of any paraphrase, and soe have attended Conscience rather than Elegance, fidelity rather than poetry, in translating the hebrew words into english language, and Davids poetry into english meetre.

Though the rationalization is obvious, the prime concerns here clearly were extraliterary.

Another early poetic effort was John Wilson's *A Song of Deliverance* (1626). Written to convey to children an awareness of God's guiding hand in the world about them, clergyman Wilson's clumsily rhymed chronicle reveals little of aesthetic value.

A more likely critical target since colonial days has been Michael Wigglesworth's lengthy versification of Calvinist theology, *The Day of Doom* (1662). Described as perhaps "the most popular poem ever written in America," it was at least New England's most widely read poem of the later-seventeenth century.

Today its verse form seems totally inappropriate to its theme, but Wigglesworth knew his Puritan audience. In 224 stanzas of septenary, "a jigging measure that flows with the rattling facility of a Mother Goose jingle," he depicts the Calvinist Judgment Day. Scriptural references abound as the assembled hypocrites, evildoers, heathen, and infants plead for mercy. The watching saints, scheduled for Paradise, express pleasure at the punishment of the wicked. As for those who died in infancy and had not "good or bad effected pers'nally," they too shared Adam's original sin:

> A crime it is, therefore in bliss
>   you may not hope to dwell;
> But unto you I shall allow
>   the easiest room in Hell.
> The glorious King thus answering,
>   they cease, and plead no longer:
> Their Consciences must needs confess
>   his Reasons are the stronger.

With the infants thus compassionately dispatched to Hell's "easiest room," their elders are hastened by angelic guards "to the Pit of Woe":

> With iron bands, they bind their hands,
>   and cursed feet together,
> And cast them all, both great and small,
>   into that lake forever,
> Where day and night, without respite,
>   they wail, and cry, and howl
> For tort'ring pain, which they sustain
>   in Body and in Soul.

Wigglesworth's theological epic caught his New England neighbors' frightened fancy. The first edition of eighteen hundred copies (one for every twenty-five persons) sold out within a year. Six editions followed before 1701 and another four by 1774. It must have been a rare New Englander who remained unfamiliar with the work. Happily, Cotton Mather's prediction that *The Day of Doom* would be the book of the ages has proved inaccurate, but it was certainly the "Book of the Era."

Wiggleworth's poetic efforts did not end with *The Day of Doom.* He published a work in 1669 with the unappetizing title of *Meat Out of the Eater; or Meditations concerning the necessity and usefulness of Afflictions unto God's Children,* which went through several colonial editions. His best-written poem, however, was *God's Controversy with New England.* He described God's goodness in transforming New England's wilderness into a thriving haven for Europe's unhappy refugees. The New World's resisting natives suffer a similar fate to those daring to oppose God's chosen:

> Those curst Amalekites, that first
> Lift up their hand on high
> To fight against God's Israel,
> Were ruined fearfully.

But like the ancient Israelites, the New Englanders reveal their ingratitude, and a wrathful Jehovah proclaims his displeasure:

> What should I do with such a stiff-neckt race?
> How shall I ease me of such foes as they?
> What shall befall despisers of my Grace?
> I'll surely bear their candle-stick away,
> And lamps put out. Their glorious noon-day light
> I'll quickly turn into a dark Egyptian night.

Wigglesworth assures his countrymen if they heed God's warnings, all yet can be well:

> Consider well and wisely what the rod
> Wherewith thou art from yeer to yeer chastized,
> Instructeth thee. Repent, and turn to God,
> Who will not have his nurture be despized.

Perhaps the first New England Puritan to write solely for literary (rather than historical, polemical, or didactic) motives was Anne Bradstreet, a pioneer wife and mother. She felt the need to express her responses to nature, which she viewed as manifesting a loving and gentle God:

> How excellent is he that dwells on high?
> Whose power and beauty by his works we know.
> Sure he is goodnes, wisdome, glory, light,
> That hath this under world so richly dight:
> More Heaven then Earth was here no winter & no night.

Her guides were the English Elizabethans and metaphysicals and the French Protestant poet Guillaume Du Bartas. A true Puritan, her prime theme was religion—but as a vehicle for conveying emotion rather than instruction or admonition. Her first collected poems were published in London, in 1650, under a long title usually reduced to *The Tenth Muse*.

Few of these poems now are anthologized, "the Prologue" excepted. Consisting of versified essays and chronicles, they reveal too clearly the influence of various Renaissance poets and "Great Du Bartas' sugared lines." Her poem "The Flesh and the Spirit" (1666?), however, has proved more durable. A "debate" in the popular medieval tradition, this poem develops St. Paul's conception of the flesh and spirit's eternal struggle (as expressed in Romans 8). The struggle was for this indomitable woman no mere poetic exercise, for in a prose meditation she describes her frequent doubts of God's very existence. Thus the Spirit's declaration to the Flesh here takes on added meaning:

> Be still, thou unregenerate part,
> Disturb no more my setled heart,
> For I have vowd, (and so will doe)
> Thee as a foe, still to pursue.
> And combat with thee will and must,
> Until I see thee laid in th' dust.
> Sisters we are, yea twins we be,
> Yet deadly feud 'twixt thee and me;
> For from one father are we not,
> Thou by old Adam wast begot,
> But my arise is from above,
> Whence my dear Father I do love.

The "debate" form was used also by the greatest of American Puritan poets, Edward Taylor. A member of the second Puritan "migration," that wave set loose by the Restoration, Taylor was pastor and physician in Westfield, Mas-

sachusetts. Heavily influenced also by the metaphysical poets,
particularly George Herbert, he employs an oratorical or
dramatic style. His poems are usually speeches or prayers in
which God, Christ, man, the soul, or Satan express themselves in the homely images and dissonant colloquial diction
used so effectively by Donne, Herbert, Crashaw, Vaughan,
Traherne, and Marvell.

Taylor's longest poem, "God's Determinations Touching
His Elect," dramatizes Puritanism's basic theological concepts. His "Preparatory Meditations" reveals Herbert's influence. These are 221 poems, of varying length. Ninety-
seven are based on Old Testament texts, with the Song of
Solomon alone providing seventy-six. The New Testament
provides the other one hundred twenty-four, with most
stemming from the gospels of John and Matthew.

In one exercise, "The Experience," Taylor overwhelmed
by fervor, orders the angels to stand aside for him:

> I'le Claim my Right: Give place ye Angells Bright:
>   Ye further from the Godhead stande than I.
> My Nature is your Lord; and doth Unite
>   Better than Yours unto the Deity.

But this note of spiritual arrogance is heard rarely. Much
more frequent is one of spiritual and artistic inadequacy.
Thus in another poem he declares his abilities insufficient to
translate the divine into finite poetic terms:

> My tatter'd Fancy; and my Ragged Rymes
>   Teem leaden Metaphors: which yet might Serve
> To hum a little touching terrene Shines.
>   But Spirituall Life doth better fare deserve.

Only when God breathes inspiration into him, will he hope to
capture the divine essence.

> Hence make me, Lord, thy Golden Trumpet Choice,
>   And trumpet thou thyself upon the same
> Thy heart enravishing Hymns with Sweetest Voice.
>   When thou thy Trumpet soundst, thy times will flame.
> My heart shall then sing forth thy praises sweet.

Thoroughly devout, Taylor introduces no new theological
ideas. But he heats the Calvinist doctrines into poetic life:

Oh! that thy love might overflow my Heart!
To fire the same with Love: for Love I would.
But oh! my streight'ned Breast! my Lifeless Sparke!
My Fireless Flame! What Chilly Love, and Cold?
In measure small! In Manner Chilly! See!
Lord, blow the Coal: Thy Love Enflame in mee.

At first glance many of Taylor's images appear unorthodox. Yet biblical precedent can be cited for almost every image of the "Meditations." His favorite source is the Song of Solomon, from which he extracted the most sensuous metaphors and similes to describe his passionate devotion to God. But when he wished, he could describe the Bible's characters and events in realistic and extremely colloquial terms and connect them effectively to the images of daily life. The result was a body of poetic experience familiar and acceptable to his Puritan audience, in terms logical and natural to it, and sanctioned by the highest possible authority.

PURITANISM GROWS CONVENTIONAL American Puritanism's first native generation revealed a perceptible lessening of interest in political matters. Not for them the obsessive compulsion to guide their contemporaries' political and social destinies. Instead, many among them rejected civil office to enjoy the New World's natural abundance by moving on to found new villages or clear new lands. They exhibited also less religious zeal, though this was not apparent at first.

These social and economic changes were evident in the curious and colorful Samuel Sewall, "the Pepys of Boston," whose life typified Puritan America's first and second native generations. Brought to America at nine, Sewall grew into a hardheaded Yankee merchant, judge, community leader, and impassioned defender of the old ways. He saw the seventeenth century become the eighteenth and deplored and recorded in his famous *Diary* the rise of that secularism that was soon to topple the theocracy. Nevertheless, Sewall rejected a religious career for law, commerce, hobbies, and pleasures.

Sewall's *Diary* covers the fifty-seven years from 1673 to

1729 (with a gap from 1677 to 1685). When it begins Winthrop, Williams, Cotton, and their contemporaries had had their day. The new period lacked the vigor, imagination, and drama of the settlement era. It was, however, more enlightened and realistic. Sewall never forgets that the most commonplace happening reflects the divine will and has to be so evaluated, as he describes vividly the steady influx of immigrants and the rapid secularization in their wake. He presents shrewd impressions of those sharply practical "Yankee" traits evolving in Boston daily life. Both his life and writings reflect the middle-class concepts and values emerging as Renaissance and Reformation give way to rationalism, commercialism, and materialism.

By the time Sewall had attained his maturity, Puritanism had become temperate, conventional, and practical. But its verities and standards persisted. Sewall spent his time as businessman, lawyer, magistrate, and the colony's chief justice, yet he never neglected his Bible, strewing his writings with scriptural references. In his *Phaenomena Quaedam Apocalyptica* (1697), he prophesied that New England would harbor the New Jerusalem. In *The Selling of Joseph* (1700), he used the narrative of Joseph and his brothers to produce America's first antislavery tract. Sewall's most famous act was his public repentance for having been one of the three presiding judges in Salem's witch trials.

Puritan domination of American letters had come to an end. Henceforth, non-Puritans (Jonathan Edwards excepted) would make the important literary contributions. Puritans now looked backward rather than forward, and their writers were not disposed to win a reader's favor or excite his imagination. They wrote principally to convey God's word. They described the most minute occurrence with dramatic vigor, but they did so to evoke a sense of its "ultimate significance."

The numerous writings of Increase and Cotton Mather exemplify this attitude. Despite having published ninety-two works (most of them sermons), Increase Mather enjoys a historical rather than literary position. Famed for his voice of "tonitrous cogency," he was Boston's best-known preacher, Harvard's president, and an impassioned advocate of the theocratic tradition. Both Mathers, in fact, devoted their lives to sustaining the outmoded and crumbling theocracy.

A commercial society based on fishing, shipping, rum, and slaves was replacing the agrarian one that had concerned itself so wholeheartedly with theological questions.

Church dominance of New England life was shattered by the new Royal Charter, which based citizenship rights on property rather than church membership. But Increase Mather was not one to surrender easily. In sermons, councils, and writings he argued for the old Puritan values. He stated and restated his conviction that New England's misfortunes were acts of divine providence, relating numerous examples of God's rewards and punishments. One backslider, he reports, was struck dead in the midst of a blasphemous oath; another plunged into a fire while intoxicated. Nothing could convince Increase Mather that the Puritans were not beset on all sides by Satan's legions.

Apparently fearful of being overshadowed by his formidable parent, Cotton Mather devoted a crowded lifetime to preaching and writing. He delivered more than a thousand sermons, published approximately 444 works, and left unpublished many others. He wrote sermons, theological tracts, biographies, religious manuals, essays, poems, fables, and letters. His principal interests were religion and politics, but he delved also into science, natural history, and medicine. His writings reveal his undeniable industry, zeal, and erudition. Yet he hardly could be accused of undue consistency, for if he showed occasional open-mindedness in science, he also revealed bigotry and rigidity in theology. And even his scientific writings are marred by unbelievable credulity and neurotic parochialism. Coloring his thought and work was a deep-rooted longing for that "old New England way" in which the clergyman's word had been virtual law.

Cotton Mather's most significant books in American literature are *The Wonders of the Invisible World* (1693), *Magnalia Christi Americana* (1702), and his *Diary*. *Wonders* is the best-known account of the Salem witch trials. Like most of his countrymen (and a good part of the civilized world), Mather was convinced that Satan's legions were hovering everywhere and that the most stringent measures should be taken against those succumbing to Satan's wiles. His compilation of "evidence" here constitutes not only an example of Puritan superstition and bigotry but a tragicomic illustration of credulity in what undoubtedly was one of New England's better late-seventeenth-century minds.

Magnalia Christi Americana, or, The Ecclesiastical History of New England, 1620–98 glorifies the Bible commonwealth and its founders in seven long books. Its jumbled fact, fable, and outright distortion are presented in a style ranging from the simple and lively to the crabbed, pedantic, and showily rhetorical, all laden heavily with scriptural and learned allusions. Whittier was to describe the *Magnalia* aptly in his "The Garrison of Cape Ann": *"In that quaint Magnalia Christi, with all strange/marvellous things/Heaped up huge and indigested, like the chaos Ovid/sings."* Modeling his chronicle upon Burton's *Anatomy of Melancholy,* Mather strove to preserve the commonwealth's principles by establishing their biblical precedents, arguing God's sustained concern with New England, and glorifying "the wonders of the Christian religion." The *Magnalia* retains its place in American literature as a memorial to that rigid yet profound Puritan mentality shaping New England's first century.

An even more incredible document is Cotton Mather's *Diary.* A diary enabled the Puritan to record his daily battle against Satan and to evaluate his chances for salvation. Mather's *Diary* again makes clear that consistency was not one of his virtues. On one page he could attack the persecution of heretics, and on the very next unquestioningly accept devils running rampant in Salem and its environs. The numerous posed, or "deliberate," passages indicate the *Diary* was meant for eventual publication.

Cotton Mather committed himself to an age that was past when he was still young. He had considerable talent and courage but experienced increasing frustration and bitterness in face of the displacement of the old by the new.

Many commentators have declared their inability to find in seventeenth-century American literature works of major artistic significance. They value colonial writings "chiefly as a study in origins and as a complex mirror of early American experience." Recent critical studies, however, give these early writings a much higher literary rating.

THE GREAT AWAKENING   The rapid social, political, intellectual, and religious changes molding eighteenth-century America were not conducive to high literary standards. Those national culture values and ideals necessary to artistic creation had not yet evolved—or even been clearly defined. The 250,000 Americans scattered among the fishing villages, trade centers, and farm communities dotting the Atlantic seaboard were just launching that agrarian-mercantile society that would soon support a wealthy cosmopolitan class, wage war successfully against England, formulate and ratify a federal constitution, and initiate a two-party political system.

By the eighteenth century's end the scattered colonies would have welded themselves into a united democracy of five million, and many of its emerging social problems would persist into the twentieth century. In 1700 most religious Americans derived their beliefs from Calvinist or Lutheran doctrines. By 1800 the country's intellectual leadership, although having led the fight against England, had absorbed the mother country's scientific deism, while the populace had been drawn to the pietism of England's John Wesley and his Methodist followers. And a professional literature slowly was bestirring itself.

Up to this point American writings had been promotional, political, and religious. But for the new United States citizen, extremely nationalistic and sensitive to foreign or domestic criticism, a strictly political or religious literature was no longer enough. As he saw it, writes Theodore Hornberger, "if poetry, fiction, and the drama were the marks of a great culture, America must have them. If, as Aristotle had asserted, epic poetry was the height of literary art, the United States must have epic poems comparable in grandeur to the North American continent and the superior political institutions of the Republic."

Newspapers and magazines were started, usually containing "United States," "American," "Columbian," or a placename, in the title. The theater became nationally popular, and a few novels were published. Stressed repeatedly was America's need to be intellectually independent, to create a literature surpassing any of the Old World. Slowly America became urbane, witty, and cosmopolitan. The next century would bring the writings of Irving, Cooper, and Poe. But in the early-eighteenth century Calvinism was not yet dead, nor were the Mathers and Samuel Sewall. In New England, Jonathan Edwards was to prolong Calvinist doctrines through another stormy generation. Religious thought and writings, however, were confined neither to seventeenth-century New England, nor Calvinism. Proof lay in the writing of the aristocratic Virginian William Byrd.

Colonel William Byrd epitomized the Southern aristocracy and the new age's quickening social and intellectual awareness. A witty scholar and practical gentleman, his world seems ages apart from that of Sewall, his New England contemporary. Supported by slave and white-servant labor, its lands protected by English primogeniture and entail laws, Virginia's Tidewater aristocracy dominated a stratified, patrician society that held itself aloof from the neighboring easygoing, uncouth North Carolina backwoodsmen.

Lawyer, statesman, and plantation owner, Byrd found time to produce both histories and secret diaries describing Virginia and North Carolina life. Byrd merits a high place in American literature, states Byrd's modern editor, Louis B. Wright, "because he introduced a new note of urbanity, ease, grace, and humor. . . . But he was more than a graceful writer. He was the colonial counterpart of the European virtuoso of the Enlightenment—with a difference." A lover of dining, dancing, and hunting, Byrd still took seriously his social responsibilities, his writing, and his religion. The library at Westover, his palatial home, housed 3,600 selected volumes.

He had been educated in England, attending the famed Felsted Grammar School, in Essex, near his grandfather's home. The Felsted School had trained Oliver Cromwell's sons, and there, late in the seventeenth century, Byrd acquired a lifelong love of Hebrew, Latin, and Greek studies. His diary entries over a thirty-year period reveal he tried to read daily from the Hebrew and Greek. As other matters often interrupted his afternoons, he read in these languages before breakfast. The entry for October 31, 1709, is typical: "I rose at 6 o'clock and read two chapters in Hebrew and some Greek in Lucian. I said my prayers and ate milk for breakfast. About 10 o'clock we went to court."

Byrd had the usual assortment of human weaknesses, but he had also a deep religious instinct, viewing religion as a prime social need. Whenever he forgot his daily prayers, he noted the fact in his diaries to help expiate his sense of guilt. Although he loved the classics, hunting, and the good life generally, Byrd, like the Puritans he disliked, was given to sermon-reading.

On the whole, however, early-eighteenth-century America experienced a decline in religious interest. The increased mingling of ethnic groups and lack of a state church blunted Protestantism's earlier zeal. On the Virginia frontier the rough, undisciplined individualists carving places for themselves were virtually untouched by the Tidewater aristocracy's formalistic Anglicanism. In New England the religious spirit that had created the Bible commonwealth was no longer pervasive. A new spiritual impetus was needed if the earlier zeal was to be revitalized. Just such an explosive spark was provided by the pietistic, evangelistic movement known as the "Great Awakening," and by its leading preacher and thinker, Jonathan Edwards. Philosopher, poet, scientist, and theologian, the fiery Edwards infused into New England a short-lived but soul-shattering resurgence of Calvinist fervor.

Edwards is described often as the country's major theologian and philosopher and as America's greatest writer before the nineteenth century. He combined a natural flair for logic and psychology with a mystic's intense love of God; to these he added a tender sensitivity for man and a severely moralistic view of human behavior. The result was the most uniquely religious mind in American intellectual history.

The son and grandson of Puritan ministers, Edwards graduated from Yale in 1720, when not quite seventeen and when the college was still dominated by traditional Calvinist doctrines. Edwards unquestioningly accepted Calvinism's theology, but into Calvinism's coldly rational dogmas he injected a mystic's intuitive insights and a poet's emotional responses. Yet his intention and response were guided always by an acute mind shaped by Lockian philosophy and contemporary psychology.

Edwards emerged as Calvinism's champion. He argued God's absolute sovereignty and the communication of truth through emotion rather than intellect. He strove to establish these ideas by the latest principles of logic and psychology, hoping to demolish the rationalist theories by proving predestination's unquestioned validity and free will's essential falseness. To these ends he addressed "A Divine and Supernatural Light" (1733), *A Personal Narrative* (1743), *A Treatise Concerning Religious Affections* (1746), and *The Freedom of the Will* (1754). Edwards insisted that free will was a delusion, that the human will was passive and subject to involuntary forces producing desires and needs causing the individual to act. (The similarity to modern theories of the unconscious is remarkable indeed.) Edwards insisted that underlying all human behavior (both good and evil) and universal events was a First Cause: God's divine will. Arguments for personal salvation rested on fallacy; God alone could make the choice. Yet the individual was not excused from striving for salvation by unremitting piety and morality.

Edwards' insistence that man's knowledge is "transcendent," "intuitive," and "immediate" was two generations later to influence Emerson and the other transcendentalists. But while this view was to drive Emerson and his followers away from Calvinist theology and strict adherence to Scripture, it only reaffirmed Edwards' orthodoxy.

Intellectually attuned to New England's first generation, Jonathan Edwards was born two generations too late. If he brought a unique mind and imagination to bear on Calvinist doctrines, he never failed to affirm their validity, thundering from the pulpit such sermons as "God Glorified in Man's Dependence" and "Sinners in the Hands of an Angry God." Edwards powerfully affected his own generation. His sermons, full of fire and brimstone, launched in 1734 a series of spontaneous "awakenings" among his Northampton congregation, particularly its younger members, that soon spread throughout the community. Northampton's inhabitants, in turn, ignited the "Great Awakening," that sequence of religious revivals that during the next seventy-five years swept the country to make "Protestant evangelicalism" America's "prevailing religion."

Edwards' *Narrative of Surprising Conversions* (1737) records the Awakening's early stirrings and his own shocked reaction to the commotion he had created. New Englanders by the hundreds "awakened" to experience a rapid transition from a sinful state to that of grace or "conversion"; this they did by admitting unworthiness, exclaiming repentance, and throwing themselves upon God's mercy.

Widespread opposition soon developed to the revivals and their accompanying trances, visions, cryings, faintings, and even mental breakdowns. Edwards realized many contorting repenters were moved more by exhibitionism than by a sense of sin, but he persisted in his preaching. He was convinced sincere conversion was vital in conveying an awareness of God's love. His faith in "experience" and intuitive knowledge helped make evangelicalism and revivalism dominant religious patterns in America.

The Great Awakening, in its American form, gained its initial impetus from Edwards, but there were several European parallels. These were part of the great pietistic reaction to increasing Lutheran and Anglican formalism and deism's natural laws. Such early Pietists as the German Lutheran Philipp Spener and the Swedish philosopher Emanuel Swedenborg were insisting religion stemmed not from the head but the heart. One greatly influenced by this emotional reaction to religious formality was the German nobleman, Count Nikolaus Zinzendorf, founder of the Moravian Brethren. Moravian emigrants migrated to Pennsylvania and introduced many of the rigorous social practices soon to be described as Pennsylvania Dutch.

The Anglican minister John Wesley and his brother Charles returned to England in 1737 after a disappointing trip to America, where they had tried unsuccessfully to convert the Georgia Colony's Indians. Having met the Moravian Brethren in England and America, the Wesleys decided to replace the formal Anglican sermon with the Moravians' fervent extemporaneous appeals. They soon attracted large crowds among England's workers who were seeking a "religious excitement and consolation" lacking in deism and the Church of England. Because the Wesleys emphasized "methodical devotion," the movement their preachings launched became known as Methodism. In their desire to appeal to Northern England's largely unlettered workingmen, the Methodists developed an evangelical stress upon Adam's fall strongly paralleling the approach of Edwards. The American tours of such great Methodist preachers as George Whitefield and Francis Asbury helped spread throughout the colonies the religious enthusiasm generated by Edwards in New England.

Eighteenth-century pietism permeated the American mind. From Massachusetts the Great Awakening moved through Connecticut and New Jersey. From there Presbyterian Samuel Davis carried it into the Virginia farmlands, where Baptists and Presbyterians were affected. In Pennsylvania, the Moravians spread their pietism, and during the next half-century Kentucky and Tennessee's frontiersmen were greatly influenced. By 1880 the colonial churches had been replaced and American thought "stamped indelibly" by Protestant evangelism. All American literature since has been conditioned, as Professor Walter Fuller Taylor points out, by this "aggressive religion" whose "moral didacticism" retarded drama and novel and which in Europe purged romanticism of its libertinism.

Thus Jonathan Edwards' stern Protestantism dominated American thought until very recently. By the late-nineteenth century evangelical "idealism, restraint, and moral decency" had hardened into those provincial pieties arousing Mark Twain's displeasure, and in the twentieth it produced the fundamentalism evoking bitter reactions from H. L. Mencken and Sinclair Lewis.

APPEALS TO REASON   During the years Edwards conveyed his explanations of the divine mysteries to all who would listen, John Woolman, a young New Jersey Quaker, turned his back on both theological disputation and material prosperity to preach God's word as it came to him by the "Inner Light."

In the early-eighteenth century the Society of Friends, or Quakers, experienced rapid growth. Their reliance upon the "Inner Light" rather than on a professional clergy, and their pacifism, humanitarianism, and tolerance, attracted large followings in the Middle colonies and Southern rural areas. John Woolman preserved much of early-eighteenth-century Quaker thought and custom in his unpretentiously eloquent and revealing *Journal*. More than thirty reprintings attest to the *Journal's* popularity, with such diverse literary practitioners as Charles Lamb, Crabb Robinson, William Ellery Channing, and John Greenleaf Whittier, among others, praising its literary quality. His writings reveal a deeply mystical nature.

Woolman's outward life seemingly was uneventful. He spent much of it touring Quaker homes and meetings from New England to the Carolinas—and even the Indian territories—to relate his interpretations of God's word.

Woolman devoted his life to man's social and spiritual betterment. Drawing upon a deep scriptural knowledge and a natural talent for appropriate quotation, he attacked, with gentle but moving fervor, colonial America's abuse of slaves, laborers, Indians, and sailors. The underlying cause of man's oppression of his fellow, as Woolman saw it, was desire for wealth, power, and luxury. Every object not an absolute necessity became to Woolman a hateful excess contrary to the divine will or wisdom. He therefore advised all those in the "honest employ" of "merchandize" to pay special heed to "that precept which the prophet Jeremiah laid down for

Baruch, his scribe: 'Seekest thou great things for thyself? seek them not.' "

Woolman's radicalism unnerved even his liberal coreligionists. He wasn't satisfied merely to argue that those of means should use their wealth to win heaven's approval; he went on to question private ownership of land, arguing that as Earth's creator God was sole owner. He advocated methods the twentieth century has come to recognize as noncooperation, passive resistance, and the economic boycott. So passionately did he plead for better working conditions for the poor that the wealthy among the Quakers became alarmed and delayed for some thirty years the publication of his views. He declared slaves to be "of the same spirit as ourselves" and endowed with identical natural rights; therefore, to keep them in bondage was an unholy act. So persuasive were his arguments to fellow Quakers that slavery among them disappeared within a few years after his opinions were published. And from then on the Quakers became ardent abolitionists.

Woolman credited his views to a continual reading of "scriptures and other good books," absorbing them to where he "felt that rise which prepares the creature to Stand like a Trumpet, through which the Lord Speaks to his flock." And whenever tempted to grumble that such total social and spiritual commitment was "heavy," he remembered "what the Almighty Said to Ezekiel, respecting his duty as a watchman."

Many of Woolman's ideas were closer to twentieth- than eighteenth-century thought. They contributed much to that stirring of national conscience that in the nineteenth century was to become acutely conscious of all human exploitation. Woolman, like Roger Williams, was among the first of America's intellectuals to question the young nation's early social practices from the point of view of a religious mystic. He regarded all men as creations of the divine and therefore equally deserving of human dignity, political liberty, and social equality.

Religious fervor did not disappear with the passing of the Great Awakening; it merely subsided. The eighteenth century's shaping influence was reason, which touched and transformed almost every human activity, eliminating in the process many venerable superstitions and institutions. Reformation theology was replaced by Diderot and Voltaire's rationalism. Revelation gave way to "enlightenment." Literally transforming both political and scientific ideas, reason also pervaded theological thought to produce a rational religion: deism.

Deism's roots lay in seventeenth-century science, specifically in Newton's view of the solar system as a perfect mechanism functioning not according to special providences but unchanging physical laws. A perfect universe indicated a flawless and benevolent Creator as First Cause, but one removed from direct daily control of His creation. God's will was revealed most clearly in physical, rather than religious, miracles. In France, England, and the United States, such science-minded liberals as Denis Diderot, Joseph Priestly, Benjamin Franklin, and Thomas Jefferson expressed deistic views in their writings.

To the orthodox of all sects Jefferson's assertion that individual reason was the "only oracle given . . . by heaven" epitomized human presumption and conceit. It convinced them that deism was a thinly disguised excuse for infidelity, atheism, and materialism. Deism's emphasis of humanitarianism rather than faith, and reason rather than Scripture, challenged the traditional roles of church and clergy as sole interpreters of God's plan for man.

Most deists were active humanitarians who equated worship and good deeds. Man's most acceptable service to God, stated Franklin, is to do good to his fellow man.

Deism was a philosophical attitude rather than a movement. American deists, though never numerous, were extremely influential at a crucial time in the nation's history. Franklin, Crèvecoeur, Freneau, Jefferson, Madison, Washington, and Paine, among others, revealed varying degrees of sympathy for deism's liberal principles. Benjamin Franklin embraced deism at an early age, having read such leading rationalist thinkers as Locke, Wollaston, Shaftesbury, and Collins. They caused him to reject revelation in favor of a rational morality and faith. However, like most deists, he never wavered in his belief in God, or the soul's immortality, or the need to help mankind.

He published his deistic views in *Dissertation on Liberty and Necessity, Pleasure and Pain* (1725) and the two "Dialogues between Philocles and Horatio" (1730). Thereafter he kept his religious views generally to himself, expressing only his admiration for the orthodox Christian churches' beneficial social influence. Yet his deistic sentiments are revealed clearly, if obliquely, in his rational morality, tolerance, humanitarianism, dislike of the irrational, and general reverence for nature's "Sacred Book."

Franklin lacked the deep spirituality of his great contemporary Jonathan Edwards, and was—as has been said—more interested in paving Philadelphia's Market Street than in the new Jerusalem's golden paving. But the eighteenth century was a practical age and America a young country badly in need of the simplest material comforts and mechanical contrivances. And however concerned with worldly needs, Franklin never forgot those of the spirit. In a letter to Ezra Stiles, written a few weeks before his death, he sums up his religious views:

> Here is my creed. I believe in one God, creator of the universe. That he governs it by his providence. That he ought to be worshipped. That the most acceptable service we render to him is doing good to his other children. That the soul of man is immortal, and will be treated with justice in another life respecting its conduct in this. These I take to be the fundamental points in all sound religion, and I regard them as you do in whatever sect I meet with them.

He adds a postscript: "I have ever let others enjoy their religious sentiments without reflecting on them for those that appeared to me unsupportable or even absurd."

Most of Franklin's political colleagues shared his reluctance to air personal religious views. One notable exception, however, was Thomas Paine. A leveling democrat and ardent deist, Paine accepted wholeheartedly deism's scientific assumptions: a precise mechanical universe guided by a benevolent Creator's immutable laws. These harmonious laws, Paine believed, could be instituted among just and rational men.

Paine's faith in the common man exceeded even that of Rousseau, from whom he drew many political views. He believed democracy could eliminate antiquated social superstitions, traditions, and institutions; the public need only determine upon reform. "That which a whole nation chooses to do," he declared in *The Rights of Man,* "it has a right to do." He therefore denied one generation's right to impose its will on succeeding ones, insisting governmental power is derived from the immediate consent of the governed. Each generation must find its social contract agreeable; if not, it possesses the moral and legal right to rebel.

Paine's political views paralleled his religious ones, and his clear vigorous style and common-sense deistic ideas proved effective weapons. Paine, like Franklin and Jefferson, rejected atheism. He stated bluntly in the *Age of Reason:*

> I believe in one God, and no more; and I hope for happiness beyond this life.
> I believe [in] the equality of man; and I believe that religious duties consist in doing justice, loving mercy, and endeavouring to make our fellow creatures happy.

He antagonized his orthodox contemporaries, however, by repudiating flatly Bible, church, and clergy:

> I do not believe in the creed professed by the Jewish church, by the Roman church, by the Greek church, by the Turkish church, by the Protestant church, nor by any church that I know of. My own mind is my own church.
> All national institutions of churches, whether Jewish, Christian, or Turkish, appear to be no other than human inventions, set up to terrify and enslave mankind, and monopolize power and profit. . . .
> Every national church or religion has established itself by pretending some special mission from God, communicated to certain individuals. The Jews have their Moses; the Christians their Jesus Christ, their apostles, and saints; and the Turks their Mahomet, as if the way to God was not open to every man alike.
> Each of those churches show certain books, which they call *revelation,* or the word of God. The Jews say, that their word of God was given by God to Moses, face to face; the Christians say, that their word of God came by divine inspiration; and the Turks say, that their word of God (the Koran) was brought by an angel from Heaven. Each of those churches accuse the other of unbelief; and, for my own part, I dis-believe them all.

Although he disavowed Scripture, Paine, to substantiate his views, often cited the nineteenth Psalm's declaration that "the heavens declare the glory of God, and the firmament sheweth His handiwork." He also paid respectful tribute to the moral code of Jesus, comparing it to those of Confucius, the Greek philosophers, and Quakers. But he underscored similarities between the Greek version of the war between the Giants and Jupiter and the Christian accounts of Satan's rebellion against God, concluding that "Christian mythology is made up partly from ancient mythology, and partly from the Jewish traditions." He found the fall in Genesis ridiculous, insisting it would be "impossible to conceive a story more derogatory to the Almighty, more inconsistent with his wisdom, more contradictory to his power, than this story is."

Paine rejected the Judeo-Christian Bible in favor of the "Scripture called the Creation," in which are discerned principles at once eternal and divine. For the God who created man also created nature and science; thus man best can encounter his Creator through these mediums.

That Paine's outspoken political and religious views excited violent hatred and condemnation in the three most liberal Western nations—the United States, France, and England—is hardly surprising. Persisting to the twentieth century, this feeling is epitomized in Theodore Roosevelt's bitter, if inaccurate, reference to Paine as a "filthy little atheist."

Thomas Jefferson, too, aroused deep and lasting hostility because of his religious views. This hostility never quite equaled that leveled at Paine, but it still was considerable and equally persistent. Jefferson's ancestral ties were within the Anglican Church, but he was from early manhood a confirmed deist. His rejection of orthodox dogmas and championing of religious freedom, combined with his deism, was enough for religious conservatives to brand him atheist and infidel. The Philadelphia Public Library refused as late as 1830 to allow his writings on its shelves. But those groups struggling for religious independence, such as the Baptists and Methodists, enthusiastically supported him.

Jefferson, like Franklin, was reluctant to air his religious views, sharing Locke's belief that "the care of every man's soul belongs to himself." And like Franklin and Paine, he had little quarrel with Christianity's moral code. "To the corruptions of Christianity," he wrote to Benjamin Rush, in April, 1803, "I am, indeed, opposed, but not to the genuine precepts of Jesus himself." Jefferson accepted Jesus as "first of human sages" and the Jewish religion's "sublime reformer," but the recording of

> his life and doctrines fell on unlettered and ignorant men; who wrote, too, from memory, and not till long after the transactions had passed. . . . Notwithstanding these disadvantages, a system of morals is presented to us, which, if filled up in the style and spirit of the rich

fragments he left us, would be the most perfect and sublime that has ever been taught by man.

A decade later Jefferson revealed to Miles King his belief in religious freedom:

> Our particular principles of religion are a subject of accountability to our God alone. I inquire after no man's, and trouble none with mine. . . . [We] have heard it said that there is not a Quaker or a Baptist, a Presbyterian or an Episcopalian, a Catholic, or a Protestant in heaven; that, on entering that gate, we leave those badges of schism behind, and find ourselves united in those principles only in which God has united us all.

Jefferson's regard for the ethical teachings of Jesus, plus his wish that they be taught to the Indians, led him to compile a series of Gospel passages presented in a continuous narrative of Jesus' life and teachings. Convinced that Paul had corrupted Jesus' clear doctrines and that the virgin birth was to be classed with Greek myth, Jefferson included only those Gospel passages not referring to Jesus' birth, miracles, or resurrection. The result was a cohesive forty-six-page account he entitled "The Philosophy of Jesus of Nazareth." Having pared away all he considered erroneous, Jefferson was satisfied what remained of the New Testament was "the most sublime and benevolent code of morals which has ever been offered to man." In 1819 Jefferson produced an enlarged "Bible" of eighty-five pages, in which Greek and Latin texts were mounted on the left-hand pages and French and English on the right. He then had it bound and retitled the *Morals of Jesus*. However, it is best (if somewhat inaccurately) known as *Jefferson's Bible*.

Although Jefferson did not hold with all the Bible contained, he paid it the respect due a great religious work, advising Peter Carr, his nephew, to "read the Bible . . . as you would read Livy or Tacitus."

Jefferson differed with those he felt had corrupted Christianity's fundamental principles. "I am of a sect by myself, as far as I know," he wrote Ezra Stiles. "It is the speculations of crazy theologists which have made a Babel of a religion the most moral and sublime ever preached to man, and calculated to heal, and not to create differences." Jefferson never "joined" any church, but as he grew older he repeatedly identified himself in private correspondence as a

Unitarian. He was attracted apparently by Unitarianism's intellectual freedom and tolerance, and its acceptance of reason as a divine means of attaining truth.

Deism, as such, was short-lived in America, for despite their political restlessness most people refused to surrender their Bibles. But deism bequeathed some of its basic tenets to Unitarianism, transcendentalism, and universalism. These doctrines shared deism's confidence in a universe rotating about man rather than God.

THE TRANSCENDENTALISTS   Toward the late-eighteenth century various factors combined to underscore man's *individual* importance. One was the rise of romanticism. Rejecting Calvinism's devaluation of human nature and deism's emphasis of reason and logic, romanticism stressed man's goodness, emotions, and imagination. Its roots rested in America's economic prosperity and in those increasingly assertive middle classes that had won a war and had replaced mercantile restrictions with the commercial individualism advocated in Adam Smith's *Wealth of Nations* (1776).

Increased prosperity enabled many Americans to acquaint themselves with the post-Renaissance ideas revolutionizing European thought. Most of these ideas emphasized man's life in this, rather than the next, world. Martin Luther had contributed to this new individualism by stressing the soul's dignity in the God-man relationship. The assumptions of Isaac Newton and the scientific deists, as well as those of such associational psychologists as John Locke, David Hartley, and Claude Adrien Helvetius, also had strengthened man's position. These theorists argued that not only could man discern God's universal principles, but that he could adjust his life to them so as to enjoy continued improvement of mind, character, and social institutions.

Also shaping romantic idealism was Jean Jacques Rousseau's impassioned insistence that human nature, untrammeled by needless social conventions and corrupt institutions, was good. The most significant factor, perhaps, was that romanticism represented an emotional reaction to the preceding Age of Reason's rigid formalism in thought, art, and manners. American romanticists, like their European counterparts, placed their faith in the individual's complete freedom of thought and action. They rejected any restriction or limitation of the human spirit.

Around 1820 romantic individualism began reviving New England's creativity; the latter had been dormant during the preceding four decades. Running true to form, New England romanticists placed special emphasis upon religious and political reform. But wherever located, American romanticists, motivated by rising emotional fervor, were attracted to varying religious groups.

Together with the Puritan-descended Congregationalists and Presbyterians, the evangelical sects—Methodists and Baptists leading the way—exerted strong influence upon nineteenth- and early-twentieth-century American morality. These religious groups determined the moral tone of the national literature.

While the evangelical groups did not accept much of Puritan theology, they did share the Puritan concern for a rigorous public and private moral code. Buttressed by a fundamentalist reverence for Scripture, they were quick to cite chapter and verse in attacking any sign of sexual license and in protecting the sanctity of marriage, home, and family. So successfully did evangelical Protestantism impose its views on literature that nineteenth-century American fiction was almost totally devoid of illicit love at a time when Europe's romantic writers were making it a central theme. When a sexual implication was introduced—as in Cooper or Hawthorne—it "was handled," writes Walter Fuller Taylor, "with such delicacy as to avoid giving offense to the most fastidious churchgoer. And woe to the author who, like Melville or Whitman, violated this convention of reserve."

In fact, the devout suspected all literature lacking a strong didactic purpose. Whittier, believing poetry should improve as well as amuse, drew heavily from the Bible to convey both beauty and morality. Mid-nineteenth-century American writing embodied more than its fair share of moral teaching—the only notable exceptions being Edgar Allan Poe and Washington Irving. Other literary figures, whether religiously or secularly inclined, tried to "elevate" as well as entertain. Many factors contributed to this didacticism, but certainly the rising middle classes, with their Bible and evangelical views, proved the dominant cause.

In terms of literary purpose, the second religious wing—

the intellectually liberal Unitarians—proved more immediately significant. Unitarianism's early stirrings occurred in pre-revolutionary New England among those rationalists who accepted liberal French ideas of human worth but were reluctant to reject scriptural guidance. In short, the Unitarians not only shared deism's individualism and humanitarianism but also accepted revelation. Having absorbed Rousseau's high opinion of human nature, Unitarians reasoned that since all men are potentially good, the individual need take to heart only the Bible and Christ's ethical precepts.

Calvinism held firm in the regions west and north of Boston, but the new Unitarian views dominated the immediate Boston area by 1800. Between them, Unitarians and Calvinists dominated New England's religious thought. However, they did not enjoy a monopoly. The transcendentalists, too, made their presence felt. The transcendentalists were a small group of New England liberals who assembled around Ralph Waldo Emerson between 1830 and 1835. They included Bronson Alcott, Theodore Parker, Elizabeth and Sophia Peabody, William Henry Channing, Henry David Thoreau, and (briefly) Nathaniel Hawthorne. While they had no formal credo they shared somewhat similar attitudes toward God, nature, and life. Most of their views were embodied in Emerson's essay *Nature* (1836), which served as guide for the movement's Transcendental Club (1836–44) and quarterly, *The Dial* (1840–44).

Highly eclectic in thought and method, the transcendentalists borrowed many ideas from German philosophical idealism, particularly as presented in Immanuel Kant's *Critique of Pure Reason* (1781). But as their knowledge of German was limited, they relied upon the English interpretations of poet-critic Samuel Taylor Coleridge and essayist-historian Thomas Carlyle. And they leavened their English-German amalgam with the ideas of Swedish theologian Emanuel Swedenborg, Platonism, and the Oriental religions.

The transcendentalists, like the Unitarians, emphasized man's basic goodness and the soundness of his moral and rational judgment in religious matters. Channing and his followers accepted unequivocally eighteenth-century rationalism; Emerson, however, did not. Distinguishing between the rational and intuitive faculties, he stressed the intuitive as much the more authoritative in all spiritual matters, insisting that it "transcended" reason, logic, and the physical senses. Emerson's complex semantics did not fire the American imagination; his glorification of the individual "soul" and intuition did. Emerson's very definition of transcendentalism as "the intuitive perception of truth" owed much to Jonathan Edwards' "divine and supernatural light." Both Edwards and Emerson rejected eighteenth-century rationalism. But Edwards viewed the individual intuitive grasp of divine truth as very limited, while Emerson saw its potential as infinite.

The transcendentalists, essentially mystics, strove to "transcend" physical phenomena and communicate directly with God, the "Over-Soul." God, they believed, revealed Himself in nature, that "beautiful web of appearances veiling . . . the Deity within," which surrounded man with divine mind and love. Thus man was linked not only to God but to nature.

Upon this mystical union of God-nature-man rested Emerson's individualism, Thoreau's nature views, and Whitman's self-image as universal man. History and tradition, church and creed became minor. Significant was man's ability to live independently, to trust his inner promptings, for he could grasp "truth intuitively" by transcending the "reach of the sense."

In Emerson's opinion, historical Christianity committed major errors in deifying Jesus and in assuming the Bible represented God's complete and final revelation. "Jesus Christ belonged to the true race of prophets," declared Emerson in his Harvard Divinity School address. "Alone in all history he estimated the greatness of man. . . . He said . . . 'I am divine. Through me, God acts; through me, speaks. Would you see God, see me; or see thee, when thou also thinkest as I now think.' " But the followers of Jesus failed to realize, argued Emerson, that difference of degree rather than kind separated him from other men. Instead, subsequent ages distorted his doctrine to mean " 'This was Jehovah come down out of Heaven. I will kill you if you say he was a man.' " On them, mankind's "divinity" was lost.

Only the Unitarians and transcendentalists, however, accepted Emerson's rejection of the divinity of Jesus. Emerson's faith in human intuition moved him to reject biblical authority too. "Make your own Bible," he admonished listeners and readers, collect those "words and sentences that in all your reading have been to you like the blast of a trumpet, out of Shakespeare, Seneca, Moses, John, and Paul." Discard all external laws, authorities, and criteria, for nothing is sacred "but the integrity of your own mind." Be grateful, of course, for the past's great religious leaders, but say, "I also am a man."

Western man needs a "new revelation," he informed his Harvard Divinity School audience. "We forget that God is, not was; that He speaketh, not spake." Love Him, "without mediator or veil," Emerson declared, and "that supreme Beauty" that moved the Hebrews to wisdom will speak also to the West. True, the Old and New Testaments "have been bread of life to millions," still they lack "epical integrity" and have proved fragmentary at best. Man now should look for the "new Teacher," he who will recognize the world as the soul's "mirror" and grasp the underlying unity of science, purity, beauty, and joy.

Emerson repeated these ideas in his other essay-lectures and poems. In "Self-Reliance," he urged greater individual independence in religion and dismissed all creeds as intellectual disorders and most prayers as "vicious" attempts to satisfy private needs. Prayer implies the duality, rather than unity, of man and God. As soon as man realized God and he are one, he would cease begging. And in such poems as "Brahma," "The Problem," "Woodnotes," and "Threnody," Emerson restated his confidence in the essential unity of God, man, and nature.

Some modern commentators (among others, Allen Tate and Robert Penn Warren) view Emerson as the prime source of the secularism that dominated post-Civil War New England. Randall Stewart has declared Emerson to be "the arch-heretic of American literature, and Emersonism the greatest heresy. By no dint of sophistry can he be brought within the Christian fold. His doctrine is radically anti-Christian, and has done more than any other doctrine to undermine Christian belief in America." For many moderns, then, Emerson symbolizes the nineteenth century's intellectual shift from a God-centered to man-centered America.

Sharing Emerson's religious views was his spiritual disciple, Henry David Thoreau. Thoreau was deeply interested in nature's varied physical forms, but he was fascinated even more by its spiritual aspects. For him, as for all transcendentalists, the material was but the spiritual made tangible—in woods, rivers, or a summer's day.

Man alone, of all God's creatures, Thoreau pointed out, attempts—or even desires—to transcend the physical. To do this involves not ritual and dogma, he believed, but living, feeling, and experiencing intensely every day. All that is eternal, true, and sublime, Thoreau insisted, is telescoped into each moment. "God himself culminates in the present moment, and will never be more divine in the lapse of all the ages."

Thoreau did not hesitate to echo Emerson's thoughts, but he was not afraid to differ from the master. In later years he developed a more negative view of human nature than that held by the older man. In a journal entry dated March 5, 1853, Thoreau declared himself not only mystic and transcendentalist, but "a natural philosopher to boot." The statement proved significant, for as he grew older he became less transcendentalist and more scientific observer. Nor was he reluctant to cite Scripture when a passage happened to strike his fancy. After describing the New Testament as a "strange . . . heretical, and unpopular" book, for instance, he selected in *A Week on the Concord and Merrimack Rivers* several scriptural admonitions calculated to shake up his tightfisted Yankee readers:

> "Seek first the kingdom of heaven." "Lay not up for yourselves treasures on earth." "If thou wilt be perfect, go and sell that [which] thou hast, and give to the poor, and thou shalt have treasure in heaven." "For what is a man profited, if he shall gain the whole world, and lose his own soul? Or what shall a man give in exchange for his soul?" Think of this, Yankees. . . . They never *were* read, they never *were* heard. Let but one of these sentences be rightly read, from any pulpit in the land, and there would not be left one stone of that meeting-house upon another.

Emerson's modern critics notwithstanding, the transcendentalist who proved the major source of postwar secularism was neither Emerson nor Thoreau—but Walt Whitman.

Thoreau absorbed, advocated, and practiced much of the Emersonian doctrine, yet Whitman was an equal, if not stronger, adherent. He too accepted and glorified all that enhanced the individual—and without Emerson's asceticism and sexual shyness. Emerson had deified the individual soul; Whitman deified the body as well. Broad, expansive, and tender, Whitman felt charitable toward all mankind. But his was not Christian charity, at least not in any orthodox sense. For he, like Emerson, rejected traditional conceptions of man's fall, atonement, and redemption—and of scriptural authority.

Whitman shared the transcendental belief that all creation is one, that God's spirit has permeated all, past and present. Heaven's stars, therefore, are no more miracle than a leaf of grass, the past's great hours no more significant than the present moment:

> Why should I wish to see God better than this day?
> I see something of God each hour of the twenty-four,
>   and each moment then,
> In the faces of men and women I see God, and in my
>   own face in the glass.

Equal in every way to star or leaf is the human body's wondrous capabilities. "I Sing the Body Electric," he stated flatly. "If anything is sacred the human body is sacred." He differed from those who saw something fearful in the universe's impersonal processes, such as evolution. These were merely God's "vital laws" unfolding cosmic purpose and promise and relentless progress. Whitman saw only "Good in all."

To express his vast hymn of America, Whitman experimented with form, diction, and structure. He rejected metrical and rhymed verse to fashion an irregular but rhythmical chant that echoed the biblical Psalms' cadences, repetitions, and parallelisms. Relying upon panoramic metaphors, he voiced repeatedly the mystic's search for God, comparing these inner explorations to those of adventurous mariners:

> O we can wait no longer,
> We too take ship, O soul,
> Joyous we too launch out on trackless seas . . .

> Thoughts, silent thoughts, of Time and Space
>   and Death, like waters flowing,
> Bear me indeed as through the regions infinite,
> Whose air I breathe, whose ripples hear, lave me all over,
> Bathe me O God in thee, mounting to thee,
> I and my soul to range in range of thee.

These were hardly the sentiments of an immoral atheist, as Whitman's contemporaries so often described him. His view of the "Inner Light" he described as "The potent, felt, interior command, stronger than words,/ A message from the Heavens whispering to me even in sleep."

To their orthodox contemporaries (and to some conservative modern commentators), the transcendentalists' insistence that man is "part and parcel of God" was an arrogant exaggeration of individualism and a deliberate confusion of Creator and created. These critics viewed the romantic identification of God and nature as undisguised paganism and pantheism. Nineteenth-century writers and poets divided in their appraisals of nature. Hawthorne looked upon forest and garden as natural locales for adultery, witchcraft, and perverted science; others shared Bryant's belief that woods and hills are "God's first temples" and more appropriate for worship than the cathedral, church, or meetinghouse.

Transcendentalism's impact upon New England, if short-lived, was varied and significant. Some were favorably disposed toward it, others mildly derisive, many bitterly scornful. Oliver Wendell Holmes viewed all religious questions with a scientist's cool detachment, as evidenced by his light-hearted "The Deacon's Masterpiece." But he was equally unsympathetic toward transcendental idealism. He inclined to the deistic view that given a proper rationalist orientation the soul might well experience continual progress.

James Russell Lowell was much more pointed. Lowell could admire Emerson for having made his contemporaries conscious of the individual soul's "supreme and everlasting originality," but he had little patience with Thoreau or transcendentalism. The very word "transcendental," he declared, was actually "the maid of all work for those who could not think."

MEN OF STATURE   While such urbane wits as Holmes and Lowell made only scattered use of religious themes in their poetry, fellow Brahmin Henry Wadsworth Longfellow was a devout Christian who throughout his poems urged complete trust in God. Longfellow wrote a trilogy of lyrical dramas entitled Christus: A Mystery; these deal with the Christian spirit as it functioned, first in the century following Christ's death, then the Middle Ages, and finally in Puritan New England. In 1851 he published the middle section first— "The Golden Legend," a nine-episode cycle of religious miracle plays. Based on the ancient German story Der arme Heinrich, it is a medieval tale of an ailing prince who is tricked by Lucifer. He is saved, however, by religious faith and his pure love for a peasant girl. Longfellow here stresses that evil, as personified in Lucifer, actually is God's means of furthering His divine plan for men. For as the vanquished Lucifer leaves, an angel comments:

> . . . Since God suffers him to be,
> He, too, is God's minister,
> And labors for some good
> By us not understood!

Longfellow waited almost two decades before publishing part three, "The New England Tragedies" (1868); it consists of two five-act closet dramas centering on the Puritans, "John Endicott" and "Giles Corey of the Salem Farms." He completed the trilogy in 1871 by publishing "The Divine Tragedy," a verse-rendering of Christ's life and passion. The three dramas illustrate Longfellow's delight in religious history, particularly that centering upon medieval Christianity.

Longfellow's major poetic achievement, however, is his sonnet series, "Divina Commedia," written while translating Dante's great work. The much anthologized introductory sonnet conveys Longfellow's belief that literature offers the world-weary that serenity of spirit otherwise found only in a cathedral:

> Oft have I seen at some cathedral door
> A laborer, pausing in the dust and heat,
> Lay down his burden, and with reverent feet
> Enter, and cross himself, and on the floor
> Kneel to repeat his paternoster o'er;
> Far off the noises of the world retreat. . . .

His elegiac Bible-referenced poem, "The Jewish Cemetery at Newport," resulted from a visit to a Sephardic cemetery:

> The trees are white with dust, that o'er their sleep
>   Wave their broad curtains in the south-wind's breath,
> While underneath these leafy tents they keep
>   The long, mysterious Exodus of Death.
>
> And these sepulchral stones, so old and brown,
>   That pave with level flags their burial-place,
> Seem like the tablets of the Law, thrown down
>   And broken by Moses at the mountain's base.

Closed are the portals of their Synagogue,
     No Psalms of David now the silence break,
No Rabbi reads the ancient Decalogue
     In the grand dialect the Prophets spake. . . .

The chief New England opponent of transcendentalism was not Holmes, Lowell, or Longfellow, but that somber Puritan heir, Nathaniel Hawthorne. Unable to throw off completely his Puritan heritage, Hawthorne rejected Emerson's religious optimism, although he liked the Concord philosopher personally and his poetry's "deep beauty and austere tenderness." But, Hawthorne insisted, he "sought nothing from him as a philosopher." Emerson too had the highest personal regard for Hawthorne, but noted in his journal that the latter's writing was "not good for anything."

Hawthorne found man's soul dark and unpromising. Like Melville, he rejected contemporary romanticism's optimistic view of man, underscoring the dangers posed by human pride and arrogance. Human suffering, conspicuously absent in Emerson and Whitman, unifies Hawthorne's tales, romances, and novels, being a chastening and expiatory force. *The Scarlet Letter*'s heroine, Hester Prynne, expresses this hope of expiation through suffering when she cries to her minister lover, "Surely, surely, we have ransomed one another, with all this woe!" And the dying Dimmesdale replies, "God knows; and He is merciful! He hath proved his mercy, most of all, in my afflictions." Hawthorne's conviction that evil is a near and constant danger colors all his writings. No character is able to overlook the taint of his humanity; Ethan Brand, Parson Hooper, the scientists Aylmer and Rappaccini, Hester Prynne, Roger Chillingworth, each realizes his moral frailty as Adam's sinful heir.

Hawthorne had little use for social reforms: not institutions but the human heart had to be changed. He probed, with the earnestness "of a scientist of the human heart," the interaction of morality and conscious wrongdoing. In such tales as "The Celestial Railroad" and "Earth's Holocaust," he expressed his low regard for Unitarian and transcendental utopian measures, arguing instead for the sinful heart's reformation. "Purify that inward sphere," he declared in "Earth's Holocaust," "and the many shapes of evil that haunt the outward . . . will vanish of their own accord."

Herman Melville was much taken with Hawthorne's dark view of life. In his well-known 1850 essay on Hawthorne, Melville admits he is unable to distinguish whether the latter's "mystical blackness" is an unconscious trace of "Puritan gloom" or a mere literary device. "This black conceit pervades him through and through." Shakespeare exhibits this same "blackness," Melville adds, and if Hawthorne is not as great as Shakespeare, "the difference between the two men is by no means immeasurable."

Modern commentators continue to stress Hawthorne's Puritan tendencies. Randall Stewart describes him as "perhaps the Puritan of Puritans among the great American writers." For although he scored Puritan cruelty and intolerance, Hawthorne in his stories has "a way of taking the Puritan side." He was a descendant, after all, of that William Hathorne who had ordered a half-naked Quaker woman whipped, and of the John Hathorne who, in 1692, had joined Samuel Sewall and William Stoughton in passing death sentences upon the Salem witches.

Hawthorne probes the Puritan character and setting, not only in *The Scarlet Letter* (1850) but in such short tales as "Endicott and the Red Cross," "The Maypole of Merry Mount," "The Gray Champion," and "The Gentle Boy." New England emerges "a land of clouded visages, of hard toil, of sermon and psalm forever," while its inhabitants appear sour, unsmiling prigs. His composite portrait produced such definitions of Puritanism as H. L. Mencken's: "the haunting fear that someone, somewhere, may be happy."

Hawthorne decried Puritanism's bigotry, yet valued its moral earnestness. He was troubled by man's brash attempts to usurp God's place by tampering with the lives of others. Aylmer, in "The Birthmark," is obsessed with removing a tiny blemish from his wife's beautiful face so that she might be perfect. His attempts result in her death. A similar fate befalls the kind and beautiful, but scientifically poisoned, heroine of "Rappaccini's Daughter."

Parallels to the Genesis myth of Eden are numerous, as Hawthorne underscored repeatedly the inevitable tragedy of intellectual arrogance and pride. Yet he was quick to emphasize those spiritual benefits resulting from exposure to and victory over an omnipresent Satan's strong temptations. Hawthorne shared Milton's low opinion of "cloistered virtue," seeing merit only in goodness that survived—or resulted from —an intense conflict with evil. The characters in "The Minister's Black Veil," "Young Goodman Brown," "Egotism, or the Bosom Serpent," and "My Kinsman, Major Molineux" gain some semblance of moral victory from traumatic encounters with Satan's forces. Several Hawthorne novels explore this theme. In *The Marble Faun* (1860), the sculptor Kenyon voices it as a question that has troubled Christian thinkers since Paul and that Milton's Adam repeated:

> Is sin, then—which we deem such a dreadful blackness in the universe—is it, like sorrow, merely an element of human education, through which we struggle to a higher and purer state than we could otherwise have attained? Did Adam fall, that we might ultimately rise to a far loftier paradise than his?

Hawthorne seems to answer his own question affirmatively in *The Scarlet Letter*. In the Massachusetts Colony of the 1630's the passionate Hester Prynne and the brilliant young clergyman Arthur Dimmesdale break the Seventh Commandment; each soon is forced to expiate the sin in radically different ways. Hester's guilt is revealed by the birth of a daughter, whom she names Pearl (from the Bible's "pearl of great price"), and she is sentenced to wear an embroidered badge of shame. Hester has nothing left to suppress. Her internal conflicts resolved, she can withstand her neighbors' criticism, and in time finds favor in their eyes and in God's.

Dimmesdale's fate is different. Forced into the role of religious hypocrite, he steadily deteriorates. Seven years of almost literal scriptural servitude render unbearable his secret sin. Mounting the same scaffold upon which Hester has been forced to stand, he confesses his adultery—and dies. His confession, Hawthorne indicates, makes possible his ultimate salvation.

For Hawthorne, then, human sin is not irrevocable. Instead, it provides the human spirit with a means of attaining redemption through atonement. Only those who (like Emerson and Whitman) deny Satan's existence find religion, in its normative Judeo-Christian form, irrelevant. And only perverse human pride and arrogance, Hawthorne makes clear, prevent God from bestowing grace upon impassioned, bedeviled man.

Herman Melville agrees. Sometimes seen as atheist, Melville is much more accurately described (as by Hawthorne) as skeptic. Melville, wrote Hawthorne, "can neither believe, nor be comfortable in his unbelief; and he is too honest and courageous not to try to do one or the other." As obsessed as Hawthorne with man's evil compulsions, Melville found transcendentalism's optimistic formulations naive and pretentious. Admitting Emerson to be something "more than a brilliant fellow," he expressed irritation with the latter's "insinuation, that had he lived in those days when the world was made, he might have offered some valuable suggestions. These men are all cracked right across the brow. . . . But enough of this Plato who talks thro' his nose."

God, the universe, life—in spite of their seeming order, Melville was convinced—are much more complex and contradictory than most rationalists and idealists seemed to realize. Most men, he informed Hawthorne, "fear God, and *at bottom dislike* Him," because they conceive Him to be lacking in "heart" and to be "all brain, like a watch." Despite God's alleged goodness, He has created a universe rampant with cruelty: "If true what priests avouch of Thee,/ The shark thou madst, yet claimst the dove."

Melville's two major works, *Moby-Dick* (1851) and *Billy Budd* (1888–91), reveal his concern with original sin as a means of probing the nature of God, fate, and the human will. Both narratives abound in scriptural allusions, images, and parallels. Melville was firmly convinced even the greatest law scholars—such as Coke and Blackstone—could not "shed so much light into obscure spiritual places as the Hebrew prophets."

Moby-Dick centers upon Captain Ahab's defiant, maniacal, and blasphemous pursuit of the great white whale, a pursuit ending in destruction of ship and crew. Ahab emerges a tragically heroic victim, a victim of his own monomania. He sees in the white whale the universe's inscrutable evil "visibly personified and made practically assailable." And assail it Ahab does to his last breath.

Moby-Dick's theme is established early. It is implied in Father Mapple's lengthy sermon describing the scriptural account of Jonah as a tale of "the sin, hard-heartedness, suddenly awakened fears, the swift punishment, repentance, prayers and finally the deliverance and joy of Jonah." The difference between Jonah and Ahab becomes clear in the mariner cleric's conclusion: "If we obey God, we must disobey ourselves; and it is in this disobeying ourselves, wherein the hardness of obeying God consists." But arrogant Ahab goes to his death rather than relinquish his thirst for revenge against the whale that has shorn his leg.

At sea, Ahab's demonic determination captivates the *Pequod*'s all-nations crew, with the single exception of Starbuck, the first mate. Starbuck warns his captain that to seek "vengeance on a dumb brute . . . seems blasphemous." Revealing obsession and excessive pride, Ahab replies: "Talk not to me of blasphemy, man; I'd strike the sun if it insulted me." To him the white whale embodies "That intangible malignity which has been from the beginning; to whose dominion even the modern Christians ascribe one-half of the worlds."

But as Moby Dick continues elusive, Ahab places himself increasingly under domination of the Satanic Fedallah, a Parsee harpooner. Their evil pact leads to inevitable disaster for all, with only the wanderer Ishmael surviving to tell the tale. Yet Ahab's pathetic attempts to strike back at a malignant universe clearly evoked Melville's sympathies, and at *Moby-Dick*'s completion he informed Hawthorne, "I have written a wicked book, and feel spotless as the lamb."

Ahab emerges a pathetically heroic figure destroyed by his alliance with Satanic influences; Billy Budd ends a tragically heroic Christ symbol, bearing a distinct resemblance both to Adam and Isaac. Young, extremely handsome, and almost unbelievably innocent, Billy is a sailor aboard a British warship during the Napoleonic Wars. But lest Billy appear too perfect to be human, Melville (influenced by Hawthorne's "The Birthmark") gives him a vocal defect. When excited, Billy tends to stutter. Despite excessive innocence and purity, then, Billy bears the mark of his humanity. This physical shortcoming causes Billy's tragic end. For when he is falsely accused of mutiny, the angry, excited, and frustrated Billy, unable to protest his innocence, lashes out at his accuser.

The blow is fatal and Billy's fate is sealed. Captain Vere discerns Billy's innocence immediately. But he realizes his is the priestly function of imposing God's law. "Struck dead by an angel of God!" he decrees sadly. "Yet the angel must hang!" Billy's innocence will have to await the Day of Judgment; the Mutiny Act still governs the British Navy.

Billy's final actions parallel closely those of Christ on the cross. About to be hanged, he cries out, "God bless Captain Vere!"

> At the same moment, it chanced that the vapoury fleece hanging low in the East, was shot through with a soft glory as of the fleece of the Lamb of God seen in mystical vision, and simultaneously therewith, watched by the wedged mass of upturned faces, Billy ascended; and, ascending, took the full rose of the dawn.

To Billy's shipmates the spar upon which he dies is "as a piece of the Cross."

The doubt and skepticism Melville personified in Ahab are transmuted in Billy Budd. Seemingly, Melville's "desire to believe" finally outweighed his spiritual doubts. Like Hawthorne, he rejected any formal dogma. Both writers countered in their fiction the romantic inflation of the individual by demonstrating the ease with which "self-reliance" becomes hubris. Melville saw man as caught in the duel God and Satan wage for his soul; yet man alone determines the victor. Ahab, having chosen Satan, suffers the dire consequences. Billy retains his purity and attains spiritual victory even in defeat. For Hawthorne and Melville, life is a spiritual battleground, but one in which God's redeeming grace is available to whoever chooses to ask for it.

THE BRILLIANCE OF A DYING CENTURY Other American romantics found religious orthodoxy easier. Sidney Lanier, who rejected a Calvinist inheritance and desired to reconcile religion with "Sweet Science," experienced no loss of faith. Nor did his almost pagan enjoyment of nature cause him to confuse it with God. His intuitive acceptance both of divine goodness and man's spiritual worth was somewhat similar to Tennyson's. In his poem "The Marshes of Glynn" he declares that nature provides man with a direct and private means of communing with God:

As the marsh-hen secretly builds on the watery sod,
Behold I will build me a nest on the greatness of God:
I will fly in the greatness of God as the marsh-hen flies
In the freedom that fills all the space 'twixt the marsh
    and the skies:
By so many roots as the marsh-grass sends in the sod
I will heartily lay me a-hold on the greatness of God.

Even Christ, he imagines, found temporary haven and solace in nature's quiet beauty. In "A Ballad of Trees and the Master," Lanier states:

> Into the woods my Master went,
> Clean forspent, forspent.
> Into the woods my Master came,
> Forspent with love and shame.
> But the olives they were not blind to Him,
> The little gray leaves were kind to Him:
> The thorn-tree had a mind to Him
> When into the woods He came.

And Lanier could, without pagan overtones, describe a summer dawn as the ante-reign

> Of Mary Morning, blissful mother mild,
> Minded of nought but peace, and of a child.

Another who retained a basic Christian faith, despite the strong Emersonian cast of her poems, was Emily Dickinson. She could turn Emerson's ironic comment that "On Sundays, it seems wicked to go to church" into an affirmation of belief:

> Some keep the Sabbath going to church;
>   I keep it staying at home,
> With a bobolink for a chorister,
>   And an orchard for a dome.
>
> Some keep the Sabbath in surplice;
>   I just wear my wings,
> And instead of tolling the bell for church,
>   Our little sexton sings.
>
> God preaches—a noted clergyman—
>   And the sermon is never long;
> So instead of getting to heaven at last,
>   I'm going all along!

Like Lanier, Dickinson rejected the extreme Calvinism of her Puritan background, but she also was totally unimpressed by the voluble, often socially pretentious, new breed of "liberal" clergymen. Of one such she wrote:

> He preached upon "breadth" till it argued him narrow,—
> The broad are too broad to define;
> And of "truth" until it proclaimed him a liar,—
> The truth never flaunted a sign.
>
> Simplicity fled from this counterfeit presence

As gold the pyrites would shun.
What confusion would cover the innocent Jesus
To meet so enabled a man!

She lacked Lanier's respect for science. She was concerned that contemporary attempts to establish a common ground for science and religion would dilute the latter. Science did not satisfy those spiritual needs that, to her, only faith could serve:

> I never spoke with God,
> Nor visited in heaven;
> Yet certain am I of the spot
> As if the chart were given.

Nor did she have much use for man's overweening habit of creating God in his own image. She implies, in "Papa Above," that if man can take such liberties so can the lowly mouse, who undoubtedly visualizes death as a cat and heaven as a cupboard amply supplied with cheese for all eternity:

> Papa above!
>   Regard a Mouse
> O'erpowered by the Cat;
> Reserve within thy Kingdom
> A "mansion" for the Rat!
>
> Snug in seraphic cupboards
> To nibble all the day,
> While unsuspecting cycles
> Wheel pompously away!

Emily Dickinson transmuted belief into first-rate poetry.

One American who saw in his world little sign either of a benevolent God or beneficent physical laws was the embittered descendant of two American presidents, Henry Adams. Some contemporaries derived solace from evolutionary forces promising both biological and social progress; Adams did not. The forces of change at work in the world seemed to him to constitute an "Evolution that did not evolve; Uniformity that was not uniform; and Selection that did not select."

Searching history for values that would introduce order into contemporary existence, Adams focused upon medieval France and the symbol of the Virgin. To him the Virgin embodied the medieval reverence and creativity which unified religious belief and produced the great cathedrals. In *Mont-Saint-Michel and Chartres* (1904), he argues that medieval "unity" has been replaced by modern "multiplicity." Using the thermodynamic principle that energy disperses from a center, Adams contrasts the Virgin with the modern dynamo; the latter, he claims, produces blind, unchanneled energy that dissipates its force toward diverse poles and causes loss of social and spiritual cohesion. The resultant individualism hastens religion's decay. Medieval Christianity's "universe," he reiterates sadly, has been replaced by the twentieth century's "multiverse": medieval man served the church; his descendants serve the "Power House."

In his autobiography, *The Education of Henry Adams* (1907), he traces the effects of this moral and spiritual disunity upon the sensitive Adams sensibility. He is troubled particularly by modern psychology's new challenge. Promising fresh insights into the emotional chaos of the unconscious, psychology gives no more evidence than religion or politics of introducing order into human existence. Both man and his universe, Adams concludes, lack coherence, control, or dignity. "Chaos was the law of nature," he declares in retrospect. "Order was the dream of man."

Henry Adams' dissatisfaction with American society is not difficult to understand. To one of his temperament late-nineteenth-century America might well have seemed a culture without form, unity, or direction. It was a society in rapid transition. Its 1870 population of thirty-eight million doubled by 1900, and many of these new Americans spread west to settle the sparsely inhabited Pacific Coast. Industrialism, meantime, shifted the nation's economic base from farm to factory—and the people followed. Large urban centers sprouted, flourished, and spread throughout New England, the Middle states, and the South.

These major social and economic changes were accompanied by even more drastic intellectual ones. While industrialism was altering the social structure, scientific determinism was transforming the older philosophic, theological, and aesthetic concepts. The national literature soon reflected these transformations by increased skepticism, religious uncertainty, and changing moral values.

The reshaping of Western literature under the influence of science was hardly new, having started during the seventeenth century. Sir Isaac Newton's mathematical theories had fashioned a cosmic harmony that soon resulted in the deism of

Franklin, Paine, Jefferson, and Freneau. But nineteenth-century scientific thought, founded on biology and geology (rather than mathematics, astronomy, and physics), impressed the popular mind more strongly. Biology and geology produced concepts that rearranged religion's traditional world picture.

The eighteenth century's static world-mechanism was demolished by Darwin's evolutionary theories of a changing universe filled with complex forms evolving, with some retrogression, from simpler organisms. Furthermore, geology established the earth as older than Genesis chronology, and astronomy pointed to an infinite universe in which man appeared insignificant. At the same time, sociologists argued that folkways and mores determined human behavior, while biologists emphasized that physical inheritance and glandular secretions made man the simple product of body chemistry.

What was the individual to believe?

The "loser" throughout was religion. For if man were only what past and present made him, where was individual responsibility? For that matter, how valid was belief in a God who revealed, not special concern for His creation man, but complete neutrality? The earlier-nineteenth-century optimism seemed hopelessly outdated. The onrushing twentieth century was going to be a different-colored century.

Literary men were influenced greatly by the mechanistic philosophy. By 1890 most of the romantic poets—all of whom had retained a basic religious faith—were dead. The American writers now influencing the public mind reflected not only the latest biological, sociological, and psychological theories, but the "realistic" and "naturalistic" continental fiction of Tolstoy, Turgenev, Balzac, Zola, and Flaubert. Viewing life darkly, such writers as Stephen Crane, Frank Norris, Hamlin Garland, Theodore Dreiser, Upton Sinclair, and Jack London reiterated man's helplessness in a universe little concerned with his fate.

Stephen Crane made this the central theme of his prose and poetry. His short story "The Open Boat" (1898) pinpoints man's helpless insignificance when caught by the physical forces of an immense, remote, and indifferent universe. He also reduced this view to a few lines of verse:

A man said to the universe:
"Sir, I exist!"
"However," replied the universe,

> "The fact has not created in me
> A sense of obligation."

Frank Norris, in his major novels, *The Octopus* (1901) and *The Pit* (1903), underlined the age's deepening pessimism as he described man's helplessness before nature's "colossal power!" Seeing wheat as symbolic of earth's generative force, he asked:

> What were these heated, tiny squabbles, this feverish, small bustle of mankind, this minute swarming of the human insect, to the great, majestic, silent ocean of the Wheat itself! Indifferent, gigantic, resistless, it moved in its appointed grooves. Men, Lilliputians, gnats in the sunshine, buzzed impudently in their tiny battles, were born, lived through their little day, died, and were forgotten; while the Wheat, wrapped in Nirvanic calm, grew steadily under the night, alone with the stars and with God.

The turn-of-the-century generation's outstanding naturalist was Theodore Dreiser. An unabashed determinist, Dreiser was convinced human existence lacked reason or meaning. His *Sister Carrie* (1900) shocked readers by presenting a heroine, Carrie Meeber, who disregards convention by calmly utilizing animal laws of survival to conquer poverty. Here, and in such later novels as *Jennie Gerhardt* (1911), *The Financier* (1912), *The Titan* (1914), *The Genius* (1915), and *An American Tragedy* (1925), Dreiser depicts a world in which "this animal called man," struggling with irrational impulses, passions, and fate, feels himself no longer the object of creation but the mere plaything of indifferent chemical-physical forces. Character then cannot be evaluated as good or bad but merely as strong or weak. Frank Cowperwood, the Nietzschean businessman-hero of *The Financier* and *The Titan,* is convinced man must "eat or be eaten."

Dreiser expressed unhesitatingly and often his opinion both of organized religion and social morality. His fiction embodies his views. Certainly early Christian training does not save ambitious but ineffectual Clyde Griffiths, of *An American Tragedy,* from being crushed by external social forces and inner amoral compulsions. All Dreiser characters struggle ineffectually against the overpowering laws of an indifferent universe from which God has absented Himself.

Another writer much taken with Darwin's harsh survival

theories was Jack London. A wanderer much more at ease out-of-doors than in the city, London produced naturalistic romances of ruthless human (and animal) warfare. In *Call of the Wild* (1903), *The Sea Wolf* (1904), *The Game* (1905), *The Iron Heel* (1907), and *Burning Delight* (1910), man and beast rely for survival exclusively upon personal courage and strength rather than upon a higher power.

The predominance of naturalism at the twentieth century's beginning did not mean optimism and sentimentality were dead, but certainly they were scarce. Many writers challenged the mechanistic philosophy. Such philosophers as Josiah Royce, William James (in his influential *The Varieties of Religious Experience*), George Santayana, and John Dewey; social critics Thorstein Veblen and Lincoln Steffens; novelist Robert Herrick; and poets William Vaughn Moody and Edwin Arlington Robinson, among others, expressed deep-rooted dissatisfaction with science's impact upon religion. And these thinkers reflected the growing social and spiritual uneasiness of the masses already living in poverty amidst the new industrialism's choking slums.

Early-twentieth-century American literature showed only occasional traces of Emersonian optimism. Late-century skepticism was heightened by the new century's cataclysmic social and technological changes and wars. During the first two decades Dreiser was joined in his unblinking social analysis by Upton Sinclair, Willa Cather, Sherwood Anderson, Carl Sandburg, Sinclair Lewis, and John Dos Passos. Together these writers continued to probe social and economic issues that had bothered William Dean Howells and Hamlin Garland. The result was an American literature more realistic and more skeptical than ever, exploring public questions and the most intimate religious and psychological ones.

THE FLOWERING OF AMERICAN LITERATURE A new American literature had emerged by 1920. Volume and quality were high as novelists, poets, playwrights, and critics experimented with new ways of expressing the moral and spiritual disappointments of a sophisticated and critically demanding generation, one made cynical by the First World

War's human costs. These writers reexamined the nation's values with honesty and almost scientific detachment.

American writings of the twenties were filled with many of the tensions, anxieties, and crises that still motivate the nation's literature. The decade proved an amazingly fruitful one for letters. Most of modern America's major literary figures emerged from 1920 to 1930. Ezra Pound, T. S. Eliot, Archibald MacLeish, John Dos Passos, Ernest Hemingway, Edmund Wilson, Sinclair Lewis, William Faulkner, F. Scott Fitzgerald, Eugene O'Neill, Robinson Jeffers, and Thomas Wolfe were gaining wide recognition as they employed all the major literary forms to comment on the loss of personal values in a confused and impersonal world.

The first quarter of twentieth-century American literature reflected the impassioned debate between the religious and nonreligious. Many new writers criticized sharply organized religion's most cherished doctrines. Despite this criticism, American churches, led by the powerful Methodists, Baptists, and Presbyterians, continued to grow. For while most Americans were troubled enough by the new ideas to revise traditional Protestant theology, relatively few were ready to discard completely Christianity's ethical code.

Less dramatic than the religious debates, but more significant intellectually, was the literary movement known as the "New Humanism." This movement rejected the modern heresies of science, romanticism, realism, and naturalism. Led by a pair of university professors, Harvard's Irving Babbitt and Princeton's Paul Elmer More, its members returned to those traditional standards of discipline and taste embodied in Hellenistic literature and art. Their prime source of values was Western civilization's two major traditions—the Greek and Judeo-Christian.

"The humanists," wrote Percy H. Boynton, "want a harmonious development of body, mind, and, in the case of the religious humanists, soul." Some saw in the movement an attempt at a pseudo-religion. Both Babbitt and More rejected this view. "It is an error," Babbitt wrote, "to hold that humanism can take the place of religion. Religion indeed may more readily dispense with humanism than humanism with religion." And in *Rousseau and Romanticism* (1919) and *Democracy and Leadership* (1924), Babbitt decried the modern loss of values such as "awe and reverence and humility." What suffers is the inner life's special control, which is then replaced by "an increasing resort to outer control."

While many contemporaries, H. L. Mencken, George Santayana, and the Southern Fugitives, were not impressed by the humanists' return to the past, others were—T. S. Eliot among them. And many an opponent shared the humanists' reverence for religious values.

The continuing religious concern influenced the resurgent poetry and drama. These forms, despite the imagist and free-verse movements, had been somewhat neglected by major American writers during the two preceding decades. Now Pound, Eliot, Jeffers, and MacLeish combed classical, European, and Oriental literatures for symbols and myths with which to express poetically modern man's troubled soul-searching.

A return by some of America's men of letters to religious orthodoxy was symbolized dramatically by T. S. Eliot's 1928 announcement that he had become an Anglo-Catholic. Eliot's spiritual progress from doubt and despair to hope and belief are traced in such poems as "The Love Song of J. Alfred Prufrock" (1917), "Gerontion" (1920), *The Waste Land* (1922), *Ash Wednesday* (1930), and *Four Quartets* (1943). In *The Waste Land,* easily the most germinal of modern poems, Eliot attempts to capture the twentieth century's spiritual aridity, a condition he attributes to Protestantism's steady decay. *Ash Wednesday* reiterates his sense of the loss of past religious faith; Eliot here declares he cannot "hope to know again/ The infirm glory of the positive hour." Man's only chance of recovering belief, he states, is to surrender completely his individual will to that of God.

The *Four Quartets* continues Eliot's thesis that modern man's basic spiritual need, in a chaotic world allowing him only "hints and guesses," is "prayer, observance, discipline, thought and action." He explores in its four poems Christian concepts in terms of time, history, and religious psychology. Eliot's Catholic sympathies find a prose counterpart in non-Catholic Willa Cather's novel *Death Comes for the Archbishop* (1927). Eliot's literary approach to religion is essentially intellectual. Miss Cather's is aesthetic and emotional. Her Father Latour declares that great love is accompanied always by "miracles." Religious miracles, he explains, lie not so much upon distant "faces or voices or healing power . . . but upon our perceptions being made finer, so that for a moment our eyes can see and our ears can hear what there is about us always."

In his verse dramas Eliot explores the various ambiguities

of man's religious plight. In *Murder in the Cathedral* (1935), he dramatizes Archbishop Thomas à Becket's death to compare the laws of God and man. He makes clear that Becket's murder by Henry II's knights gives the king a mere temporal victory and that Becket's is the final spiritual triumph. And in *Family Reunion* (1939) and *The Cocktail Party* (1949) Eliot deals in a modern context with the same spiritual themes of martyrdom and humility, commingling as he does mysticism, science, comedy of manners, and psychiatry. Differing sharply from those contemporaries advocating rejection of religion's "shackles," Eliot has argued for almost a half-century that "In the end it is the Christian who can have the more varied, refined, and intense enjoyment of life; which time will demonstrate."

Eliot has been far from alone in dramatizing man's spiritual condition. At this century's turn, in fact, American drama already had become an effective vehicle for the examination of public and private problems. Influenced by the analytical plays of Ibsen, Strindberg, Hauptmann, and Shaw, American dramatists strove for psychological analysis and expressionistic symbolism in exploring modern man's moral deterioration. In spite of their "scientism" and hard-eyed realism, many retained a surprisingly constant religious affirmation, seeking to establish, through their plays, a basis for man's spiritual rejuvenation.

Play after play explored modern man's encounter with hostile nature, community, and parents—and his usual external defeat. But the playwrights were taking their cue from Maxim Gorky's character in *The Lower Depths* (1902) who declares that "Everybody lives for something better to come." They emphasized repeatedly the internal victory possible for those seeming victims who seek rapport with the divine.

Religious conflict pervades such early-twentieth-century plays as poet-dramatist William Vaughn Moody's *The Great Divide* (1906) and *The Faith Healer* (1909). Between the two World Wars it became an even more prevalent theme. Paul Green's *The Field God* (1927) presents a farmer condemned by his religious neighbors for what they consider the crime of lust. Don Marquis' "passion play" *The Dark Hours* (1933) broke theatrical convention by presenting Jesus on stage; its central figure, however, is Judas, whose motives for betrayal are explored.

Man's quest for values higher and insights deeper than those discernible in ordinary existence also knits together

Maxwell Anderson's verse tragedies. In *Winterset* (1935), Esdras, the embittered old evolutionist, glimpses the human spirit's indomitability in the young couple's love and courage. Looking out at the dark, cold night, he declares:

> In all these turning lights I find no clue,
> only a masterless night, and in my blood
> no certain answer, yet is my mind my own,
> yet is my heart a cry toward something dim
> in distance, which is higher than I am
> and makes me emperor of the endless dark
> even in seeking.

D'Alcala, the blind father of *Key Largo* (1939), expresses a similar view. At play's end the old man proclaims man's challenge to be

> .... to take this dust
> and water and our range of appetites
> and build them toward some vision of a god
> of beauty and unselfishness and truth—
> could we ask better of the mud we are
> than to accept the challenge, and look up
> and search for god-head?

Other dramatists focused more clearly on the inner self to justify religious belief. This inward view resulted—during the late Thirties and the Forties—in psychoanalytic and religious dramas using fantasy, dreams, and illusions to probe the unconscious with both humor and seriousness. Philip Barry's plays—such as *Hotel Universe* (1930), *The Joyous Season* (1934), and particularly *Here Come the Clowns* (1938)— reveal these elements. Barry underlines man's need for God even though his faith has been eroded by reality's superficial and illusionary masks. With much less tension, William Saroyan—in *The Time of Your Life* (1939), *The Beautiful People* (1941), and *Jim Dandy, Fat Man in a Famine* (1947)—stresses the underlying unity of life, faith, dreams, God's love for man, and man's love for his fellow. As America approached World War II, the parallel ideas of compassion and tribulation—and their religious overtones—were sounded in Clifford Odets' *Night Music* (1940) and Robert Sherwood's *There Shall Be No Night* (1940).

Some recent American playwrights have chosen to express their religious ideas more directly, dramatizing in modern psychological terms biblical or pseudobiblical events. Philip Barry's *John* (1927), Marc Connelly's *Green Pastures* (1930), Maxwell Anderson's *Journey to Jerusalem* (1940), and even more recently Archibald MacLeish's *J. B.* (1958) and Paddy Chayefsky's *Gideon* (1961) are a few notable examples. The somewhat related theme of demonology is depicted in Chayefsky's *The Tenth Man* (1959).

The composite human portrait these contemporary religious dramas create is both frightening and reassuring. Caught in a world coldly indifferent to human aspiration, modern man (as here presented) has found surprising internal strength. He has learned to reshape his external existence into the image of an inner conception of faith. While this reapproachment has not solved his spiritual dilemma, it has enabled him to continue striving for belief in God and himself.

A telling dramatic analysis of this inner vision is found in the plays of Eugene O'Neill. Like Hawthorne and Melville, O'Neill explored the soul's fears and uncertainties, yet he retained unfailing faith in man's essential dignity. His intention was to depict "man's self-destructive struggle" for expression in terms of the life-force. O'Neill therefore concluded his own prime concern should be not the relationship between man and man, but that between man and God.

To illuminate contemporary man's uncertain spiritual condition, O'Neill employed Freudian insights into the subconscious, modern fiction's stream-of-consciousness techniques, romantic fantasy, and expressionistic symbolism. A succession of experimental, challenging, and frequently obscure dramas resulted. In *The Great God Brown* (1926), O'Neill strives to strip bare materialism's basic emptiness by contrasting pagan indulgence and religious denial. He uses masks to reveal his characters' internal and external personalities, particularly those of Dion Anthony (in whom Dionysus and St. Anthony do battle) and William A. Brown, an empty product of a success-bent age. The play's credo is voiced by the prostitute Cybel, who cradles and assures the dying Brown of God's existence and that love is man's only reality and hope.

O'Neill followed this with *Lazarus Laughed* (1927), a drama celebrating love and joy's triumph over the fear of death and centering upon the biblical figure Jesus raised from the dead. Lazarus returns from the dead echoing "the laughter of God" and bearing a message of God's love and death's negation. He champions a joyous rejection of self and acceptance of God's universal life-scheme. "Laughing we lived with our gift," he declares, "now with laughter give we back that gift to become again the Essence of the Giver." Even when martyred he cries out, "Fear not life. You die—but there is no death for man!" Yet O'Neill here preaches not so much Christian immortality as man's need for faith and spiritual insight into his existence.

He repeats this idea in *Dynamo* (1929), in terms reminiscent of Henry Adams. O'Neill makes the electric dynamo a deity symbol that not only replaces the biblical God but that proceeds to destroy its own worshipers. In *Days Without End* (1934), he again expresses man's need to believe in his own spiritual goodness. Cynical John Loving learns that in a morally deficient age, one which has reduced man to "a badly driven mechanism," a saviour is needed to illuminate faith. Guided by a Catholic priest, Loving discovers that to believe in Christ's love is to attain a victory of the spirit over the worldly forces of corruption and decay.

The degree and kind of O'Neill's "faith" is still being debated, but there is evidence that he found in the Christian tradition some solace from the personal demons that continually plagued him.

While America's playwrights have experienced and expressed much of the century's spiritual confusion, the nation's poets have shared their plight. Many poets harbor the uneasy conviction that God does not exist and that in a Godless universe to expect moral and ethical responsibility is fruitless. They are torn by doubts, confusion, and a desire to believe. Some have attempted to bridge this inability and desire to believe by focusing upon the figure of Jesus. A sizable literature has resulted rejecting creedal Christianity but centering upon the life of Jesus.

This concern with Jesus early became an effective symbolic means of giving religious (but unorthodox) expression to demands for social change and justice. In the 1890's, Richard Watson Gilder, for instance, saw in Jesus:

> Not the Christ of our subtle creeds,
> But the brother of want and blame,
> The lover of women and men,
> With a love that puts to shame
> All passions of mortal ken.

Edwin Arlington Robinson sounded the same note in "Calvary":

But after nineteen hundred years the shame
Still clings, and we have not made good the loss
That outraged faith has entered in his name.
Ah, when shall come love's courage to be strong!
Tell me, O Lord—tell me, O Lord, how long
Are we to keep Christ writhing on the cross!

Generalized social protest soon took a strongly political, particularly Marxian, turn. Typical was this excerpt from Sarah N. Cleghorn's "Comrade Jesus":

Thank to Saint Matthew, who had been
At mass-meetings in Palestine,
We know whose side was spoken for
When Comrade Jesus had the floor. . . .

Ah, let no Local him refuse!
Comrade Jesus has paid his dues.
Whatever other be debarred,
Comrade Jesus has his red card.

And Edna St. Vincent Millay's sonnet "To Jesus On His Birthday" might have been written only yesterday, scoring the materialistic despoiling of Christmas:

For this Your mother sweated in the cold,
For this You bled upon the bitter tree:
A yard of tinsel ribbon bought and sold;
A paper wreath; a day at home for me.
. . . . Less than the wind that blows
Are all your words to us you died to save.

A few American poets resisted all religious doubts. Vachel Lindsay, "Christianity's unofficial poet laureate," objectified his belief in such evangelistic poems as "General William Booth Enters into Heaven," "The Illinois Village," "The Unpardonable Sin," and in "Heart of God":

Heart, dear heart of God,
Beside you now I kneel,
Strong heart of faith. O heart not mine,
Where God has set His seal.

Wild thundering heart of God
Out of my doubt I come,

And my foolish feet with prophets' feet,
March with the prophets' drum.

For every Lindsay, however, there were several poets whose hearts entered the church but whose heads remained outside. Robinson's "The Children of the Night" voices this "reverential skepticism":

If there be nothing, good or bad,
    But chaos for a soul to trust,—
God counts it for a soul gone mad,
    And if God be God, He is just.

And if God be God, He is Love;
    And though the Dawn be still so dim,
It shows us we have played enough
    With creeds that make a fiend of Him. . . .

It is the faith within the fear
    That holds us to the life we curse;—
So let us in ourselves revere
    The Self which is the Universe!

Let us, the Children of the Night,
    Put off the cloak that hides the scar!
Let us be Children of the Light,
    And tell the ages what we are!

Poets closer to the present have continued to externalize their spiritual turmoil. Allen Tate, in his "Sonnets at Christmas," has expressed this conflict that often takes the form of a troubled conscience:

Therefore with idle hands and Head I sit
In late December before the fire's daze
Punished by crimes of which I would be quit.

Years later, torn by the same duality of belief and doubt, he protests almost angrily:

Ten years are enough time to be dismayed
By mummy Christ, head crammed between his knees.

Modern man's excessive reliance upon mind, states theologian Amos Wilder, has made him a mere "critic, observer, analyst, scientist"; it has placed a seal upon his impulse and "myth-

believing faculties." Modern intellectualism has weakened
that intuitive and spontaneous sense of life man should retain
always as God's creature.

A more specifically anti-Christian view than Tate's is found
in Wallace Stevens' "Sunday Morning." Stevens here leveled
against religion the common modern complaint of a "false
asceticism" which denies life's natural beauty and goodness.
The woman narrator finds herself unnerved by the "En-
croachment of that old catastrophe," the Christ story, with its
harsh tones of "blood and sepulchre." She wonders:

> Why should she give her bounty to the dead?
> What is divinity if it can come
> Only in silent shadows and in dreams?

Furthermore, she reasons, religion's legends have not "en-
dured/ As April's green endures." This convinces her:

> "The tomb in Palestine
> Is not the porch of spirits lingering.
> It is the grave of Jesus, where He lay."

Hence she will seek spiritual contentment not in abstract
religious faith but in concrete physical beauty.

Some modern poets are harsher critics of religion than
Stevens. Influenced by English writers such as George Bernard Shaw and William Butler Yeats, they have charged
Christianity with leading man to commit—in God's name—
the most heinous deeds. Elder Olson, in *The Cock of Heaven,*
declares "that this long night,/ This cold eclipse, is shade
cast from Christ's cross." Indeed this "hanged staring Man/
Strung like a hanged worm in spider-string" foretells "foul-
ness; foul graves for Nero and Charlemagne,/ Crowned
Frederick, gowned Gregory, Dolfuss, Fey, Stalin."

This view of Christianity's sanguinary influence was shared
by Robinson Jeffers. Hammering at what he considered
Christian mythology's morbid concern with suffering, Jeffers
(clearly influenced by Shaw and Yeats) attributed Christ's
two-millennia hold on mankind to man's fascination with
cruelty and pain. Christ's "personal anguish and insane solution," he declares, "have stained an age; nearly two thousand
years are one vast poem/drunk with the wine of his blood."
Despite his low opinion of mankind in general and organized
Christianity in particular, Jeffers expresses respect for the

man Jesus and the tragedy of man's fall. (He was here at one with his literary contemporaries Faulkner, Eliot, Auden, and Warren.) His "Shine, Perishing Republic," describes Christ as one of the world's "noblest spirits" and one who suffered the misfortune of being caught in that "trap" that is the "love of man."

In *Dear Judas*, Jeffers develops more fully the Jesus-as-victim idea. Jesus here disregards Lazarus' warnings that involving himself in man's affairs can end only in disaster. Jesus recognizes clearly—and somewhat sardonically—that his power over men's minds will derive from human masochism and sadism:

> Oh, power
> Bought at the price these hands and feet and all
> this body perishing in torture will pay is holy.
> Their minds love terror, their souls cry to be
> sacrificed for: pain's almost the God
> Of doubtful men, who tremble expecting to
> endure it. Their cruelty sublimed. And I
> think the brute cross itself,
> Hewn down to a gibbet now, has been worshipped;
> it stands yet for an idol of life and
> power in the dreaming
> Soul of the world. . . .
>
> I frightfully
> Lifted up drawing all men to my feet: I go a
> stranger passage to a greater dominion,
> More tyrannous, more terrible, more true, than
> Caesar or any subduer of the earth
> before him has dared to dream of.

As events take their fateful course, Lazarus reassures Mary that "Your son has done what men are not able to do,/ He has chosen and made his own fate." But it is Jesus who expresses the poem's theme when, following his betrayal, he comforts the guilt-ridden Judas that all merely have fulfilled predestined roles:

> Dear Judas, it is God drives us.
> It is not shameful to be duped by God. I have
> known his glory in my lifetime, I
> have *been* his glory, I know
> Beyond illusion the enormous beauty of the

torch in which our agonies and all
are particles of fire.

Neither Jeffers, Tate, nor Stevens rejects the religious
impulse itself. (Tate, in fact, has converted to Catholicism,
and in "The Cross" he describes the impact of Christ's coming upon man's imagination.) They protest only what they
consider Christianity's cold and uninspired aspects. They are
often—as Amos Wilder points out—heretical and misguided;
still they criticize only that which is restrictive and discour-
aging to faith. They actually demand that the "yea-saying
impulse of the biblical faith and its moment of creative play
be given their due place, and that this 'yea' should be spoken
not only to the spirit but also to the flesh."

Despite their negativism, the concern of America's major
poets with the God-man relationship signifies their desire to
share in the spiritual values of the Judeo-Christian tradition.

This same religious concern is to be found in most of the
more important contemporary American novelists. They too
have rejected formal theological or ecclesiastical dogmas for
the simpler, more fundamental God-man dialogue. Darwinian
ideas had convinced such early naturalists as Crane, Norris,
and Dreiser that man's old universal myths (as presented in
the Bible) were useless—if not dead. To them and their immediate successors it seemed modern technology and its
mechanical mass media were eroding not only regional differences but personal identity. Increasingly disturbed, America's
novelists tried to check this purposeless drift and anonymity
by turning either to science or religion, or both. But they
soon decided that neither, alone, provided all the answers to
the frightening questions of modern existence.

The Scopes trial crystallized the intellectuals' growing
resentment of "Bible" religion. Sinclair Lewis' novels exemplify the near-hysterical revulsion to fundamentalism. Strongly influenced by Mencken's dismissal of religion as an outmoded relic of human immaturity, Lewis published in *Elmer
Gantry* (1927) an excoriating indictment of evangelical
Protestantism. Dedicated "To H. L. Mencken, with profound
admiration," the novel details the unsavory exploits of an
immoral and hypocritical exangelist. A few years later James
T. Farrell, the last of America's major naturalists, in his
Studs Lonigan trilogy (1932–35), stressed the inability of
church, home, or school to prevent his young hero's progressive corruption.

A DEEPENING INTEREST IN RELIGION'S VALUES

While fundamentalism and parochialism fared poorly with America's novelists of the Thirties, science did little better. By the mid-Thirties any lingering hope they may have had that science would liberate mankind had been replaced by a fear of its tendency to mechanize and impoverish the human spirit. And in their deflation of science they soon included such concomitants as naturalism and Marxism. In recent years naturalism's decline has resulted from and added to the deepening interest in religion's values. Recent Southern fiction, especially, is concerned with original sin. Its heroes, having retained a sense of moral responsibility for their actions, are not the hapless, innocent victims of deterministic forces.

Certainly William Faulkner's heroes are neither completely hapless nor "innocent." Faulkner, like Hawthorne and Melville, is both moralist and social historian. He is interested not only in the subtle machinations of heart and mind but in the social context shaping them. With Faulkner this means the internal-external conflicts arising from attempts to preserve traditional Southern values in a rapidly shifting modern society. And he is interested not merely "in one generation, but in many generations in their interlocking continuity."

Faulkner, too, is a noncreedal Christian who uses scriptural myth to give his stories form, meaning, and depth. He shares with Hawthorne and Melville (not to mention Henry James and T. S. Eliot) a deep concern with evil's relationship to the "truths of the heart." He rejects all simple solutions to fundamental human problems. He does not view the transcendentalists' faith in self-reliance, or "humanistic optimism," or "science and humanity" as adequate substitutes for an outmoded Christian tradition. Faulkner's characters are Adam's children struggling valiantly with dark inner compulsions. Like Ahab, Roger Chillingworth, and even Hester Prynne, they combine a "satanic monomania with an appealing heroism."

Faulkner forces religious and nonreligious readers to scrutinize their own values. He weaves into his tales such

Christ figures as Benjy Compson, Joe Christmas, Ike Mc-Caslin, and the Corporal, in *A Fable,* and themes of sin and damnation, suffering and possible redemption. These themes are to be seen in early tales like "Out of Nazareth," "The Kingdom of God," and "The Rosary," and in the novels from *Soldiers' Pay* (1926) to *The Mansion* (1959). Although a sense of troubled—even inadequate—religious faith afflicts most of his characters, Faulkner makes clear that no adequate substitute for faith exists.

Deeply sensitive to the fanaticism embodied in normative theology, Faulkner favors rejection of encrusted ecclesiastical distortions for a return to the simple ethics of Jesus. In *The Sound and the Fury* (1929), for instance, Quentin Compson is obsessed by Christian ideals of purity and chastity; thus their violation by his relatives (particularly by his sister, Caddy) drives him to suicide. Faulkner conveys his lack of patience with such warped religiosity. Quentin's was "some Presbyterian concept of eternal punishment; he, not God, could by that means cast himself and his sister both into Hell, where he would guard her forever and keep her forevermore intact amid the eternal fires."

Faulkner decries the tyranny of outmoded codes of honor, status, and sexual behavior and the twisting of positive religious values into negative, self-destructive forces. His quarrel is not with religion, but with its petrified and distorted forms. While he scores Christianity's destructive capacity in Quentin Compson's suicide, he emphasizes its spiritual and moral strength in the maid Dilsey, who has kept the Compson family together and functioning for many years. Dilsey's belief saves her from the despair engulfing the Compsons. Its persistent note of religious affirmation has caused critic Hyatt Waggoner to place *The Sound and the Fury* in "a rather small category, the class of great Christian novels."

Faulkner again relies upon religious materials in *As I Lay Dying* (1930), which he fills not only with scriptural images and symbols, but with allusions to the Anglican Prayerbook's Holy Communion service. But here, too, and again in *Absalom, Absalom!* (1936), Faulkner makes clear he is much more concerned with human behavior than with dogmas, doctrines, or creeds. He may lean heavily upon the Christian theme of suffering, but he does not promise the inevitable attainment of total perfection or even love. Indeed, his frequent denial of ultimate faith or salvation makes his work essentially tragic. Like those of Melville, many of Faulkner's characters—as in *Sanctuary* (1931) and *Pylon* (1935)—are filled with unadulterated despair.

Such later works, however, as *Go Down, Moses* (1942), *Intruder in the Dust* (1948), and *Requiem for a Nun* (1951) do reveal a definite emphasis upon faith and compassion as the sole means of erasing past error and justifying future hope. The redemptive theme is developed also in Ike McCaslin, who unifies the *Go Down, Moses* stories and is the hero of the most acclaimed of these, "The Bear." Like *Moby-Dick* (and to a lesser degree and in a different way, like Ernest Hemingway's fishing story "Big Two-Hearted River"), "The Bear" centers upon a hunt. But this hunt is pursued according to a ritualistic code possessing definite religious overtones. Ahab's maniacal, blasphemous anger is missing; instead, the hunters view their almost supernatural quarry, "Old Ben," with a respect verging on piety. And from their respectful observance of hunting and fishing's traditional verities, Ike McCaslin and Nick Adams learn courage, humility, and patience. By passing along his acquired piety and compassion to others, Ike strives to atone for the collective past guilt of community and family.

Intruder in the Dust (1948) displays again Faulkner's moral concerns. Its frighteningly realistic lynching story poses a number of religious and ethical questions. His fiction takes on even deeper religious tones in such later works as *The Fable* (1954) and *Requiem for a Nun* (1951). *The Fable* recasts allegorically the Gospel story of Passion Week; in *Requiem* the thrice-cursed "Negro, dopefiend, whore" Nancy Mannigoe serves as redemptive instrument for the fallen heroine, Temple Drake. Temple's experiences emphasize Faulkner's belief in the possibility of salvation for the most degraded, provided there is recognition and confession of sin. His principal theme obviously is compassion. For even his most negative characters (Nancy, Popeye, Joe Christmas, Jason Compson) are as much victims as perpetrators.

Faulkner is no "believing" Christian in any orthodox sense. He points instead to that cleansing inner struggle of evil and virtue as heroic, tragic, sinful man's sole hope for spiritual improvement. Only discipline, dignity, courage, and sacrifice enable the individual to gain a measure of divine grace. To depict this inner struggle as he sees it, Faulkner makes constant use of biblical images and analogues—moving Randall Stewart to describe him "as one of the most profoundly Christian writers in our time. There is everywhere in his writings the basic premise of Original Sin; everywhere the conflict between the flesh and the spirit."

Robert Penn Warren is another who explores evil's various forms in modern man's character and psyche. His is a morality somewhat similar to Faulkner's. In *Night Rider* (1939), Percy Munn compromises with evil in a futile attempt to do good; the inevitable result is moral deterioration and destruction. In *All the King's Men,* Dr. Adam Stanton and narrator Jack Burden mistakenly feel they can avoid or reject corruption, but realistic Willie Stark grasps and capitalizes on human nature's inherent villainy. "Goodness. Yeah, just plain, simple goodness," Willie declares to Stanton. "Well you can't inherit that from anybody. You got to make it, Doc. If you want it. And you got to make it out of badness. Badness. And you know why, Doc? . . . Because there isn't anything else to make it out of."

Warren reiterates in verse as well as fiction his belief that man cannot avoid a legacy of evil. His poem "Original Sin: A Short Story" is a searching lament for lost innocence, while his lengthy verse narrative of murder, *Brother to Dragons* (1953), analyzes the degree of responsibility, fallibility, and guilt involved in the human condition. Set in "No Place" and occurring at "Any Time," *Brother to Dragons* attacks the American Revolution's romantic optimism, especially its leaders' inflated views of man's goodness and democratic institutions. A number of historical figures act as speakers, including Thomas Jefferson, and Warren himself. Warren expresses the poem's theme that man cannot even hope for the inner strength to rise above human selfishness until he recognizes and accepts his moral frailty.

CULTURAL PARADOXES Clearly, the American intellectual tradition reveals numerous paradoxes, if not outright contradictions. New England, for instance, the fount of New World Puritan rigidity, was transformed within two centuries into a center of liberal thought. For there such varied religious and political dissenters as Williams, Hutchinson, Hooker, Woolman, Channing, Emerson, and Thoreau introduced those heretical ideas that during the nineteenth century became part of the national heritage. Conversely, such Southern colonies as Virginia and South Carolina—both founded by worldly and relatively liberal Anglicans—were converted into a fundamentalist "Bible Belt" by the strong moral pietism of the evangelic Methodists, Baptists, and Campbellites.

In recent years, however, another cultural reversal has taken place. Today, the South again serves as arena for the intellectual confrontation of old and new. Much that is most significant in American literature is being originated by Southern writers. But where New England liberals created a literature of religious protest and change, Southerners are producing "a literature of acceptance." Faulkner and Warren, for instance—like Hawthorne—tend to be descriptive and analytic rather than critical or reformist.

This doesn't mean Southern fictionists have remained uninfluenced by those naturalists who saw man as a mere passive victim of heredity and environment. Yet in an anxious age, one in which old scientific certainties seem much less certain, the evangelic emphasis upon Scripture has regained much of its earlier luster. Hence Faulkner and Warren, among others, in striving to underscore modern man's moral responsibility and tragic shortcomings, are continuing Hawthorne and Melville's essentially religious view of man as imperfect, fallible, and incapable of solving his moral and spiritual problems by science and technology alone.

Southern writers, if seemingly dominant, are far from alone in their religious affirmation. Even those secular writers most vociferously demanding religious and social changes have derived their own moral values from the Judeo-Christian tradition, although frequently unaware of the fact. Certainly few of the shapers of American literature have urged anything contrary (when closely examined) to the biblical verities.

Indeed, the one truth emerging from a survey of American literature's religious themes is that the sensitive artist is not impeded but inspired by the spirit and flesh's seeming dichotomy. He fuses them into a dramatic structure reflecting their complex, paradoxical, yet basically interrelated aspects. And he does so in a manner enriching the reader's vision of human nature in action.

BIBLIOGRAPHY

PILGRIMS, PURITANS, AND THE NEW ISRAEL

Ashton, Robert (ed.). *The Works of John Robinson*. 2 vols. London, 1851.

Banvard, Joseph. *Plymouth and the Pilgrims*. Boston, 1851.

Barlow, William. *The Summe and Substance of the Conference . . . at Hampton Court,* January 14, 1603. London, 1605.

Bradford, William. *History of Plymouth Plantation 1606–1646*. Ed. by W. T. Davis. New York, 1959.

Burlingame, Roger. *The American Conscience*. New York, 1957.

Burrows, Millar. "Democracy in the Hebrew-Christian Tradition; Old and New Testaments," in *Science, Philosophy and Religion: Second Symposium*. Ed. by Lyman Bryson and Louis Finkelstein. New York, 1942.

Calvin, John. *Institutes of the Christian Religion*. Trans. by John Allen. 3 vols. Philadelphia, 1813.

Campbell, Douglas. *The Puritan in Holland, England and America*. New York, 1902.

Cotton, John. "God's Promise to his Plantation," in *Old South Leaflets*. No. 53. Boston, 1896.

Curti, Merle. *The Growth of American Thought*. New York, 1943.

Earle, M. *The Sabbath in Puritan New England*. New York, 1891.

Elton, Romeo. *Life of Roger Williams*. New York, 1952.

Green, J. R. *Short History of the English People*. New York, 1888.

Gregory, J. *Puritanism in the Old World and in the New*. New York, 1896.

Lowell, J. R. *Among My Books*. Second Series. Boston, 1876.

Macaulay, T. B. "John Milton," in *Critical and Historical Essays*. London, 1923.

MacDonald, William (ed.). *Select Charters . . . of American History, 1606–1675*. New York, 1904.

Manion, Clarence. "The Religious Background of Democratic Ideas," in *Science, Philosophy and Religion: Second Symposium*. Ed. by Lyman Bryson and Louis Finkelstein. New York, 1942.

Marsh, D. L. *The American Canon*. Nashville, 1939.

Mather, Cotton. *Magnalia Christi Americana; or, The Ec-clesiastical History of New-England*. Hartford, 1820.

Miller, Perry (ed.). *The American Puritans: Their Prose and Poetry*. Garden City, N. Y., 1956.

Miller, Perry. *The New England Mind: From Colony to Province*. Cambridge, 1953.

————. *The New England Mind: The Seventeenth Century*. Cambridge, 1954.

Miller, Perry and T. H. Johnson (eds.). *The Puritans*. New York, 1938.

Morgan, Joseph. *The Nature of Riches, Shewed From the Natural Reasons of the Use and Effects Thereof. . . .* Philadelphia, 1732.

Morton, Nathaniel. *New Englands Memoriall; or, A Brief Relation of the most Memorable and Remarkable Pas-sages of the Providence of God . . . 1669*. Boston, 1855.

Neuman, A. A. *Relation of the Hebrew Scriptures to American Institutions*. New York, n.d.

New England's First Fruits with Divers other Special Mat-ters concerning that Country. 1643.

Palfrey, J. G. *A Compendious History of New England*. 4 vols. Boston, 1858–90.

Perry, Bliss (ed.). *The Heart of Emerson's Journals*. Boston, 1926.

Perry, R. B. *Puritanism and Democracy*. New York, 1944.

Schneider, H. W. *The Puritan Mind*. New York, 1930.

Selbie, W. B. "The Influence of the Old Testament on Puri-tanism," in *Legacy of Israel*. Ed. by E. R. Bevan and Charles Singer. Oxford, 1927.

Stephenson, G. M. *The Puritan Heritage*. New York, 1952.

Straus, O. S. *The Origin of Republican Form of Govern-ment in the United States of America*. New York, 1926.

Tennant, F. R. *The Sources of the Doctrines of the Fall and Original Sin*. Cambridge, 1903.

Tillyard, E. M. W. *Studies in Milton*. London and New York, 1951.

Tyler, M. C. *A History of American Literature 1607–1765*. Ithaca, N. Y., 1949.

Walker, Williston. *The Creeds and Platforms of Congrega-tionalism*. New York, 1893.

BIBLE, CHURCH, AND STATE

Adams, C. F. (ed.). *The Works of John Adams, Second President of the United States*. 2 vols. Boston, 1850–56.

Baldwin, A. M. *The New England Clergy and the American Revolution*. Durham, N. C., 1928.

Bates, E. S. *American Faith: Its Religious, Political and Economic Foundations*. New York, 1940.

Becker, Carl. *The Declaration of Independence: A Study in the History of Political Ideas*. New York, 1942.

——. *The Heavenly City of the Eighteenth-Century Philosophers*. New Haven, Conn., 1932.

Bigelow, John (ed.). *The Works of Benjamin Franklin*. 11 vols. New York, 1904.

Brattle, William. *MS Sermons*. Harvard College Library.

Byington, E. H. *The Puritan in England and New England*. Boston, 1896.

Cotton, John. *The Way of the Churches*. 1645.

Cousins, Norman (ed.). *"In God We Trust"; The Religious Beliefs and Ideas of the American Founding Fathers*. New York, 1958.

Curti, Merle. *The Growth of American Thought*. New York, 1943.

Dearden, R. R., Jr. and D. S. Watson. *An Original Leaf from the Bible of the Revolution and an Essay Concerning It*. San Francisco, 1930.

Dobschütz, Ernest von. *The Influence of the Bible on Civilization*. New York, 1914.

Elliot, Jonathan. *The Debates in the Several State Conventions on the Adoption of the Federal Constitution.* . . . 5 vols. Philadelphia, 1836–1845.

Ernst, James. *Roger Williams, New England Firebrand*. New York, 1932.

Fast, Howard. *The Selected Work of Tom Paine and Citizen Tom Paine*. New York, 1946.

Fitzpatrick, J. C. (ed.). *Writings of George Washington*. 5 vols. Washington, 1932.

Foote, H. W. *Thomas Jefferson, Champion of Religious Freedom, Advocate of Christian Morals*. Boston, 1947.

Gregory, J. *Puritanism in the Old World and in the New, From its Inception in the Reign of Elizabeth to the Establishment of the Puritan Theocracy in New England*. New York and Edinburgh, 1896.

Headley, J. T. *The Chaplains and Clergy of the Revolution*. New York, 1864.

Humphrey, E. F. *Nationalism and Religion in America, 1774–1789*. Boston, 1924.

Hunt, Gaillard. *History of the Seal of the United States*. Washington, 1909.

Hutchinson, Thomas. *History of the Colony of Massachusetts*

Bay from its First Settlement in 1628 to the year 1750. 4 vols. Boston, 1764–1828.

Journals of the Continental Congress. Ford Edition. 13 vols. Washington, 1904–37.

Knowles, J. D. *Memoir of Roger Williams, the Founder of the State of Rhode Island.* Boston, 1834.

Lecky, W. E. H. *History of the Rise and Influence of the Spirit of Rationalism in Europe.* 2 vols. New York, 1888.

Maine, H. J. S. *Popular Government: Four Essays.* New York, 1886.

Mather, Increase. *The Order of the Gospel, Professed and Practised by the Churches of Christ in New England....* Boston, 1700.

Mayhew, Jonathan. *Sermon to Young Men.* London, 1767.

Rider, S. S. *Soul Liberty, Rhode Island's Gift to the Nation . . . in Rhode Island Historical Tracts.* Second Series, No. 5. Providence, 1897.

Sidney, Algernon. *Discourses Concerning Government.* London, 1704.

Simms, P. M. *The Bible in America; Versions that Have Played Their Part in the Making of the Republic.* New York, 1936.

Stokes, A. P. *Church and State in the United States.* New York, 1950.

Sweet, W. W. *Religion in the Development of American Culture, 1765–1840.* New York, 1952.

Swift, Lindsay. *The Massachusetts Election Sermons.* Cambridge, 1897.

Thornton, J. W. *The Historical Relation of New England to the English Commonwealth.* Boston, 1874.

Thornton, J. W. (ed.). *The Pulpit of the American Revolution: Or, The Political Sermons of the Period of 1776.* Boston, 1860.

Walker, G. L. *Thomas Hooker: Preacher, Founder, Democrat.* New York, 1891.

Washington, H. A. (ed.). *The Writings of Thomas Jefferson: Being his Autobiography, Correspondence, Reports, Messages, Addresses, and Other Writings, Official and Private.* 7 vols. Philadelphia, 1869–71.

Weigle, L. A. "The Religious Background of Democracy," in *Science, Philosophy and Religion: Second Symposium.* Ed. by Lyman Bryson and Louis Finkelstein. New York, 1942.

Wertenbaker, T. J. *The First Americans 1607–1690.* New York, 1927.

Williams, Roger. *Major Butler's Fourth Paper.* London, 1652.

Winthrop, R. C. *Life and Letters of John Winthrop.* 2 vols. Boston, 1869.

Wise, John. *Law of Nature in Government: A Vindication of the Government of the New England Churches.* Boston, 1717.

Zollmann, Carl. *American Church Law.* St. Paul, Minn., 1933.

LAW AND THE BIBLE:
THE STRUGGLE FOR RELIGIOUS FREEDOM

Adams, C. F. (ed.). *Antinomianism in the Colony of Massachusetts Bay, 1636–1638.* Boston, 1894.

————. *Three Episodes of Massachusetts History.* Boston, 1893.

Bates, E. H. (ed.). *Quarter Sessions Records for the County of Somerset.* London, 1907.

Bowers, C. G. *Jefferson in Power: The Death Struggle of the Federalists.* Boston, 1936.

Bradshaw, William. *Several Treatises of Worship and Ceremonies.* Cambridge and Oxford, 1660.

Bryce, James. *The American Commonwealth.* 2 vols. New York, 1927.

Butts, R. F. *The American Tradition in Religion and Education.* Boston, 1950.

Calder, I. M. "John Cotton and the New Haven Colony," in New England Quarterly III (1930), No. 82.

Calendar of State Papers, Colonial America and West Indies, 1677–1680.

Cobb, S. H. *The Rise of Religious Liberty in America: A History.* New York, 1902.

Cobbet, Thomas. *The Civil Magistrates Power In Matters of Religion Modestly Debated, Impartially Stated According to the Bounds and Grounds of Scripture.* London, 1653.

Coke, Sir Edward. *The Third Part of the Institutes of the Laws of England: Concerning High Treason, and other Pleas of the Crown, and Criminal Causes.* London, 1664.

Commager, H. S. (ed.). *Documents of American History,* New York, 1950.

Cotton, John. *A Briefe Exposition of the Whole Book of Canticles, or Song of Solomon.* London, 1648.

————. *The Keyes of the Kingdom of Heaven and Power Thereof, According to the Word of God. Tending to*

Reconcile Some Present Differences about Discipline.
London, 1644.

————. *Moses his Judicials,* in *Collections of the Massachusetts Historical Society* (1798). First Series. V. 173ff.

————. *The Result of a Synod at Cambridge in New England, Anno 1646. Concerning The Power of Magistrates in Matters of the First Table. The Nature & Power
of Synods.* London, 1654.

Dunning, W. A. *A History of Political Theories From
Luther to Montesquieu.* 3 vols. New York, 1923.

*Examen Legum Angliae: or, the Laws of England Ex-
amined, By Scripture, Antiquity, and Reason.* London,
1656.

Farrand, Max (ed.). *The Book of the Lawes and Libertyes of
Massachusetts.* Cambridge, 1929.

Foote, H. W. (ed.). *The Cambridge Platform of 1648.* Boston,
1949.

Greene, M. L. *The Development of Religious Liberty in Connecticut.* New York, 1905.

Hardy, W. J. *Calendar to the Sessions Records for the County
of Somerset.* London, 1935.

Haskins, G. L. "Codification of the Law in Colonial Massachusetts: A Study in Comparative Law," in *Indiana Law
Journal XXX* (1954), No. 3.

————. *Law and Authority in Early Massachusetts: A Study
in Tradition and Design.* New York, 1960.

————. and S. E. Ewing, III. "The Spread of Massachusetts Law in the Seventeenth Century," in *University of
Pennsylvania Law Review CVI,* No. 413, (1958).

Hening, W. W. (ed.). *Statutes at Large of Virginia.* 12 vols.

Hoadly, C. J. (ed.). *Records of the Colony or Jurisdiction
of New Haven, from May, 1653 to the Union.* Hartford,
1858.

Hosmer, J. K. (ed.). *Winthrop's Journal: History of New
England, 1630–1649.* New York, 1908.

Howard, Leon. "The Puritans in Old and New England," in
*Anglo-American Cultural Relations in the Seventeenth
and Eighteenth Centuries.* Los Angeles, 1958.

Hubbard, William. *The Happiness of a People.* Boston,
1676.

Hull, John. "The Diaries of John Hull," in *Transactions
and Collections of the American Antiquarian Society*
(1857).

Hunt, Gaillard (ed.). *The Writings of James Madison.* 2 vols.
New York, 1901.

Kittredge, G. L. *Witchcraft in Old and New England*. Cambridge, 1929.

Leland, John. *The Rights of Conscience, Inalienable, and therefore Religious Opinions not Cognizable by Law*. New London, 1791.

Lerner, Max. *America as a Civilization: Life and Thought in the United States Today*. New York, 1957.

Levy, B. M. *Preaching in the First Half Century of New England History*. Hartford, 1945.

Mather, Increase. *An Essay for the Recording of Illustrious Providences*. Boston, 1684.

———. *A Further Account of the Tryals of the New-England Witches. . . .* London, 1693.

Mather, Richard. *Church-Government and Church Covenant Discussed, In an Answer of the Elders of the Severall Churches in New England to Two and Thirty Questions Sent Over to Them by Divers Ministers in England*. London, 1643.

McCloskey, R. G. (ed.). *Essays in Constitutional Law*. New York, 1957.

McNeill, J. T. "Natural Law in the Teaching of the Reformers," in *Journal of Religion* XXVI (1946).

Miller, Perry. *Orthodoxy in Massachusetts, 1630–1650: A Genetic Study*. Cambridge, 1933.

Morton, Thomas. *New English Canaan*. Ed. by C. F. Adams. Boston, 1883.

Neal, Daniel. *History of the Puritans*. 3 vols. London, 1837.

Niebuhr, Reinhold. *Pious and Secular America*. New York, 1958.

Norton, John. *The Heart of N—England Rent at the Blasphemies of the Present Generation*. Cambridge, 1659.

Notestein, Wallace. *A History of Witchcraft in England from 1558 to 1718*. Washington, 1911.

Oakes, Urian. *New-England Pleaded with, and Pressed to Consider the Things which Concern her Peace, at least in this her Day*. Cambridge, 1673.

O'Hara, Edwin. "A Catholic Social Order," in *Catholic Action* (June, 1938).

O'Neill, J. M. *Religion and Education under the Constitution*. New York, 1949.

Osgood, H. L. *The American Colonies in the Seventeenth Century*. New York, 1904.

Penn, William. "The Great Case of Liberty of Conscience Once More Briefly Debated and Defended by the Authority of Reason, Scripture, and Antiquity," in *The Select Works of William Penn*, 3 vols. London, 1782.

Perkins, W. *The Order of the Causes of Salvation and Damnation.* Cambridge, 1957.

Records of the First Church in Dorchester in New England. Boston, 1891.

Sewall, Samuel. *Diary of Samuel Sewall, Collections of Massachusetts Historical Society.* Fifth Series. V.

Shurtleff, N. B. (ed.). *Records of the Governor and Company of Massachusetts Bay.* 3 vols. Boston, 1853–54.

Smith, A. E. "Catholic and Patriot: Governor Smith Replies," in *The Atlantic Monthly* CXXXIX (May, 1927).

"The Social Creed of the Churches," in *The Social Ideals of the Churches.* Federal Council of Churches, 1932.

Thorpe, F. N. (ed.). *The Federal and State Constitutions, Colonial Charters and Other Organic Laws of the States.* 3 vols. Washington, 1909.

Trumbull, J. H. and C. J. Headly (eds.). *Public Records of the Colony of Connecticut 1636–1665.* 4 vols. Hartford, 1850–90.

Upham, C. W. *Salem Witchcraft; with an Account of Salem Village, and a History of Opinions of Witchcraft and Kindred Subjects.* Boston, 1867.

Ward, Nathaniel. *The Simple Cobler of Aggawam.* Ed. by David Pulsifer. Boston, 1843.

Weeden, W. B. *Economic and Social History of New England 1620–1789.* 2 vols. Boston, 1890.

Wertenbaker, T. J. *The Puritan Oligarchy: The Founding of American Civilization.* New York, 1947.

Whitmore, W. H. (ed.). *The Colonial Laws of Massachusetts.* Boston, 1889.

Winslow, Edward. *New-Englands Salamander, Discovered by an Irreligious and Scornefull Pamphlet, Called New-Englands Jonas.* London, 1647.

Winsor, Justin (ed.). *The Memorial History of Boston.* 3 vols. Boston, 1884.

RELIGION, THE BIBLE, AND THE SCHOOLS

Adams, Brooks. *The Emancipation of Massachusetts.* Boston, 1887.

Adams, J. T. *The Founding of New England.* Boston, 1921.

Bay Psalm Book. Cambridge, 1640.

Beard, Charles A. and Mary R. *The Rise of American Civilization.* New York, 1927.

Box, G. H. "Hebrew Studies in the Reformation Period and After," in *The Legacy of Israel.* Ed. by E. R. Bevan and Charles Singer. Oxford, 1927.

Brown, J. H. *Elizabethan School Days.* Oxford, 1933.

Burns, J. A. *The Growth and Development of the Catholic School System in the United States.* New York, 1912.

Chauncy, Charles. *Gods Mercy shewed to his people in giving them a faithful Ministry and schooles of Learning for the Continual supplyes thereof.* Cambridge, 1655.

Cobbet, Thomas. *A Fruitfull and Usefull Discourse touching the Honour due from Children to Parents and the Duty of Parents towards their Children.* London, 1656.

Cohen, A. *Everyman's Talmud.* New York, 1949.

Commager, H. S. *The American Mind: An Interpretation of American Thought and Character Since the 1880's.* New Haven, Conn., 1950.

Confrey, Burton. *Secularism in American Education: Its History.* Washington, 1931.

Cooper, C. H. *Annals of Cambridge.* Cambridge, 1842–53. III, 95–101.

Cotton, John. *Milk for Babes, Drawn out of the Breasts of both Testaments Chiefly for the Spirituall Nourishment of Boston Babes in either England.* London, 1646.

———. *A Practical Commentary, or An Exposition with Observation, Reasons and Uses upon the First Epistle Generall of John.* London, 1656.

Coughlan, Robert. "Religion and the Schools," in *Life* (June 16, 1961), pp. 110–122.

Crook, M. B. *The Bible and Its Literary Associations.* New York, 1937.

Cubberley, E. P. *Public Education in the United States.* Boston, 1934.

De Sola Pool, David. "Hebrew Learning Among the Puritans of New England Prior to 1700," in *Publications of the American Jewish Historical Society.* XX (1911), pp. 31–83.

Dexter, F. B. *Documentary History of Yale University, 1701–1745.* New Haven, Conn., 1916.

Dierenfield, R. B. "The Extent of Religious Influence in American Public Schools," in *Religious Education* (May–June, 1961), pp. 173–79.

Eliot, John. *The Harmony of the Gospels.* Boston, 1678.

Ellis, J. H. (ed.). *The Works of Anne Bradstreet.* Charlestown, Mass., 1867; New York, 1932.

Fletcher, H. F. *Milton's Semitic Studies and Some Manifestations of them in his Poetry.* Chicago, 1926.

Foxcroft, Thomas. *Cleansing Our Way in Youth.* Boston, 1719.

Gabel, R. J. *Public Funds for Church and Private Schools.* Washington, 1937.

Gollancz, H. *Pedagogics of the Talmud and That of Modern Times.* Oxford, 1924.

Green, E. L. *A History of the University of South Carolina.* Columbia, S. C., 1916.

Gudemann, M. "Education—In Talmudical Times," in *The Jewish Encyclopedia.* Ed. by Isadore Singer. New York, 1925. Vol. V, pp. 43–44.

Hamilton, O. T. *The Courts and the Curriculum.* New York, 1927.

Handlin, Oscar. "Federal Aid to Parochial Schools: A Debate," in *Commentary* (July, 1961), pp. 6–11.

Hanford, J. H. (ed.). *The Poems of John Milton.* New York, 1936.

Hertzberg, Arthur. "The Protestant 'Establishment.' Catholic Dogma, & the Presidency," in *Commentary* (October, 1960), pp. 277–85.

Honeywell, R. J. *The Educational Work of Thomas Jefferson.* Cambridge, 1931.

Hoole, Charles. *New Discovery of the Old Art of Teaching School.* Ed. by Thiselton Mark. Syracuse, N. Y., 1912.

Jernegan, M. W. *Laboring and Dependent Classes in Colonial America, 1607–1783: Studies of the Economic, Educational, and Social Significance of Slaves, Servants, Apprentices, and Poor Folk.* Chicago, 1931.

Johnson, A. W. *The Legal Status of Church—State Relationships in the United States, with Special Reference to the Public Schools.* Minneapolis, Minn., 1934.

Johnson, Samuel. *An English and Hebrew Grammar, Being the First Short Rudiments of Those Two Languages Taught Together, to Which is Added a Synopsis of all the Parts of Learning.* London, 1767.

Joseph, Morris. "Education (Jewish)," in *Encyclopedia of Religion and Ethics.* Ed. by James Hastings. New York, 1912. Vol. V, pp. 194–8.

Kohler, Kaufmann. "Education—Biblical and Pre-Talmudical Data," *The Jewish Encyclopedia.* Ed. by Isadore Singer. New York, 1925. Vol. V, pp. 42–3.

Lawson, Deodat. *The Duty and Property of a Religious Householder.* Boston, 1693.

Leach, A. F. *Schools of Medieval England.* London, 1910.

Lipscomb, A. A. and A. E. Berg (eds.). *The Writings of Thomas Jefferson. Monticello Edition, Containing his Autobiography, Notes on Virginia, Parliamentary Man-*

ual . . . and Other Writings. . . . 15 vols. Washington, 1904–05.

Lischka, C. N. *Private Schools and State Laws. . . .* Washington, 1924.

Mann, Horace. *Annual Report, 1845–1848.* 5 vols. Boston, 1891.

Mather, Cotton. *Corderius Americanus. An Essay upon the Good Education of Children.* Boston, 1708.

———. *Help for Distressed Parents.* Boston, 1695.

Mitchell, W. F. *English Pulpit Oratory from Andrewes to Tillotson.* London, 1932.

Moehlman, C. H. *The American Constitutions and Religion; Religious References in the Charters of the Thirteen Colonies and the Constitutions of the Forty-Eight States. . . .* Rochester, N. Y., 1938.

———. *School and Church: the American Way; An Historical Approach to the Problem of Religious Instruction in Public Education.* New York, 1944.

Moore, C. C. *Compendious Lexicon of the Hebrew Language.* 2 vols. New York, 1809.

Morgan, E. S. *The Puritan Family: Essays on Religion and Domestic Relations in Seventeenth-Century New England.* Boston, 1944.

Morison, S. E. *Builders of the Bay Colony.* Cambridge, 1930.

———. *The Development of Harvard University since the Inauguration of President Eliot, 1869–1929.* Cambridge, 1930.

———. *The Founding of Harvard College.* Cambridge, 1935. II.

———. *Harvard College in the Seventeenth Century.* Cambridge, 1936.

———. *The Intellectual Life of Colonial New England.* Ithaca, 1960. This work was published originally as *The Puritan Pronaos: Studies in the Intellectual Life of New England in the Seventeenth Century.* New York, 1936.

———. *Three Centuries of Harvard 1636–1936.* Cambridge, 1936.

Murray, J. C. "Law or Prepossession?" in *Essays in Constitutional Law.* Ed. by R. G. McCloskey. New York, 1957.

Myers, E. D. *Education in the Perspective of History.* New York, 1960.

Nye, R. B. *The Cultural Life of the New Nation 1776–1830.* New York, 1960.

Parsons, Wilfrid. *The First Freedom: Considerations on Church and State in the United States.* New York, 1948.

Pfeffer, Leo. *Creeds in Competition: A Creative Force in American Culture.* New York, 1958.

Prizer, J. B. "Some Aspects of the Influence of Cambridge Men and their University in the American Colonies," in *Historical Publications of the Society of Colonial Wars in the Commonwealth of Pennsylvania.* Philadelphia, 1956. Vol. VIII, No. 9.

Schneider, Herbert and Carol (eds.). *Samuel Johnson, President of King's College: His Career and Writings.* 4 vols. New York, 1929.

Small, W. H. *Early New England Schools.* Boston, 1914.

Smith, S. M. *The Relation of the State to Religious Education in Massachusetts.* Syracuse, N. Y., 1926.

Stewart, Jr., George. *A History of Religious Education in Connecticutt to the Middle of the Nineteenth Century.* New Haven, Conn., 1924.

Van den Haag, Ernest. "Federal Aid to Parochial Schools: A Debate," in *Commentary* (July, 1961), pp. 1–6.

Wadsworth, Benjamin. *Exhortation to Early Piety.* Boston, 1702.

———. *The Well-Ordered Family.* Boston, 1772.

Watson, Foster. "Scholars and Scholarship, 1600–60," in *The Cambridge History of English Literature.* Ed. by A. W. Ward and A. R. Waller. New York, 1911. Vol. VII, pp. 345–67.

Wright, L. B. *The Cultural Life of the American Colonies 1607–1763.* New York, 1957.

Wrong, G. M. *Conquest of New France.* New Haven, Conn., 1918.

GOD, THE PHYSICIAN, AND HYGIENE

Abrahams, Israel. *Jewish Life in the Middle Ages.* London, 1932.

Atkinson, D. T. *Magic, Myth and Medicine.* Cleveland, 1956.

Beall, Jr., O. T. and R. H. Shryock. *Cotton Mather: First Significant Figure in American Medicine.* Baltimore, 1954.

Bernstein, Abraham and H. C. "Medicine in the Talmud," in *California Medicine* LXXIV, (April, 1951).

Blake, J. B. "The Inoculation Controversy in Boston: 1721–1722," in *New England Quarterly* XXV, (December, 1952), pp. 489–506.

Campbell, D. E. *Arabian Medicine and Its Influence on the Middle Ages.* London, 1926.

Castiglioni, Arturo. *A History of Medicine.* Trans. and ed. by E. B. Krumbhaar. New York and London, 1947.

Cowles, E. S. *Religion and Medicine in the Church.* New York, 1925.

Frank, Johann Peter. *A Complete System of Medical Polity.* 6 vols. Mannheim, 1779–1817.

Fitz, R. H. "Zabdiel Boyleston, Inoculator," in *Johns Hopkins Hospital Bulletin* XXII, (September 1911).

Friedenwald, Harry. *The Jews and Medicine: Essays.* 2 vols. Baltimore, 1944.

Garrison, F. H. *An Introduction to the History of Medicine.* Philadelphia, 1929.

Glenn, J. B. "Consumption of Fat and Longevity," in *The Jewish Forum* (March, 1960), pp. 41–42.

Gold, H. R. "Psychiatry and the Bible," in *The Jewish Digest* (November, 1958), pp. 61–65.

Gordon, H. L. (ed.). *The Preservation of Youth by Maimonides.* New York, 1958.

Gordon, M. B. *Aesculapius Comes to the Colonies.* Ventnor City, N. J., 1949.

Green, S. A. *History of Medicine in Massachusetts.* Boston, 1881.

Greenstone, J. H. "Hospital," in *The Jewish Encyclopedia.* Ed. by Isadore Singer. New York, 1925. Vol. VI, pp. 479–80.

———. "Hospitality," in *The Jewish Encyclopedia.* Ed. by Isadore Singer. New York, 1925. Vol. VI, pp. 480–81.

Haggard, H. W. *Devils, Drugs, and Doctors.* New York, 1929.

Haneman, F. T. "Medicine—In Post-Talmudic Times," in *The Jewish Encyclopedia.* Ed. by Isadore Singer. New York, 1925. Vol. XIII, pp. 414–22.

Isaacs, Nathan. "The Influence of Judaism on Western Law," in *The Legacy of Israel.* Ed. by E. R. Bevan and Charles Singer. Oxford, 1953.

Jakobovits, Immanuel. *Jewish Medical Ethics.* New York, 1959.

Kittredge, G. L. "Some Lost Works of Cotton Mathers," in *Proceedings of the Massachusetts Historical Society.* XLV, 427.

Lecky, W. E. *History of European Morals.* 2 vols. London, 1911.

Loewe, Herbert. "Disease and Medicine," in *Encyclopedia of Religion and Ethics.* Ed. by James Hastings. New York, 1955. Vol. IV, pp. 755–57.

Mather, Cotton. "The Angel of Bethesda," in *Cotton Mather: First Significant Figure in American Medicine.* Ed. by O. T. Beall, Jr. and R. H. Shryock. Baltimore, 1954.

———. *The Great Physician, Inviting Them that are Sensible*

of their Internal Maladies to Repair Unto Him for His Heavenly Remedies. Boston, 1700.

McKinney, L. M. "Medical Ethics and Etiquette in the Early Middle Ages," *Bulletin of the History of Medicine* (1952). 25:5.

Munter, Zussmann (ed.). *Perek Moshe.* Jerusalem, 1959.

Neuberger, Max. *Geschichte der Medizin.* Stuttgart, 1906.

Osler, William. *The Evolution of Modern Medicine.* New Haven, Conn., and London, 1921.

Oursler, Will. *The Healing Power of Faith.* Kingswood, Surrey, 1958.

Preuss, Julius. *Biblisch—talmudische Medizin.* Berlin, 1911.

Puschmann, Theodor. *A History of Medical Education from the Most Remote to the Most Recent Times.* Trans. by E. E. Hare. London, 1891.

Rawlinson, George (trans.). *The History of Herodotus.* New York, 1928.

Riesman, David. *The Story of Medicine in the Middle Ages.* New York, 1935.

Robinson, Victor. *The Story of Medicine.* New York, 1931.

Sigerist, H. E. *Man and Medicine.* Trans. by M. G. Boise. New York, 1932.

Spivak, C. D. "Medicine—In Bible and Talmud," in *The Jewish Encyclopedia.* Ed. by Isadore Singer. New York, 1925. Vol. VIII, pp. 409–14.

Sudhoff, Karl. *Essays in the History of Medicine.* Ed. by F. H. Garrison. New York, 1926.

Taylor, G. R. *Sex in History.* New York, 1955.

Thorndike, Lynn. *Science and Thought in the 15th Century.* New York, 1929.

Tobey, J. A. *Riders of the Plague: the Story of the Conquest of Disease.* New York, 1930.

White, A. D. *A History of the Warfare of Science with Theology in Christendom.* 2 vols. New York, 1955.

Zung, Leopold. "Jewish Moralists," in *Hebrew Characteristics.* New York, 1875.

AMERICAN LITERATURE AND
THE RELIGIOUS TRADITION

Adams, Henry. *The Education of Henry Adams: An Autobiography.* Boston, 1918.

————. *Mont-Saint-Michel and Chartres.* Boston, 1936.

Anderson, Christopher. *Annals of the English Bible.* Ed. by Hugh Anderson. London, 1862.

Anderson, Maxwell. *Eleven Verse Plays, 1929–1939.* New York, 1940.

Babbitt, Irving. *Democracy and Leadership*. Boston, 1927.
————. *Rousseau and Romanticism*. Boston, 1919.
Baroway, Israel. "The Imagery of Spenser and the Song of Sons," in *Journal of English and Germanic Philology* XXXIII, (April, 1934), pp. 23–45.
Battenhouse, R. W. "Measure for Measure and Christian Doctrine of the Atonement," in *PMLA* LXI, (1960), pp. 1029–59.
————. "Shakespeare Tragedy: A Christian Interpretation," in *The Tragic Vision and the Christian Faith*. Ed. by N. A. Scott, Jr. New York, 1957.
Baxter, Richard. *Poetical Fragments*. London, 1821.
Boynton, P. H. *The Challenge of Modern Criticism*. Chicago, 1931.
Braswell, William. *Melville's Religious Thought*. Durham, N. C., 1943.
Brinton, Crane and J. B. Christopher and R. L. Wolff. *A History of Civilization: 1715 to the Present*. Englewood Cliffs, N. J., 1955.
Bruce, F. F. *The English Bible: A History of Translations*. New York, 1961.
Bryant, W. C. *Poetical Works of William Cullen Bryant*. New York, 1922.
Cather, Willa. *Death Comes for the Archbishop*. New York, 1931.
Chambers, E. K. *Elizabethan Stage*. 4 vols. Oxford, 1923.
Channing, W. E. *The Works of William E. Channing*. Boston, 1891.
Clark, T. C. (ed.). *The Master of Men, Quotable Poems About Jesus*. New York, 1930.
Cleghorn, S. N. *Poems of Peace and Freedom*. Rome, N. Y., 1945.
Cook, A. S. *The Authorized Version of the Bible and Its Influence*. New York, 1910.
Cotton, John. *A Reply to Mr. Williams: His Examination, and Answer of the Letter Sent to Him by John Cotton*. London, 1647.
————. *The Controversies Concerning Liberty of Conscience in Matters of Religion Truly Stated*. London, 1646.
Cowley, Malcolm (ed.). *After the Genteel Tradition: American Writers Since 1910*. New York, 1937.
Cowley, Malcolm (ed.). *The Portable Hawthorne*. New York, 1948.
Crane, Stephen. *The Collected Poems of Stephen Crane*. New York, 1956.

Crook, M. B. *The Bible and Its Literary Associations*. New York, 1937.

Crowe, M. F. and E. J. Slack (eds.). *Christ in the Poetry of Today* New York, 1928.

Davidson, Donald. *Still Rebels, Still Yankees, and Other Essays*. Baton Rouge, La., 1957.

Davis, M. R. and W. H. Gilman. *The Letters of Herman Melville*. New Haven, Conn., 1960.

Dickinson, Emily. *The Poems of Emily Dickinson*. Ed. by M. D. Bianchi and A. L. Hampson. Boston, 1941.

Dreiser, Theodore. *Dawn: A History of Myself*. New York, 1931.

Dunster, John and Richard Lyon. *The Psalms, Hymns and Spiritual Songs of the Old and New Testament, faithfully translated into English metre*. Cambridge, 1651.

Eaton, T. R. *Shakespeare and the Bible*. Norwich, Conn., 1957.

Edwards, Jonathan. *A Careful and Strict Inquiry into the Modern Prevailing Notions of That Freedom of Will Which Is Supposed To Be Essential to Moral Agency, Virtue and Vice, Reward and Punishment, Praise and Blame*. Boston, 1754.

————. *A Faithful Narrative of the Surprising Work of God in the Conversion of Many Hundred Souls. . . .* Boston, 1738.

————. *The Great Christian Doctrine of Original Sin Defended*. Boston, 1758.

————. *Two Dissertations, I. Concerning the End for which God Created the World. II. The Nature of True Virtue*. Boston, 1765.

Eliot, T. S. *Idea of a Christian Society*. New York, 1949.

————. *Collected Poems 1909–1935*. London, 1936.

————. *The Complete Poems and Plays 1909–1950*. New York, 1958.

————. *Essays, Ancient and Modern*. London, 1936.

Emerson, E. W. (ed.). *The Complete Works of Ralph Waldo Emerson*. Boston, 1903.

Emerson, E. W. and W. E. Forbes (eds.). *Journals of Ralph Waldo Emerson*. 6 vols. Boston, 1911.

Emerson, R. W. *Essays: First Series*. Boston, 1856.

Farmer, J. S. (ed.). *The Dramatic Writings of John Bale*. London, 1907.

Faulkner, William. *New Orleans Sketches*. Intro. by Carvel Collins. New Brunswick, 1958.

————. *The Sound and the Fury and As I Lay Dying*. New York, 1946.

Faust, C. H. "The Background of the Unitarian Opposition to Transcendentalism," in *Modern Philology* XXV (February, 1938), pp. 297–320.

Foerster, Norman (ed.). *Humanism and America: Essays on the Outlook of Modern Civilization.* New York, 1930.

Ford, P. L. (ed.). *The Works of Thomas Jefferson.* New York, 1905.

Gaebelein, F. E. *Down Through the Ages; the Story of the King James Bible.* New York, 1925.

Gelb, Arthur and Barbara. *O'Neill.* New York, 1962.

Gilder, R. W. *The Poems of Richard Watson Gilder.* Boston, 1908.

Gould, W. D. "The Religious Opinions of Thomas Jefferson," *Mississippi Valley Historical Review* (1933–34), XX, 204.

Grattan, C. H. (ed.). *The Critique of Humanism: A Symposium.* New York, 1930.

Gummere, A. M. (ed.). *The Journal and Essays of John Woolman.* New York, 1922.

Halliwell, J. O. *Dictionary of Old English Plays.* London, 1860.

Haraszti, Zoltan. *The Enigma of the Bay Psalm Book.* Chicago, 1956.

Hawthorne, Nathaniel. *The Works of Nathaniel Hawthorne.* 2 vols. New York, n.d.

Jeffers, Robinson. *Dear Judas and Other Poems.* New York, 1929.

————. *Roan Stallion, Tamar and Other Poems.* New York, 1925.

————. *The Selected Poetry of Robinson Jeffers.* New York, 1938.

Jefferson, Thomas. *The Jefferson Bible, Being the Life and Morals of Jesus Christ of Nazareth.* Greenwich, Conn., 1961.

Johnson, Edward. *Wonder-Working Providence, 1628–1651.* New York, 1910.

Johnson, T. H. (ed.). *The Poetical Works of Edward Taylor.* New York, 1939.

Jones, H. M. *America and French Culture, 1750–1848.* Chapel Hill, N. C., 1927.

————. "The European Background," in *The Reinterpretation of American Literature.* Ed. by Norman Foerster. New York, 1929.

Kernodle, G. R., "Patterns of Belief in Contemporary Drama," in *Spiritual Problems in Contemporary Literature.* Ed. by S. R. Hopper. New York, 1957.

Krumpelman, J. T. "Longfellow's 'Golden Legend' and the 'Arme Heinrich' Theme in Modern German Literature," in *JEGP* XXV (1926), pp. 137–92.

Krutch, J. W. *The Modern Temper: A Study and a Confession*. New York, 1929.

Landrum, G. W. "Spenser's Use of the Bible and His Alleged Puritanism," in *PMLA* XLI (September, 1926), pp. 517–44.

Lanier, M. D. (ed.). *Poems of Sidney Lanier*. New York, 1906.

Lindsay, Vachel. *Collected Poems*. New York, 1930.

Longfellow, H. W. *The Complete Writings of Henry Wadsworth Longfellow*. 5 vols. Boston, 1904.

Lowell, J. R. *Selected Literary Essays from James Russell Lowell*. Boston, 1914.

Luccock, H. E. *Contemporary American Literature and Religion*. Chicago, 1934.

Malone, Kemp. "Religious Poetry: Caedmon and His School," in *A Literary History of England*. Ed. by A. C. Baugh. New York, 1948.

Mather, Cotton. *The Diary of Cotton Mather, 1681–1724*. 2 vols. Boston, 1911–12.

———. *A Faithful Man, Described and Rewarded*. Boston, 1705.

———. *Memorable Providences Relating to Witchcraft and Possessions*. 1689.

———. *The Wonders of the Invisible World*. 1693.

Mather, Increase. *Brief History of the Warr with the Indians in New-England*. 1676.

Mather, Increase. *A Relation of the Troubles which have hapned in New-England by reason of the Indians there. From the Year 1614 to the year 1675*. 1677.

Matthiessen, F. O. "Michael Wigglesworth, A Puritan Artist," in *New England Quarterly* I (October, 1928).

Melville, Herman. *Billy Budd and Other Prose Pieces*. Ed. by R. W. Weaver. London, 1924.

———. *The Works of Herman Melville: Standard Edition*. 8 vols. London, 1922.

Millay, Edna St. Vincent. *The Buck in the Snow and Other Poems*. New York, 1928.

Milton, John. "An Apology for Smectymmuus," in *The Student's Milton*. Ed. by F. A. Patterson. New York, 1933.

Murdock, K. B. (ed.). *Handkerchiefs from Paul, Being Pious and Consolatory Verse of Puritan Massachusetts. . . .* Cambridge, 1927.

———. *Literature and Theology in Colonial New England*. Cambridge, 1949.

————. *Selections from Cotton Mather.* New York, 1926.

Noble, Richmond. *Shakespeare's Biblical Knowledge and Use of the Book of Common Prayer.* London, 1935.

Norris, Frank. *The Octopus: A Story of California.* Garden City, N. Y., 1947.

Olson, Elder. *The Cock of Heaven.* New York, 1940.

O'Neill, Eugene. *The Great God Brown, The Fountain, The Moon of the Caribbees, and Other Plays.* New York, 1926.

————. *Lazarus Laughed 1925–26: A Play for an Imaginative Theatre.* New York, 1927.

Pearson, N. H. (ed.). *The Complete Novels and Selected Tales of Nathaniel Hawthorne.* New York, 1937.

Robinson, E. A. *Children of the Night: A Book of Poems.* New York, 1914.

————. *Sonnets, 1889–1927.* New York, 1928.

Rowlandson, Mary. *The Soveraignty and Goodness of God . . . being a Narrative of the Captivity and Restauration of Mrs. Rowlandson.* Cambridge, 1682. Republished as *The Narratives of the Captivity and Restoration.* Boston, 1930.

Sewall, Samuel. *The Selling of Joseph.* 1700.

Smith, Bernard (ed.). *The Democratic Spirit.* New York, 1941.

Squires, Radcliffe. *The Loyalties of Robinson Jeffers.* Ann Arbor, Mich., 1956.

Stafford, W. T. (ed.). *Melville's Billy Budd and the Critics.* Belmont, California, 1961.

Stevens, Wallace. *Harmonium.* New York, 1947.

Stewart, Randall. *American Literature and Christian Doctrine.* Baton Rouge, La., 1958.

Tate, Allen. *Reactionary Essays on Poetry and Ideas.* New York, 1936.

————. *Selected Poems.* New York, 1937.

Taylor, John. *The Scripture Doctrine of Original Sin Proposed to a Free and Candid Examination.* London, 1740.

Taylor, W. F. *A History of American Letters.* New York, 1947.

Thompson, Lawrence. *Melville's Quarrel with God.* Princeton, N. J., 1952.

Thoreau, H. D. *Walden; Or, Life in the Woods.* Boston, 1900.

————. *A Week on the Concord and Merrimack Rivers.* Boston, 1893.

Thorp, Willard. *American Writing in the Twentieth Century.* Cambridge, 1960.

Thorp, Willard (ed.). *Representative Selections from Melville.* New York, 1938.

Untermeyer, Louis (ed.). *The Poetry and Prose of Walt Whitman.* New York, 1949.

Waggoner, H. H. "William Faulkner's Passion Week of the Heart," in *The Tragic Vision and the Christian Faith.* Ed. by N. A. Scott, Jr. New York, 1957.

Walter, Henry (ed.). *Doctrinal Treatises and Introduction to Different Portions of the Bible.* Cambridge, 1848.

Warren, R. P. *All the King's Men.* New York, 1946.

———. *Brother to Dragons: A Tale in Verse and Voices.* New York, 1953.

Wegelin, Oscar. *Early American Poetry.* New York, 1930.

Welde, Thomas and John Eliot and Richard Mather. *The Whole Booke of Psalmes Faithfully Translated into English Metre.* Cambridge, 1640.

Wharton, Edward. *New England's Present Sufferings under their Cruel Neighbouring Indians.* London, 1675.

Wheeler, Thomas. *A Thankefull Remembrance of Gods Mercy to several Persons at Quabaug or Brookfield.* . . . Cambridge, 1676.

Wigglesworth, Michael. *The Day of Doom, Or a Poetical Description of the Great and Last Judgment.* Ed. by K. B. Murdock. New York, 1929.

———. "God's Controversy with New England, Written in the time of the great drought Anno 1662, in *Proceedings of the Massachusetts Historical Society* XII, (1859–), pp. 82–93.

Wilder, A. N. *Theology and Modern Literature.* Cambridge, 1958.

Williams, Roger. *The Bloudy Tenent of Persecution for Cause of Conscience, discussed in a Conference between Truth and Peace.* London, 1644.

Wilson, John. *A Song of Deliverance.* London, 1926; Boston, 1860.

Wright, L. B. "The Scriptures and the Elizabethan Stage," in *Modern Philology* XXVI (August, 1928), pp. 47–56.

———. "William Byrd: Citizen of the Enlightenment," in *Anglo-American Cultural Relations in the Seventeenth and Eighteenth Centuries.* Los Angeles, 1958.

Wright, L. B. and Marion Tinling (eds.). *The Secret Diary of William Byrd of Westover, 1709–1712.* Richmond, Va., 1941.

Wright, Nathalia. *Melville's Use of the Bible.* Durham, N. C., 1949.

INDEX